WOMEN
LEADING THE WAY

COMPILED BY
PEACE MITCHELL & KATY GARNER

Women Changing the World Press acknowledges the Elders and Traditional owners of country throughout Australia and their connection to lands, waters and communities. We pay our respect to Elders past and present and extend that respect to all Aboriginal and Islander peoples today. We honour more than sixty thousand years of Indigenous women's voices, stories, leadership and wisdom.

Copyright © Peace Mitchell and Katy Garner
First published in Australia in 2023
by Women Changing the World Press
an imprint of KMD Books
Waikiki, WA 6169

All rights reserved. No part of this book may be used or reproduced by any means, graphic, electronic or mechanical, including photocopying, recording, taping or by any information storage retrieval system without the written permission of the copyright owner except in the case of brief quotations embodied in critical articles and reviews.

Because of the dynamic nature of the Internet, any web addresses or links contained in this book may have changed since publication and may no longer be valid. The views expressed in this work are solely those of the author and do not necessarily reflect the views of the publisher and the publisher hereby disclaims any responsibility for them.

Edited by Tracy Regan

Typeset in Adobe Garamond Pro 12/17pt

A catalogue record for this work is available from the National Library of Australia

National Library of Australia Catalogue-in-Publication data:
Women Leading the Way/Peace Mitchell and Katy Garner

ISBN:
978-0-6457858-2-1
(Paperback)

ISBN:
978-0-6457250-6-3
(Ebook)

This book is dedicated to the next generation of women leading the way. May they have the courage and support to step into their magnificence, follow their callings and make the world a better place for us all!

CONTENTS

INTRODUCTION IX

CONFIDENT ENOUGH TO LEAD THE WAY
Amy Jackson 1

WINNING OR LEARNING
Anna Barwick 12

DEMYSTIFYING MY LIFE
Dr Aparna Baruah 21

FIND YOUR PEOPLE
Allison Rahman 31

SOMETIMES IT CAN COME OUT OF NOWEHERE ...
Clare Reilly 40

LEAD YOURSELF FIRST
Dr Emma Barrett 49

LEADERSHIP IN STEM
Fiona Holmstrom 59

DEAR GEORGIA ...
Georgia Graham.. *69*

DON'T BE DEFINED BY YOUR OWN STORY. WRITE YOUR OWN
Helen Whait... *78*

EVERYTHING IN LIFE HAPPENS FOR A REASON
Irina Castellano.. *90*

MORE THAN SKIN-DEEP
Judy Cheung-Wood.. *100*

TAKE TWO – RESETTING HISTORY
Julie Okely *113*

THE ROLE OF WOMEN IN MODERN LEADERSHIP
Karen Weaver *131*

NATURAL-BORN LEADER
Lisa Walker *139*

DARE TO BECOME MORE THAN MEDIOCRE
Megan Harrison *148*

JOURNEY OF AN AIRLINE PILOT TURNED CLIMATE TECH FOUNDER
Captain Molly Fullee *158*

GETTING UNSTUCK
Niti Nadarajah *170*

INTUITION IN LEADERSHIP
Dr Olivia Ong.. *181*

WE RISE BY LIFTING OTHERS
Peace Mitchell *191*

COPRENEURS
Petina Tieman *200*

THE FLOWER
Robina Savidis *212*

OUTWARD BOUND
Sarah Cremona *222*

LEADING WITH HEART
Sharon Collon *233*

SHARE YOUR DREAMS WITH THE WORLD
Sonia Marta *245*

USING CORE VALUES TO LEAD
Stacey Barrass *254*

LOOSENING THE GRIP OF ANXIETY
Sue Stevenson *264*

FORGING MY OWN PATH
Dr Tanya Unni *276*

PURSUIT OF YOUR PASSION THROUGH PERSEVERANCE AND PRIDE
Dr Vanessa Atienza-Hipolito *285*

PERFECTLY IMPERFECT
Wadzanai Nenzou *296*

INTRODUCTION

*'Where are the women? I started asking that question early on.
Why was a woman never mentioned in my history classes in grade school?
Why were there no women up in front of the congregation
when we sang and prayed?
Why were there no women in the photographs on the
front page of the newspaper?'*
Tara Mohr, author of *Playing Big*.

When women wholeheartedly step into their magnificence as leaders, powerful things happen. Countless studies have found that women make excellent leaders in paving a brighter future for us all. Women bring a different set of experiences and perspectives to the table than men, formed by thousands of years and generations of women seeing the world in a different way and being taught to nurture, care for and protect the earth, plants, animals and people. This unique perspective often leads to better decision-making, problem-solving and solutions which benefit everyone.

Today, more than any time in history, we have more educated and articulate women than ever before; yet despite the clear benefits of having more women in leadership positions, progress has been slow.

The lack of women in leadership positions is a persistent issue that has plagued society for decades. Despite significant progress in the fight for gender equality, women remain significantly underrepresented in leadership roles across various sectors. This is a problem that has far-reaching implications, not only for women but for society as a whole.

We still aren't seeing women fully embracing their potential as leaders, and women aren't represented equally in important places such as government, tech and science industries and Fortune 500 companies. According to a 2021 report by McKinsey & Company, women make up just 29% of senior management roles globally. This figure drops even further when we look at women in top leadership positions such as CEOs and board directors.

Women make up half of the population, so why aren't we seeing more women in leadership positions? It comes down to a complex host of reasons including gender bias, lack of role models, family responsibilities, workplace culture, societies expectations, doubt, fear of failure and structural barriers.

Encouraging more women to embrace leadership roles is essential if we are to address this imbalance. This involves addressing the root causes of gender bias and stereotypes, as well as providing more support and opportunities for women to advance in their careers. Companies and organisations can take concrete steps to support women in leadership, such as implementing gender-neutral hiring processes, providing flexible work arrangements and mentoring and sponsoring women in leadership roles.

But encouraging women to embrace leadership roles is not just the responsibility of companies and organisations. Women themselves must also be supported and encouraged to step up and take on leadership roles. This means challenging their own self-doubts and fears, as well as seeking out opportunities to develop their leadership skills. As Beyoncé once famously said, 'Power's not given to you. You have to take it.' Women must be willing to take risks and put themselves forward for leadership positions, even if they don't feel 100% ready.

There are incredible women role models who are finding their way into leadership, and I believe these are the ones we all have so much to learn from, listen to and be inspired by.

The world needs greater representation of women's voices, ideas and perspectives, and this book follows the journeys of twenty-seven exceptional women who have walked the path – overcoming challenges, setbacks and self-doubt to become leaders across a range of fields.

Women Leading the Way is an important anthology that highlights the critical importance of women's leadership in today's world. By exploring the unique qualities that women bring as leaders and the positive impact this has on our world, as well as showcasing the achievements of women in leadership roles and exploring the barriers that still exist, this anthology aims to inspire and empower more women to step up and take on leadership roles. Together, we can create a more equitable and just world where women's leadership is valued and celebrated.

CONFIDENT ENOUGH TO LEAD THE WAY

AMY JACKSON

It's 3am, my heart is racing and I'm convinced I can't do it.

I know this thing is super important. It's important for the work I want to do, the people I want to help, the business I want to grow.

I know I need to do it. It matters. I want to – really, I do – but I'm not sure I *can*. The nerves are building, the thoughts are whirling and I just wish it could be over already.

I'm circling deeper and deeper into my thought that *there's no way I can do that tomorrow.*

There have been some days when I can't. When I've called in sick or rescheduled because the weight of *I can't* has just been too heavy.

But most days, we get up and do it anyway. Especially if we want to lead. Leadership requires us to do hard things all the time. Things that feel unpleasant, impossible and way outside our comfort zones. If we are driven to do meaningful work – the stuff that really has an impact to change the world – it's going to be hard, and it's going to be uncomfortable. It's going to require me to keep picking myself up again and again, in those moments when I'm not sure if I can, but I do it anyway.

Most people I work with, including myself, wish we were more confident. We have this vague sense that *someone who was more confident would do things differently/better/faster/more effectively than me*. But the people who lead the way don't wake up one day feeling confident. Instead, they have tools to step in anyway, despite the lack of confidence. It still feels uncomfortable and difficult, but they learn how to keep themselves afloat, so they can take the first step.

We grow our confidence, not through magic transformation, but through noticing when we aren't feeling confident, grabbing a life raft and doing it anyway!

I wake and step into my day. At 10am, I'm ready for the big moment. The nerves are there, I feel the resistance, I'm not suddenly confident. But I work at it. As I feel myself being pulled under, I grab my floaties and step in. Not transformed, but ready to try.

Let's think about that really hard thing for you. The thing you most want to do today, this month, this year. Towards that thing you really want to do this lifetime. The big conversations, the key relationship-building, the *just getting started* on the new idea. I invite you to think about what it is that holds you back – the thinking, the feeling, the busyness, the procrastinating. Let's get specific about your version of *if I were more confident I would …* so that you can.

I want to step in. I feel the *I can't*. It's big/scary/messy. Someone might get angry/upset/hurt. They'll judge me. I might not be able to do it perfectly. I don't think I can do it at all.

KNOW MY NOT ENOUGH

Build your awareness of what *not confident enough* looks like for you so that you can catch it when it's holding you back. Think about one of those moments when the nerves were overwhelming you – what was going on in your:

- Feelings – What's the physical sensations you experience? (For me,

my shoulders reach my ears and my stomach churns!)
- Thoughts – What's the pattern of thinking for you? (For me, *Who am I to do this? I haven't got enough experience/skills/time.*)
- Communication – How do you communicate in these moments? (For me, I get really fast and superficial! Oh, and I snap at people I trust.)
- Action – What do you do in these moments? (For me, I put things off for another day! Or do it too fast just to get it finished!)

Write these down for yourself. (If you haven't already, grab a new notebook, you're going to want to do some journalling to capture your thinking through this …)

I need to do the thing. I wish I were more confident. I wish I was feeling like I did on that day when everything was easy.

KNOW MY CONFIDENCE

Build your own awareness of you at your best, so that you can reach for it in the moments you're going to need it. So, this time – think about a moment when you felt like *I've got this!* What was going on in your:
- Feelings – For me, I stand tall, my shoulders drop – I feel energised but calmer.
- Thoughts – My fog is gone, it's like I can see all the pieces of the puzzle at once. The curtains are open, and the spotlight is on. I get to choose what's on the stage of my thinking!
- Communication – I speak more slowly. I pause more. I listen before I jump in.
- Action – I just give it a go; I get started. I focus on doing something rather than waiting until it's perfect.

Confidence is a constantly shifting state, not a destination. The more I see myself, the more I can choose my state.

In the moments we need to do something hard, there are microseconds in which we can change our brain state. To shift our state of confidence, we practise the habit of noticing we're drowning, and pausing a moment to reach for a floatation device to keep us above water, and then we are ready to try.

In that difficult moment, if I 'pause', I get to lead. I get to choose to respond rather than react. (Sometimes I have to notice my reaction, then pause, say sorry and try to respond – especially with my team who know me best!)

KNOW MY INTENTION

Your reaction comes from your brain trying to protect you, to keep you safe. We don't want to be judged, rejected, embarrassed. Your response comes from choosing that the risk is worth it.

To do this, you need to know your intention. Why this thing is worth taking the risk for. This is the kind of thinking that is hard to access in the moment. You need to do it in advance, in depth, so you can grab it quickly when you need it.

Who do you want to be as a leader? What's the impact you want to have? What makes these hard things worth being uncomfortable for?

I'm in the moment – I want to move from reaction to response. I see my reaction bubbling.

Catch my reaction in the net!

To help catch your *I can't* quickly, you need to notice your reaction. What's the first signal you're going to be able to use to identify that you're heading for the whirlpool?

For me it's the excuses that start playing in my head about why I shouldn't do this thing right now! Or my heart racing (depending how big the thing is).

I see it. I notice my heart is racing, the fog has set in, my curtains are closed. I'm ready to go do anything but this! I hear that I'm talking super fast. I can feel I'm hunched over. I choose to pause.

PAUSE AND BREATHE

How do you pause? You simply take a breath. Just one breath. Well, ideally three, but one is enough. In that breath, that moment of pause is your access to the confidence you need to step in. To choose your response instead of your reaction. One breath.

Breathe in and slowly breathe out. It doesn't matter how, just notice that you are. Feeling unsure? Always start with the breath.

I take a breath. I slow for just a moment. I see my thoughts racing and notice the story that tells me to run! *Now! You don't have to do this!* Then I grab a safety ring to round up my thoughts.

I SEE YOU

These runaway thoughts are essentially your brain trying to protect you from getting hurt. That's great, super helpful. But if you want to lead, then you must be willing to take the risk you might get hurt when you're doing the stuff that really matters to you in the world. Your brain will only learn that it doesn't hurt if you take the chance when it might.

So instead of fighting with your brain, have the briefest of conversations with yourself. I simply say *I see you*. I know it might hurt, but let's give it a go anyway. Short and sharp. Shuts down the story and helps me shift state in that moment.

(I do this a lot now, because I understand that helpful conversations are great for my mental health. The harsh critic jabbering away at me, not so much. But the kind, gentle me that talks to everyone else is super valuable when she talks to me too!)

I take a breath. I chat with my brain. I can still feel the bubbling, but it's starting to whirl less. My body is still feeling super wobbly though. I'm still looking for the blanket to hide under!

SHIFT MY BODY

To help bring your thinking back online, you can use your body to get you there. When you step into what *confident enough* physically looks like for you, you both reassure yourself and appear more confident to others. This shift in posture acts to calm both ourselves and others involved in this difficult moment.

Look back at what happens for you physically in the moments you feel like *you can*. Practise stepping into that. For me, this is standing tall. Shoulders back, head up. For some it is unfolding, pulling their head up towards the sky.

My favourite way to practise is to sit or stand in my nervous pose. Then take a deep breath and shift into my confident pose. I always end up with a smile on my face! Then step back again. Step forward and up. Move yourself into that confident position. Practise. And practise again. And again – build your muscle memory of confidence.

I've noticed. Paused. Taken a breath, seen my brain, stood up tall. Okay, I can feel the spotlight is back on. But I still can't quite gather my thoughts! *Why, oh why, am I putting myself through this?*

CONNECT WITH MY INTENTION

In the really hard moments, connect back with your intention. What makes this thing worth doing, right now?

I do this as a question to myself, or as a five-minute journal scribble before the hard thing.

Sometimes I want to hide in my shell in these moments, protect myself. For me, that's quite literally hiding out in the toilet! Sometimes the life raft I need is someone else. I'm trying to close myself off to protect myself, but the thing that will bring me back out is connection with others.

I don't like this one. I resist it a lot. But when I reach out, when I send that message and ask for help – it changes everything. I get braver than I ever thought I could be.

CONNECT WITH MY HUMANS

Human connection helps reduce the stress response in the moment. In connecting with another human, you turn on a different brain pathway that helps reduce the stress.

Who might help you reach the floatie you need in that moment? One friend might help you dive in. One might help you float around for a moment and think clearly. One might help you see the waves differently.

My trusted people are my fast contacts in my phone. I message when I'm locked in the cubicle. A quick message, simply, *I'm not sure I can do this*. I get back the words I need to hear. *Yes you can. What you share is what these people need in this moment. Go be you.* I breathe again, it feels like a hug from a distance.

I've noticed the downward pull. I've paused. Pulled myself up. Connected out. One more deep breath, and I dive in. Wow! I can do it.

And it's over, I did it! Woohoo!

But then I forget. I forget that I stepped in, even though I thought I couldn't. I forget that I actually rocked it. I block out that it even happened! I miss the chance to reward myself for doing the hard thing!

CELEBRATE STEPPING IN ANYWAY

To take advantage of practising confidence in the moment, to build confidence over time, you need to pay attention to the hard thing you did and encourage yourself to do it again!

I write a note to myself in my daily planner – *I did it, woohoo!* If I have ten minutes, I sit with my coffee (and ideally a view) and my journal, and write a little thank-you note to myself. If I'm in an Uber on my way to the next appointment, I message my trusted people – *I did the hard thing and I survived!*

Sometimes, after I've stepped into a really difficult moment, instead of celebrating, I get caught in the whirlwind of judgement of everything I didn't do perfectly. I cycle around and around on the *shouldas!*

DITCH RUMINATION AND DEBRIEF INSTEAD

When you replay or worry about what might have gone wrong over and over again, it actually strengthens that negative memory in your brain, making it more likely you will fear it again next time. Instead, build your confidence over time, by constructively debriefing and rehearsing the alternative.

Rather than whirling thoughts, I sit with a journal (you could try a spreadsheet/database/speech-to-text, whatever format works for you) and capture my responses to these questions:

- What did I do well? (Acknowledgement.)
- What could I have done differently? (Learning.)
- What do I want to remember for next time? (Consolidating.)

Instead of replaying the same thing again and again, I practise my leadership like a sports star. I imagine the same scenario and how I would replay it if I had my time again.

Every time you practise any of these tools, you make it more likely that the alternative responses, and the confidence to try, will be available for you next time.

One warning about buoyancy. All your floaties need to live in a boat of self-care. My days of giving in to *I can't* are rare now, and I see they are usually telling me *I need to rest*. If I'm super tired, running on caffeine, sugar and stress, then my access to all these tools in the moment is pretty limited. In my self-care lies the buoyancy for my confidence to float. If I neglect this, I'm adrift.

WOMEN LEADING THE WAY

What do you choose next to be *confident enough* to lead? For me, I need to practise and pay attention every day.

My confidence grows every year, but so does the size of the seas I want to throw myself into! The floaties keep coming out, so I can sail into the next storm and lead towards a different way.

AMY JACKSON

Amy Jackson, B Psych (Hons I), PCC, helps women to pause in the moments day-to-day when the world needs them to do hard things, to have the impact needed to create change. She helps them to build the skills to pause, shift their body and nudge their thinking forward with kindness, learning to feel confident enough to take the next step. Cultivating habits of practical *confident enough* action, she nurtures their confidence and capacity to lead the way.

Amy loves to speak in front of an audience and energises every room she walks into! When she steps offstage people say, 'Wow I wish I could speak like you do.' She used to say, 'Wow, thank you,' with grace, whilst on the inside being terrified that someone might find out how nervous she was onstage! This pattern wasn't limited to the stage, but played out in every space in which she thrived – she was waiting to be caught out for not being the real deal, because she looked confident, but on the inside felt like a churning mess!

Noticing that this wasn't helping anyone, and inspired to step into vulnerability, Amy started sharing her story. 'Actually, I'm terrified up there, but I care deeply about the work I do so I have worked really hard to wrangle my nerves and build my confidence and trust in myself over time.' This opened up much more interesting conversations! 'How do you do that? But you look so in control, could I do that?!' Amy stopped hiding behind the pretence of confident and started nurturing *confident enough* in herself and everyone she works with. Through thousands of conversations over the last fifteen years, Amy has honed a rich and pragmatic tool kit to help everyone she works with understand the impact they wish to have as a leader, how they want to do that and how to take the action needed every day to actually do hard things that matter, despite the discomfort and without losing yourself in the process.

Amy is a leadership coach, facilitator and speaker. Coaching since 2007, her business, Nurturing Confidence, helps emerging and high-potential leaders think more strategically, communicate more effectively, and lead themselves and others flexibly for greater impact on the world. She coaches mid-level leaders one to one and in small groups or focused cohorts, and works with teams in complex environments to transform the way they work together through uncertainty. Amy specialises in highly interactive and pragmatic learning experiences focused on building the confidence, resilience and wellbeing needed to stand out as an effective leader in high pressure workplaces.

With a qualification in psychology and experience of leadership in complex workplaces, Amy is a professional certified coach with the International Coaching Federation, with extensive professional expertise and accreditation including conversational intelligence, team coaching and mindfulness coaching. Amy's clients include state and federal governments in Australia, universities and mid-level business leaders from Michigan to Melbourne via Mauritius.

Website: nurturingconfidence.com.au
LinkedIn: linkedin.com/in/amyjackson

WINNING OR LEARNING
ANNA BARWICK

You are either 'winning or learning' in life. Or so said cowboy, Rip Wheeler, from the TV show *Yellowstone*.

But what does this actually mean … and how can leaders live by it? Here is my indispensable advice – yes, that is a pharmacist pun!

MINDSET MATTERS

Mindset can be your superpower. It is something I have been aware of, since I was a teenager, that has resulted in some amazing accolades as I have made my way through life.

My parents are farmers, and my mother is also a primary school teacher. They instilled in me a sense of equity and giving back to community. They set a wonderful example as volunteers on many committees and groups that supported local people to achieve common goals. They have also been advocates of healthy living by being aware of what you consume and how often you move your body. I am very grateful for their influence, and it has encouraged me to stand up for, and with, others to achieve a positive outcome. However, you can also choose to do this no matter what start you had in life.

A beautiful family friend became an unofficial grandmother and mentor to me when my own nan unexpectedly passed away in her sleep as a result of undiagnosed heart disease when I was sixteen. Pam was a maths teacher and remains an inspiration to me. We would meet weekly during my senior school years, sometimes for maths tutoring, but mostly to chat over a cup of tea and a biscuit.

She gifted me this wonderful quote by Napoleon Hill, just before I sat my final exams, and I have continued to use it throughout my life:

'Sooner or later the one who wins is the one WHO THINKS they CAN!'

It really encapsulates the need for a positive mindset. I often think of it when I'm experiencing imposter syndrome in new situations. I applied it when involved in the Sydney Royal Showgirl competition over a decade ago. On the first day of judging, in a week-long process, I introduced myself to a woman during the introductory social event. I could tell she was uncomfortable chatting and she finally admitted to being a judge. I was convinced I didn't have a chance of winning after the awkward interaction but I also decided to continue to take the opportunities presented to me. As a result, I enjoyed my time immensely and didn't spend time discussing what I should do to perform in front of the judges, as many of the others did. I realised I was being genuine and interested, which made all the difference. So convinced was I, that I told my partner at the time, who is now my husband, not to attend the presentation ceremony! Despite being the only participant at my local show level, I went on to be announced as the overall winner in 2008. I already was a winner before I arrived, so I was grateful and believed I could be an ambassador for rural women.

A mindset model that is often used in coaching is '*Be, do, have.*' It encourages people to first focus on who they have to *be* to reach a specific goal. Only then should you consider what you need to *do* to succeed. And afterwards, what you will *have* as a result. To be a leader, you need to act that way. You can be kind, generous, focused, energetic and passionate. Then you can do things like discuss goals with your team, celebrate your team wins and mail out thank-you cards or gift vouchers to team members who deserve it. As a leader, you will win when your team members win, and you will be recognised for it, earning accolades or financial success as a result.

When I started my own telehealth business, I labelled myself as the CEO (funnily enough, this is just a title that you don't have to justify to anyone, particularly as a startup company), and advertised positions on a profession-focused Facebook page. My team grew, as highly motivated pharmacists recognised their own goals in what my business offered. I promoted independent and flexible working conditions, the ability to apply education and skills, and the ultimate goal of the business – to help people where they are. I still have pharmacists contacting me weekly about employment opportunities, as they have become disillusioned with the system they are currently working in but want to use their experience and knowledge as medication experts to improve health outcomes. Being able to lead outstanding pharmacists to achieve even more has allowed me to develop and grow as a person and a professional. We are now seeing growth and investment in the business that I planned for, even when the business was only a concept. *Be, do, have* happened here; I was the leader, formed a cracking team, and we have now achieved success in many areas.

However, this didn't happen smoothly.

THE COURAGE TO FAIL

Putting yourself forward in situations where you will be the leader can be confronting. It will make you feel uncomfortable, and you will often question your ability to do what needs to be done. This is normal and a part of your growth as a leader. It will make you more empathetic and aware of yourself and your team members.

As CEO of a startup, many failures have and continue to occur.

Some have been out of our control, but all have been our responsibility. To begin a telehealth company required a steep learning curve on my part. I was not familiar with technology platforms that could be used and met the strict health and privacy guidelines required. I knew I had to try a number to find one that could do most of what we wanted. This was an expensive learning exercise, as each required a subscription and extensive set-up times. We have had to land on two different platforms to cover the requirements of our clients. Service outages have occurred, resulting in unhappy clients and wasted wages. Even though these events have happened, we have learned from them and implemented strategies to avoid them in the future. Had I been too worried about failures happening in the first place, I would never have been able to help people around the country with their medicines and health.

Put some skin in the game. Take a chance and try something new.

Maintain Your Curiosity

Becoming a mother after infertility struggles has made me busier than ever. But I have never been so aware and intentional. This is a direct result of seeing the world through my children's eyes. My children notice things I often miss. They will come and get me when I'm working to look at a rainbow or to show me a new bug they have found in the grass. And they will really look at people when we are in social situations, often asking about what they notice in the moment.

It has made me more mindful as a leader as well. I slow down when I am speaking to my team members and read their body language to ensure the messages match. Although we are located in different parts of the country, we video chat at least fortnightly. This enables us to address issues as they arise. I can check on their wellbeing and offer options if they are unable to complete a shift due to caring responsibilities or sickness. I also ask for their feedback on what I can do to make their job easier. Being curious about their thoughts and suggestions has resulted in new service offerings that have been very successful. I am able to learn more about what motivates them and offer incentives in different ways. We share resources and encourage one another to apply for funding and training that may be of benefit.

Curiosity helps you to learn and try.

LIFELONG LEARNING

Academia is well-known for this phrase. Obviously, there is a financial reason for institutions to push this, as it encourages formal learning and qualifications. But this isn't always necessary, particularly in leadership. I have learnt so many skills by building an innovative business without needing an MBA!

It is important to take advantage of training and grants that may assist you as a leader. Governments at all levels often encourage this through webinars, seminars or asynchronous online learning platforms. These are often discounted or fully subsidised. You can also find local business incubators that offer support and advice as well, to develop your entrepreneurship and leadership skills.

As a current PhD candidate, lifelong learning is a necessity. I have to be organised and make my way systematically through reems of papers and research to find the information that is needed. The PhD process also builds leadership skills, as it is a very independent journey, with advice from experienced academics. I have been invited to speak on my research into telepharmacy at a number of conferences and events. But I know once I achieve this goal, I will need to continue to evolve and learn to ensure I build my legacy.

You can never know enough.

GET HELP

Mentors and coaches – get yourself one or many!

I have been assertive in organising mentors to guide my leadership journey. Some have been formal, through professional organisations I am a part of, and others I have identified in social situations where I recognise an emotionally intelligent person. Mentors can provide an alternative point of view or identify the cause of an issue that you can't see as a result of your proximity to it. I have had mentors who are similar to me and ones who are very different. The best ones are those who will be truthful and don't just tell you that you're doing a great job. My mentors have identified areas of weakness and then we are able to discuss strategies for reducing or eliminating this.

This can also mean getting other people to do tasks you don't have the time to do. It took me a long time to realise I am not the only one who can grow my business. I have been able to assign roles to staff members who have a particular affinity with a task or want to build their skill set in a new area. I have also paid consultants to help with particular areas, such as marketing, where I don't have the space to build these skills myself. Often, consultants can help you to learn as well, so they are a good investment.

As you can see, when you push yourself beyond your comfort zone, you have two outcomes: you will either achieve what you set out to or you will gain skills and knowledge that will help you to do so in the future. Get out there – you will be winning or learning!

ANNA BARWICK

Anna Barwick is a senior lecturer in the School of Rural Medicine at the University of New England, Armidale, NSW. Anna is currently working on her PhD in telepharmacy at the University of Queensland, holds a Master of Clinical Pharmacy, is a practising consultant pharmacist, researcher, diabetes educator and immuniser.

Originally from Peak Hill, Anna, together with her husband Mathew, manage King's Pharmacy in Walcha, NSW, servicing a large regional population of more than three thousand people. They have two children, Evie (seven) and William (five), and live on a rural property raising Australian stock horses and miniature dachshunds in their spare time.

Anna is passionate about improving the health of all Australians through education, advice and advocacy. Anna's vision is to put a pharmacist into every household in the country, twenty-four hours a day, whenever people need help. Equipping and encouraging people to be able to advocate for themselves in the health system is an important legacy that she intends to leave behind.

Anna's research interests focus on women's health, including medical termination of pregnancy, domestic and family violence support, gestational diabetes, along with telehealth services and deprescribing of potentially harmful medication.

Anna was announced as the 2022 NSW Premier's Woman of the Year and the 2022 NSW Mineral's Council Regional Woman of the Year for her health and wellbeing innovation. Anna has been recognised as the PSA 2021 NSW Pharmacist of the Year and 2021 UTS Innovative Pharmacist of the Year. Anna is also a 2023-24 Science & Technology Australia Superstar of STEM.

Anna founded PharmOnline, an online advisory video telehealth service, to connect people with experienced pharmacists to discuss their medication. Inspired by her own limited access to health care in a rural area, Anna developed PharmOnline to be particularly valuable to people who are isolated and unable to easily access their local health services. PharmOnline was recently announced as the 2021 Outstanding Start Up in the New England Northwest and was runner-up in the AusMumpreneur Digital Innovation award.

PharmOnline is currently pioneering programs in Tasmania through the Pharmacist After Hours Advice Line (PAAL) through the Pharmaceutical Society of Australia supported by the Tasmanian Government and the national Gestational Diabetes Thrive Program supported by the NSW Government.

PharmOnline is unique as it centres on advice rather than product supply, unlike most existing pharmacy competitors. PharmOnline helps to reduce harm from medications through support from the medication experts: pharmacists. Our team includes qualified pharmacists located across Australia with a range of specialties. PharmOnline aims to offer twenty-four-seven access to pharmacists when and where people need them. We are able to achieve this by employing pharmacists across the country and taking advantage of different time zones to cover night availability. PharmOnline is building consumer products tailored to the needs of specific users. We are creating B2B products to build value and support the commercial ambitions of our business partners. PharmOnline solves the problem of access to convenient medication and health advice for people who are isolated or time-poor by offering online video telehealth access to pharmacists who can provide advice and care. Using a fee-for-service model, we can reduce the pressure on taxpayer-funded health care in Australia.

Website: pharmonline.com.au

DEMYSTIFYING MY LIFE
DR APARNA BARUAH

I am curious, and I love learning. I enjoy life in all its splendour. I enjoy the sound of rain, hot cups of tea, freshly baked cakes, laughing aloud, fashionable clothes, luxury abundance, dancing and having fun.

I also enjoy the complex stuff – metaphysical concepts, mystical texts, mind-boggling complex medicine and how to evolve with pain. I am sensitive, anxious, a perfectionist and gullible. I trust others easily and am influenced by opinions. The universe has provided me with assignments, from which I have seen a fair share of victories, as well as challenges and pain.

So far, I have been a radiologist, mother of two teenage boys, a daughter torn by pain, a pampered and supporting wife, a compassionate sister, a part-time professional musician, an author, an empathetic human and a spiritual seeker.

A decade ago, I was not the person I am today. Parts of my life were a myth. I was a product of my conditioned past and anxious future. I ticked all the 'right' boxes with a drive to excel. I was a high achiever, successful and smart. Yet, I had a void within me. I held on to pressures and expectations. I felt I was not my authentic self and kept searching for something. Something which would make me complete. I was unsettled, confused and agitated. I think I was happy but was always searching for something. Deep down I knew there was more to life, the way I had visualised, when all my ambitions were fulfilled. I questioned my vulnerability and pondered on my spiral of unhappiness. Nothing soothed me – the accolades, the achievements, motherhood, holidays, the increasing luxury. It was a golden cage.

I was born in an upper-middle-class Bengali family in India. I am the youngest of three siblings. My father was a civil engineer by profession. An honest man who was quiet and timid. My earliest memories of him are of his unfailing sun salutation every morning and praying to his late mother before leaving for work. My mother was a quintessentially Bengali woman as described by the Nobel Laureate Rabindranath Tagore. She was an example of emergence of the middle-class woman. She was revolutionary in her own right and represented autonomous self-development.

We lived in a small hill station Shillong, the capital of the north-eastern state of Meghalaya meaning 'Abode of Clouds'. As the name suggests, the lacy white clouds kissed the tall pines amongst the rolling hills. This was best appreciated as we drove down to the plains, through the curvilinear hilly terrain. The terraced cultivated farming lands, strewn with happy villages, amongst ragged hill-stones and inconspicuous waterfalls were serene to the eyes. We breathed cold air with a scent of pine.

Nature blessed Shillong with her love, lush green hills, plenty of rains, happy people. It was the winter capital for the British for the state of Assam. They brought in their culture, and Shillong became a mix of cultures, taking the best of all – elegant, cosmopolitan and vibrant.

I loved school and made friends easily. It was a common scene during lunch where I was surrounded by groups of girls. Some watching keenly, some critically and some rolling in laughter to my ever-evolving mimicry of our teachers. We hushed as soon as the nuns strolled by. They never forgot to remind us to tidy our skirt pleats and our half-opened red ribbons – even at recess.

WOMEN LEADING THE WAY

I was ambitious, conscientious and worked hard to maintain A grades. I loved performing on stage. In school, I sang hymns in the school choir and was actively involved in drama production and scriptwriting. At home, under the guidance of my mother, I was groomed in Indian classical and contemporary music. Travel, literature, art and culture were strewn into our daily lives. I actively participated in various talent competitions in our town, ranging from music to fashion shows. Our parents provided us with diverse experiences. My mother made us believe that you can pursue your passions avidly whilst maintaining academic accomplishments. She led by example and took every opportunity, even in her grey days, to actively participate in local community events.

My parents claimed that an essay from year four clearly described my ambition of being a doctor. I graduated school with meritorious results and migrated to a new state, Assam, to pursue my medical degree. I was eighteen and nervous to leave home for the first time. But I was ready. I was ready to wear the white coat, make new friends and be challenged by an inexhaustible curriculum. Five years of university flew past, and I graduated as a doctor. My eagerness to enhance my career led me to New Delhi, the capital of India. I had already left home and little did I know that I would soon depart my country for new beginnings.

In Delhi, while at work, I met my future husband. He was gentle, affectionate and genuinely cared for me. I knew my heart was ready to compromise everything. We dated for a short stint of three months. He flew overseas to pursue postgraduate education and left his heart with me. Soon after, we got married and wandered off to the UK, much further from home.

Everything in a marriage feels new. I was adjusting well into the new life of an immigrant, whilst learning the rhythm of being in a marriage. Like all other migrants, I had similar challenges of being a minority. Loss of connection, adapting to a new social set-up, in addition to pursuing postgraduate medicine, did overwhelm me at times. But by now, I had some opportunities to experiment with persistence and resilience; values instilled in childhood, and some I earned after leaving home.

Home became a distant past, and it was the comfort which remained whilst listening to our parents' voices, squabbling with siblings, and chatting for hours with dear friends, over the phone. We had a glorious decade and a half in the UK. Our lives were enriched with a mixture of challenges and victories. We were now eager to venture new lands, with a deeper desire to slow down the velocity of life. Perth promised us endless summer days, azure blue skies, foamy waves, kangaroos, jacaranda and all sounded exotic. Most importantly, I craved for work-life balance, completely unaware of the dimensions of life unfolding.

We migrated to Perth in September 2009. Perth was my true landing. I was now adapting to new challenges which were predominantly personal. I was juggling with motherhood and an ambitious career, whilst craving to pursue my hobbies. Life was getting more comfortable. I was now a consultant radiologist with a well-paid job. We had a good social circle and a stable family life with two wholesome boys. But there was a feeling of inadequacy. I was not satisfied with the life I had created. There was something missing. It was the *essence.*

I decided to work part-time and consciously create time to pursue the illusive meaning, the answer to the void I have always carried. This meant I had to create a new normalcy. Motherhood and career should no longer consume me. I still should have enough energy after work to run around with the boys to their swimming, tennis and piano lessons. I should have time for me and my hubby. I wanted time to indulge in morning teas, walks and yoga with my friends. I wanted time for creativity, especially music, which was a part of my being.

To successfully multitask, I created routine and discipline. Not only for the family but predominantly for myself. I also learned to delegate, trust babysitters and ask for help when needed. I consistently charted out time for my music, dance and yoga lessons. I factored in fun and involved friends and the community to join in group activities. I mentored, volunteered, taught whatever I knew. However, spare time did make me nervous. I wanted to escape time by doing mindless activities. Sometimes I did things I didn't enjoy and drained my energy but kept me busy mentally. This confused and agitated me. I was desperate to find solace. I had to come back home to myself – and the gateway was within me.

We all have certain traits in our personalities which distinguish us. Some we inculcate and some are engraved at a cellular level. I was always curious to understand life at a deeper level, and I delved into the spiritual path. I read, tried various meditation practices and attended a few retreats, but all argued with the intellect. Reluctantly, I persisted which did open up insights, revealing guidance. The most pertinent one for me was to dedicate work for the happiness of others.

The teal green diary with light blue stripes protected my dreams to live fully. A decade ago, it took the brunt of my bitterness, frustrations and confusions sporadically. But over the last few years, it's my prime witness of the pain of losing both parents over a short two years.

I lost my parental home, my identity of being someone's child, and I felt rudderless. I needed an anchor. Loss brings moments of introspection for us to heal. The inner journey of self-realisation and coming to terms with the profound reality of *'death'* opens up channels of personal growth. My inner journey had begun without my realisation, and I went with the flow.

The process started deconstructing my thoughts. For starters, I realised I was accountable for my happiness. It was no longer someone else's fault. I was tired of justifying, blaming and feeding my negative state of mind. I was ready and determined to flourish and contribute in meaningful ways in all aspects of my life, whilst maintaining stability within the family. I started choosing to do things which gave me meaning and purpose.

Teaching and mentoring gives me purpose and pleasure. I actively participate in teaching activities and mentoring junior doctors. I volunteer in medical universities to engage in the selection process of medical students. My minimal contribution in optimising the selection of best health care advocates gives me satisfaction. I feel gratitude and a deep sense of contribution sharing my life lessons. I feel privileged where I can make a change. As a career woman, I realised I don't have to jump into every opportunity that comes my way to enhance my career. I can choose what suits my goals and my visions.

It was February 2020, and we were still enjoying summer in Perth. We were aware of a spreading Chinese virus but had no imagination of the aftermath. Soon, lockdowns, social distancing and masks were the new norm. Borders were closed and socio-economic infrastructure was changing fast. Time was again created, and it definitely slowed down the momentum of our fast-paced lives. I was already more present, with spirituality as my companion. Regular meditation and yoga did enhance my creative faculties and I started exploring.

I started online music lessons from a famous vocal coach in Mumbai and had an unexpected opportunity to make music videos. Little did I know, becoming a professional musician in the new millennia has its own set of challenges. I had to be become savvy with social media platforms. I learned quickly, but surely, how intimidating it is to be in the public eye. I was unsure of how this would work and if I could deliver what was expected. I had a secure life with all the comforts, and I had lots of questions within me. Will things fall apart whilst pursuing my passion? I also knew questions were being asked.

These are pivotal moments of your life which make or break you. On one hand you have opportunities knocking, on the other hand, you lack an infrastructure of support.

But I decided to show up for myself, breaking the norms of security and comfort. I wanted to redefine my successful life. I wanted to take risks and live the life of my dreams. Six music videos including two original songs were created in this unplanned journey over two years.

I realised that comfort, stagnation and lethargy can too be your teachers. They give you space. I grew from the space of being adequate, being comfortable, being abundant.

I have now been married for just over two decades. My husband is a busy medical practitioner and an explorer with an entrepreneurial mindset. A big risk-taker at heart, he always treaded unknown waters. We are radically different in our approach to life, likely secondary to our upbringing and experiences. He sorts out problems within himself and loves solitude. On the contrary, I love company and need solutions to my problems instantaneously by discussing matters with my trusted friends and family. In my second and third decade, I gravitated towards believing that a woman had to slow down, create space and stability in the family when the spouse is in the ascending curve of his career. This self-sacrificing attitude is an accolade for women and validated as a general norm in our society. I questioned this as I introspected my life. I deeply wanted a balance with my ascending career and a stable family life whilst pursuing my hobbies. This was my vision of my richest life, as I got ready to live the life of my dreams.

I surprised myself driving simultaneously in an ascending career, whilst managing home and a family. I focus on quality rather than quantity. I share responsibility with my spouse and strive to make my boys independent. We made some ground rules too. The most pertinent one is that every night we share dinner as a family. No matter how exhausted, frustrated, happy or bored our days are, we aim to share our stories and emotions at the dining table, no matter how brief they are. I want my boys to believe in the value of family support, which in turn gives us the confidence to be limitless.

As you become a reflector of your life, you start owning parts of yourself which are vulnerable, faulty and inauthentic. This is courage.

But when you do, the magic unfolds and allows your true authenticity to bloom. You give yourself permission slips to do things which make you happy. Have diverse experiences in all facets of life which enrich you. You don't have to choose or limit yourself to just one thing. If you have the immense energy bestowed on you and the capacity to juggle different opportunities at once, you can keep shining and become unstoppable. It's your energy of manifestation which will inspire and empower others. They will see they too can break open new paths for themselves by following their inner voices and trusting the wisdom of their hearts. Don't question why you do what you want to do. As long as it excites you and makes you feel alive – go for it! You are a unique masterpiece, so celebrate yourself by demystifying your life.

My journey so far is one of self-realisation and self-discovery. I learned to lean in and grow with pain and pleasure alike. I am grateful to my parents and my family who love me unconditionally. I am blessed with a career which gives me countless opportunities to make a difference every day. I thank India for my roots and heritage. The two chosen countries have provided us the lives we lead today, with bags full of memories and experiences. When I look back, I am amazed to see how far I've come. I was brought up in a small place in north-east India, where a foreigner needed a special permit to visit until two decades ago. It was remote and non-progressive compared to other flourishing parts of India. Yet I always thought I had an edge, a head start in life, being brought up there. This was not only because of the quality of education or the cosmopolitan culture. We were cushioned in the comforts of a caring home and community, which knew 'how to give, more than to get'.

I realise I have a deep sense of personal responsibility to encourage people to dream. Dreaming and yearning can carry people forward. Today I am adorned with my faults, failures, victories, growth, healing and evolvement. I am work in progress …

DR APARNA BARUAH

Dr Aparna Kahali Baruah is a consultant radiologist, currently working at Sir Charles Gairdner Hospital, Perth, Western Australia. She graduated from India and migrated to the UK to pursue further training and now lives in Perth, Australia.

Aparna has multifaceted interests and currently she is pursuing music professionally and has her own YouTube channel. She is passionate about dance, yoga and meditation. As a woman of multidimension, mother of two, working part-time, having diverse interests with a parallel career in professional music, Aparna is passionate about engaging and guiding the newer generation. A role model to show that one can pursue their passions and have a healthy work-life balance. Her mantra is: create the life you want in your vision board first and we can have it all.

Her creative facets along with her spiritual mindset took her to an inward journey during COVID-19 days. The feeling of losing control as a doctor, as a human and losing parents conceived a book within her. She wrote a collection of short stories, a catharsis for her soul, and was guided by intuition, synchronicities and a deeper knowing.

DR APARNA BARUAH

Dr Aparna Kahali Baruah is the author of the book *Forget Me Not*, a collection of short stories. Like the flower, the stories embody good memories, love and joy.

FIND YOUR PEOPLE
ALLISON RAHMAN

The title of this book, *Women Leading the Way,* is very intimidating in some ways. One of my best friends told me I needed to be a part of this book and when I asked why, her response was, 'Because you're a leader, you need to tell your story, it will be good for you, therapeutic.' I had a think about it – and well, here I am.

The word 'leader' got me thinking. What is a leader and why are some of us leaders and others not? What does it take to be a leader or are we born that way? I don't think it's something I ever put too much thought into until now. But to be honest, I've had several people over the years tell me *I lead*. One person at work even used the words, 'People are drawn to you and seem to follow you.' So, I started to think, am I like that in my personal life too, or is this all a facade? Do I act one way at work and another in my personal life? Do I have two personalities, and do I need a diagnosis?

So, before I go and interrogate all the people I work with, my friends and partner, or run to the doctor for a diagnosis, I decided it would be wise to write down why I think I am a leader; what made me the person I am today.

The short story began in London. Born and bred British in the 1980s, my memories of my childhood are a mix of positive and negative.

ALLISON RAHMAN

I grew up in a Bengali culture full of fancy Indian clothes and jewellery, however, I always looked a little bit different from my cousins and other family members – you see, my skin colour was lighter. I was the lighter one, while everyone else had darker skin. I was always welcomed by my extended family and accepted, although always looked slightly out of place wearing my Indian clothing standing next to my cousins. From the age of three to nine, I lived with my father, however, I spent most my time with my cousins. I grew up in a culture that didn't respect women. Women were the ones who raised the kids, kept the house and did whatever the husband requested. Children were seen but not heard. Women were beaten if they 'got out of line, or in the way'. I also have two older siblings – a brother, nine years older, and a sister, eight years older. When I was three, a decision was made to migrate to Australia. This didn't quite work out and I returned to London with my father and brother. I never really understood or questioned the reasons why. It never even occurred to me to ask those details. At forty-two years old, I have now started to put all the pieces together.

I grew up without a mother. Tragic, right? Well, as you will learn, it was probably for the best as she chose a life in Australia that didn't involve me. She chose fun, affairs and a life without much responsibility. Growing up in London was challenging. Most memories are negative, to be honest. Looking back now, I believe I was treasured by my father, however, I lived a life of loneliness and not-belonging, which only got worse at the age of nine when my father remarried. I often felt like a hindrance to the evil stepmother. I was an extra. She just wanted my father, and I was an unfortunate part of the package – much like cardamon pods in curries, it's necessary for the flavour but not pleasant when you bite into one.

So now that I have compared myself to a cardamon pod, I will move on to tell you that the next four years, I was living a life in constant fear, wondering whether I was in trouble for something and being hit repeatedly with a wooden spoon for simple things such as spilling rice on the table during dinner or just basically being who I was. I didn't have the same skin colour as them and didn't fit in. Was I a leader then? Certainly not. I was an outcast.

During the next four years I was isolated from my extended family. I was no longer able to see the people I grew up with and eventually made the choice to move to Australia to meet the mother I never knew, the person I had no memories of and the person who chose a life without me in it. Flying alone to Australia at age thirteen, the air hostesses were responsible for me. I spent the entire trip sick, physically vomiting. The hostesses took me to a doctor in Bangkok to get me something to stop the vomiting. I didn't take the large pink pills for fear they would knock me out and someone would kidnap me to sell me for my parts. I was thirteen and had a large imagination, but I now realise my body was reacting to the stress of moving to another country with no knowledge of what was ahead of me, as I didn't know the people I was going to be living with.

At thirteen, travelling across the world alone to meet someone I didn't know was scary. My life in Australia was good at first; it was promising. I met my mother, my soon-to-be stepfather, my brother and sister, and all her family. I was welcomed, and life was good. I was living without fear, I had a good group of friends at school and started to discover boys. I felt cared for and had a relatively normal life – if there is such a thing. At the age of fifteen, things changed for me when my stepfather touched me sexually. I shut down after this and stopped talking to people. He drove me to work one day and told me to, 'Get over it and start behaving.' So once again, I did as I was told. I was able to put it behind me and move on. Life was different for me emotionally, again. Was I a facade? Was I living a life that was fake? Was I not allowing my emotions to tell the truth? I certainly wouldn't have considered myself a leader.

ALLISON RAHMAN

LEARN FROM YOUR MISTAKES

Without having anyone to really trust or rely on in life, I was forced to rely on myself at an early age. I became a leader of my own life. At the age of eighteen, I moved out of home during the last week of school, with my then boyfriend, later my husband. We spent some time in Brisbane before moving to Darwin after we got married at the young age of twenty-three. I may have moved across the world to live with people I didn't know, but moving across the country to start again was surprisingly more challenging. I soon found out how bad I was at spelling. I was shit at my job and was on the brink of being fired. So, what do you do in these circumstances? I don't know if it was fear of being without a job or the feeling of being ashamed of my lack of skills that drove me to work harder, to step up, but I started to bring my work home, re-read my work and essentially taught myself to spell. I was learning from my own mistakes. I ended up loving my job and the people I worked with. I was surrounded by strong women, leaders; my first real role models. Life was pretty good. My husband and I were growing and establishing our life together. This is the time of my life where I believe I became the most resilient. This job ended way too soon. After four and a half years we moved back to Brisbane, where life was going to change drastically.

My husband and I bought a house around the corner from my mother and stepfather, which changed the dynamics of my relationship with my husband. My husband was now hanging out with my stepfather almost every day. This is where I saw the changes in my husband, as he became more like my stepfather. I was again feeling lonely. My stepfather owned a small business in the care industry. On the face of it, the business was going well for him. I did a few casual shifts in the business to help them out during Christmas and New Year periods and I was also working my nine-to-five role in a law firm. I was on maternity leave when the call came – the call that put me in a position where

I would need to step it up once again. I would become responsible for a business overnight.

CREATE OTHER LEADERS

'We have a situation!' I was told when I got to my mother's house. She was there with my stepfather and his sister. I was juggling a nine-month-old on my hip as I sat down to listen to the drama unfold. My stepfather threw his hands in the air and ran, split town, and disappeared. The business was in significant debt. The directors at the time were draining it of money. It was a failing business, full of dishonest dealings and debt. The business had potential for a good income stream, however, my stepfather and his business partner were still able to drive it into the ground.

With a strong amount of dedication and hard work, I managed to pull the broken business out of the dirt. I paid back the debt and eventually grew the company to have a turnover in the millions. This was success. This was what it was like to lead a company. I was responsible for over eighty employees. I had to be a leader, right? That was what it was all about after all. Is a leader defined as a person who commands a group or organisation? No! Being a leader isn't about being a boss, it's not about making money. As I continued to find out, being a successful leader is natural when you have a true passion in everything you do. Trusting in yourself first and then encouraging others to do well, even if that means one day those people become your competition. Leadership is about creating other leaders, and you do this by showing faith in others and challenging them and accepting challenges when you are faced with them.

There were many challenges running this business. I was not only dealing with a man who had ruled by intimidation and scare tactics to get his way. I was dealing with something much worse. Someone who was looking for her way in at every turn. Someone driven by greed, so much so, anyone that stood in her way and said no would bear the wrath of her evil ways. If I didn't have a wicked stepmother to deal with, I had something worse. Cruella at her finest, also known as, MY MOTHER.

Not long after my divorce, I stopped talking to my stepfather. I still held his secret, however, I had chosen not to allow him in my life. He knew his bread was buttered as he was set to receive a handsome six-figure salary once he returned to work, as did Cruella. But both only worked sixteen hours per fortnight. Cruella whinged about her husband; he was a gambler, a smoker, a drinker. I'd heard it all before but continued to listen as she joked about him dying and giving her all the money. She would joke about divorcing him. As time went on, the continued pressure from Cruella to talk to him was unbearable, so I told her. He had done something to me that I could not forgive. The truth was out.

SHOW COURAGE WHEN NEEDED

I received the call from Cruella: 'Can you come over now? I want this all out in the open.' So, off I went over to their house to confront the secret I had been holding for far too long. I had no reason to keep this secret anymore. Cruella taped the conversation without us knowing and used this against him, and later against me. She gained his shares in the business – and bam, there you go, half the shares in a business worth millions, while she did nothing to get there.

It didn't take long before the true colours of Cruella came out. The visits to the office became more frequent. She would hang around like some bad smell. The demands continued. 'What is all that money doing in the bank? What are you keeping it there for? I want more money.' As if the current six-figure salary was not enough for sixteen hours of work per fortnight. You see, Cruella was used to getting her own way. Continued demands soon turned to baiting me, pointing, and demanding more money, taping conversations that she later used in an Australian national news show. She claimed she was the poor, hard done by grandmother whose business was stolen from her. Several death threats followed directed towards me and my children. I still wonder how an Australian national news show can air a one-sided story without the producers being responsible for the consequences, including the mental health issues and threats to children's safety. How could this not be a concern to them? They got their juicy story; whether it was true or not did not seem to matter.

FIND YOUR PEOPLE

Cruella transcribed the taped conversations of the sexual assault for the world to see and served them to me at home on a Friday night. After reading the documents, claiming I caused her divorce and fabricated a sexual assault, I decided enough was enough. I attempted to take my own life. I was fortunate enough to have three wonderful strong women in my life at the time. The support they gave me throughout is something phenomenal. These three women saved my life. I will never forget the moment I woke up in hospital and saw one of my best friends sitting next to me. I had no idea where I was or how long I had been there. All I can say is, I was thankful she was there, a familiar face. I was sent home with her, with strict instructions for her to stay with me. These women banded together to nurture, support and hold me up. They went into damage control with the business and spoke to my lawyers. However, I was not going to be held down; people needed me to show up. The Monday morning, I left home and drove to work. With puffy eyes and wobbly legs, I will never forget the look on their faces when I turned up to work. They stared at me as I walked past them as if nothing happened. 'Morning,' I said as I let myself in and sat at my desk, ready for a busy week ahead. Having these women in my life was what held me together. People were relying on me; I was not going to let anyone down.

Fast-forward three years, I am lucky enough to have a wonderful partner who saw through the misinformation in the press, who loves and supports me with everything I do. Behind every leader is a network that provides the foundations of support. Leadership is about learning from your own mistakes, creating other leaders that then go on to lead and show courage when needed. This can only be done with the support of 'your people' – the people who believe in you and what you stand for.

ALLISON RAHMAN

As an entrepreneur and mother of two, I have had the pleasure of creating many businesses and helping people thrive. I am driven by the ethos of working hard gets you what you want and always stand up for what is right. I have had a successful career starting out in the legal industry and later moving into the human services sectors. I am currently running several successful businesses including a disability support organisation and I am also an assessor within the Human Services Quality Framework and the National Disability Insurance Scheme. My goal is to share knowledge, create other leaders and stand up for what is right. My ethos is to lead by example even when faced with hard times. I believe life throws us many challenges, however, it is easier to face those challenges when you choose to surround yourself with people who genuinely support you. In return you support and hold up others when needed. Family and friends can be chosen, sometimes you need courage to make the choice and sometimes you are forced to make the choice, however, when you do choose the right people to be in your life, you will find success and strength comes naturally.

SOMETIMES IT CAN COME OUT OF NOWEHRE ...
CLARE REILLY

Leading the way can smack you in the face like a brick; you can see no other option but to take the steps into the limelight. It can happen this way, but for me it was a very different and very slow process.

Growing up, I had a passion for nature and being outdoors. I went on to become a professional outdoor educator. I was active. I rock-climbed, white-water paddled, camped and hiked. This is how I spent my private time and how I earnt a living.

When I received my multiple sclerosis diagnosis, I heard it through a tin-can phone, distant and echoey. The words, unclear. Wading through mud, I made the confused, quick and ill-informed decision as to which medication I would take to suppress my immune system from attacking itself, I then put my head firmly in the sand.

A month later, my husband, our two-and-a-half-year-old son and I uprooted our lives and moved a five-hour drive away from everything we knew to start a new job. We were to direct an off-grid, no electricity, remote outdoor education centre, where we would be in charge of managing a staff team, coordinating staff training, managing the sixty-acre hobby farm (with sheep, alpacas and a vegetable garden bigger than the footprint of our home), booking the calendar with school programs, liaising with schools, teachers, parents and local community members, coordinating Monday-to-Friday school programs, and being on call twenty-four seven in case of emergencies when our staff and participants were out in the field on hikes.

The centre was nestled on a river flat, at the base of the Victorian Alpine National Park. To one side, an inaccessible hill rose straight up to the sky. The other edge of the river flat was hugged by the wild McAlister River, leading to the gorge. No vehicle access to the property made provisioning difficult, carrying 20kg bulk bags of oats and flour from our cars up a short rocky track to load onto the platform of a flying fox. When the platform was full, a staff member would find a seat amongst the staples, the flying fox would get released, and *WHOOSH*, it would zoom for 100m across and 50m above the river.

For those years, I felt the stress of long work hours and internalised ableism weighing down on me and my MS symptoms.

Up until this point, my symptoms were primarily invisible. They were predominantly pain and shame. The shame of 'letting' this happen to me. The shame of not being able to control my body and this disease. The shame of not being able to win out over my body. Questions echoed in my thoughts. *Why did this happen to me? What is my future going to look like? Will I be able to continue living the life I have dreamed of? How am I going to parent?* I had so many questions that no-one could answer.

While I pottered in the 100sqm vegetable garden, all I wanted was to hear stories of other people with multiple sclerosis, living whole, full lives; not letting anything stop them. I wanted a podcast I could plug in and listen to on my own, to grieve the life I had planned and learn how others lived with this debilitating, incurable disease.

After our two-and-a-half-year contract ended, we moved home to our sweet seaside community. It was there that, finally, I could no longer hide from my diagnosis. As my husband began to feel refreshed, resting from the exhaustion of the last couple of years, I still felt pain and crushing fatigue. I sobbed with grief, I screamed with anger and withdrew from myself.

Ever so slowly, I came back to myself. I began to utilise medical professionals from whom I had previously hidden. I gained access to the National Disability Insurance Scheme, which financially supported my medical needs.

And I found myself in a position where I felt emotionally stronger and more confident with myself and my diagnosis. I was able to start facing what I had needed when I was first diagnosed with the debilitating incurable disease.

This is where I fell into leading; into being an advocate for those living with MS and other invisible autoimmune diseases.

RESPECTFUL CURIOSITY

I was curious. About multiple sclerosis. About people living with it. About disability. About the symptoms people live with. I had so many questions about people and the world around me that I'd never even considered before. To find answers, I was going to need to be a detective of the most genuine and kind sort. I was going to need to be a news reporter and interview people on this sensitive topic, with respectful curiosity. I was intensely curious, and with my long list of questions, I was ready to find answers.

Leading and being curious about the world around you go hand in hand. Regardless of who you're speaking with, what their ailment is, where they're from, their background, religion, gender or beliefs, leading with respectful curiosity is the key. Curiosity alone isn't enough. Curiosity alone can be confronting, rude and offensive. Enquiring about other human beings requires gentle curiosity. And leading requires knowledge about your audience, your peers, colleagues and staff.

Starting conversations with questions like:
- Can I ask about …?
- Do you want to talk about …?
- Am I allowed to ask about …?
- Do you want to share more about …? Please feel free to tell me to shove it if this is not the right time or place.

These are all brilliant ways of treading gently and enquiring respectfully about people's life situations. This is the way you are going to get to know your community and lead with gentle, respectful curiosity. With the information you can garner, you can determine what more is needed in your field, business, workplace or how to be a better leader.

When speaking with people from across the globe, I met their stories with gentle, respectful curiosity. I learnt about their symptoms, how they lived their lives, what impacted them the most and how they stayed positive while experiencing their bodies declining. And all the while, I remained greatly curious. Curious about how my life would look, looking for stories I could relate to, and if there would be any reflection of my life in their stories.

I was then able to share these stories with my audience (with permission, of course), and the feedback was testament that this was something the community needed.

Creating what I needed, stories of others living with multiple sclerosis, was borne out of respectful curiosity.

CREATE WHAT YOU NEED

After spending two years in grief after receiving my diagnosis, spending that time in shame and stressing wildly about the unknown, I felt able to create what I needed to more-effectively manage my health; something I should have done when I was first diagnosed. I found help medically and emotionally through a wonderful medical support team filled with physiotherapists, an occupational therapist, psychologists and an MS nurse. I knew there was still a place in the world for what I needed when I had been first diagnosed. Relatable stories from real people living their life with MS.

I needed to hear the stories of others living a whole, beautiful and full life with MS. If I hadn't been through the initial shock of diagnosis, if I hadn't craved relatable stories, I wouldn't have been able to visualise and put myself in the position of those who would be following in my footsteps. Diagnosis of a chronic illness is terrifying, and for someone to be providing exactly what I needed when I was diagnosed was key.

By creating what you need, you know there will be someone else out there craving the same thing. So, I set to work building what I knew was missing from our community.

The messages and feedback I have received have confirmed that others have been seeking exactly what I needed and have created. While it wasn't available when I needed it, it'll be out there for others to utilise when they need a friendly voice to tell them that, while their diagnosis sucks, it's absolutely not the end of the world. Just the end of the world as they know it.

YOU DO YOU, BOO

Forget what everyone says about you not being your brand. These days the individual is absolutely what the audience is following. When leading, you need to be 100% yourself and lead as only you can.

Your style of leadership and your brand are going to stand out because – you are you! There could be hundreds of other people doing the same thing but no-one has your style.

There may be something out there very similar to what you are creating but no-one will be able to do it like you. No-one will be able to advertise like you; no-one will be able to share like you; no-one will have your stories to share with the world, allowing different people to relate to what you're producing.

DIVE ON IN

Jump in! Do it! Even if you don't think you're ready, or are waiting for some other penny to drop, as Nike says, 'Just Do It', because what you are creating is needed in the world. When I became a leader in the disability and multiple sclerosis community, I had no idea what I was doing. But thinking about creating *what I needed* and creating it with respectful curiosity, I knew it was time. I stepped up and started sharing my experiences and my stories, and people related to them.

However, there is a limit to this. I wasn't emotionally ready to create, to lead and to share my story with the world when I was initially diagnosed. Only when I had the medical and emotional support and had begun to come to terms with my diagnosis was I able to share what I knew needed to be released into the world. I needed to be leading myself first. So, I waited until I was ready, emotionally, but when I was, I dove in headfirst.

I didn't know what it would take to be a leader. I didn't know what it would take to create what I wanted to share. With a lot of googling and reaching out for help, I was able to share the stories. When you're asking for help, all people can say is 'yes' or 'no'; you have a 50% chance of people helping you out. And if you're doing something with purpose, creating what you know needs to exist, then others will see that too.

Initially, I reached out to quite well-known people in the multiple sclerosis community, people who had no reason to help me, but who saw what I was going to create would help so many others in the same position we'd been in.

As a leader in the disability community, you can only do it your way.

You can only share what you know, as everyone's experiences are different. You need to be open to this as a leader in any space; you only know your experiences and can only lead from a space of knowledge.

Leadership comes in many shapes and sizes. My diagnosis led me down the path to create a resource I wished was available when I was first diagnosed. It led me down a path of leadership and disability advocacy. I created a resource that has now been utilised across the globe, something I never could have imagined when I set to work developing what I had needed.

Treating my peers living with multiple sclerosis with respectful curiosity was key to being able to kindly share their stories with my audience. Sharing my stories was key to creating and supporting my newly diagnosed self. To hear real stories from other people living with multiple sclerosis had the wonderful added benefit of these stories resonating with an audience too. I honestly believe there's only one way to lead in the current climate and that is to be yourself – *full stop*. Your audience may resonate with your product but YOU and your personality, who you are, your story and the connections you make with them are what is going to sell it to them. And finally, start before you're ready. You'll make mistakes, you'll stumble along the way, but only then are you going to be able to get to the good stuff.

More than ever before, I am now confidently myself. With the grey fog of a chronic illness diagnosis clouding my everything, I have rediscovered my why, my purpose and my passions. They have shone through the fog, like sunshine clearing the morning mist over the ocean.

CLARE REILLY

Clare Reilly (she/her) was diagnosed with multiple sclerosis (MS) in April 2017. With a background in outdoor education, Clare loves to spend time outdoors, albeit slightly differently these days. Clare lives on the Bellarine Peninsula, near Geelong, with her husband and son, and loves an early morning dip in Port Phillip Bay. Clare is a creative, who loves to try her hand at various arts and crafts, including painting, ceramics, book nooks (seriously, check them out) and is passionate about stepping lightly on the planet and sharing really good food with loved ones.

Clare is an advocate for those living with MS and other chronic illnesses. She shares funny, sometimes confronting and thought-provoking posts and Reels on Instagram and TikTok. Clare hosts the podcast *MS Understood* – conversations about multiple sclerosis with people from all over the world. She loves the community feel and support she both gives and receives via Instagram and through the podcast. A question Clare asks at the end of every podcast episode is, 'What is the best thing to have happened because you were diagnosed with MS?' Clare's answer is the incredible community that she has discovered, the empathy she has developed and the self awareness and confidence that has emerged since diagnosis.

When Clare began creating and hosting the *MS Understood* podcast, she had no idea how to produce a podcast, let alone invite high-profile people to be guests and share their stories on a wide platform. But after diving in feet first, there are now almost one hundred episodes available to listen to. The hope being that people who are newly diagnosed with the autoimmune disease can find a story they relate to, that gives a spark in the dreary, overwhelmed world of the newly diagnosed and to help family and friends understand what their loved ones might be going through.

Guests on the *MS Understood* podcast have included Tim Ferguson of The Doug Anthony All Stars, Chantelle Otten, award-winning sexologist, and Emily Padfield from Netflix *Win the Wilderness*, as well as incredible people who shared the stories of living MS so vulnerably.

Clare was awarded the Gold Disabled Business Excellence award for Victoria and the Silver Disabled Business excellence award for Australia in the AusMumpreneur Awards 2022. Clare has written a chapter in an anthology *Renewal – Lived and Learned Advice To Give.*

In the future, once Clare has finished her Bachelor of Psychological Science she hopes to work one on one with people who have a new disability or chronic illness diagnosis in a therapy and counselling capacity and hopes to write a novel with her name on the cover.

Website: clarereilly.com
Instagram: instagram.com/Clare.Reilly
TikTok: @clarereilly
LinkedIn: linkedin.com/in/clare-reilly-85a3301ba
Email: clare@clarereilly.com

LEAD YOURSELF FIRST
DR EMMA BARRETT

I remember sitting in the doctor's office, my face was red and my scrub shirt wet from tears.

I had recently had my second baby, fourteen months after my first. When my newborn was three weeks old, the only other vet practice within a 500km radius closed their doors, leaving me as the sole vet in the whole region.

In addition, my mum had recently been diagnosed with breast cancer; news that came as a crushing blow.

Both babies needed me throughout the night, as did many pets, their owners desperately calling for help at all hours. I was working seventy to eighty hours a week and hadn't slept for as long as I could remember. Hormones were wreaking havoc on my body and the emotional and physical stress had taken its toll.

I had reached complete burnout.

Not that you would have known from the outside. I was great at wearing a mask of bravado – a smile that said, everything is fine.

Just keep working, working, working, bury yourself in busyness and it's got to get better, right?

After I had poured my heart out, my doctor looked at me. I could see the sadness and genuine concern in her eyes. She calmly said, 'You need to slow down, you need to take a break.'

It wasn't the first time I'd heard it, but it was the first time I really admitted to myself that I needed help. What I was doing was not working. All the things I was juggling were about to come crashing to the ground because, as the one who was keeping all the balls in the air, I was drowning.

I was being torn in all directions and failing to show up for myself. By the time I had given to my children, family, team and clients, there was nothing left. The problem was, I was not giving anyone anywhere near the best version of me.

I needed to lead myself before I was able to lead anyone else. I had driven myself into my current reality, so I was responsible for driving myself out. I just wasn't sure how!

I was born in the spring of 1984 on a banana plantation in the Gascoyne. The first child for my parents, who worked long hard hours on the farm. Our livelihood depended on so many uncontrollable external factors and the hard work was often for little financial reward. Still, my parents made endless sacrifices to ensure their children were educated and never went without. They wanted more for us.

From my very earliest memories of childhood, I wanted to be a vet. I worked hard at school and put in extra hours of study to ensure I gained a first-round placement in my chosen degree.

All my life, it had been evident to me that the only road to success was to work, and when you were done, to work some more.

In 2006, I was honoured to don my cap and gown as I accepted my graduate certificate in Bachelor of Science and Bachelor of Veterinary Medicine and Surgery from Murdoch University. My parents beamed with pride, and I felt invincible, with stars in my eyes.

My career as a vet was very nearly over before it began.

I felt as if I had won the career lottery, doing what I loved and giving back to the small community who had supported me throughout my life.

Within a month of graduating, I was sent on a locum placement to the Pilbara region of Western Australia to be a sole charge vet in three branch practices.

I had never even completed a full surgery on my own and I was expected to run three clinics – alone and without any support! The pressure quickly took its toll and after a few weeks, I had lost over 10kg and was admitted to hospital suffering severe anxiety and heart arrhythmia; a full breakdown was imminent.

This was not the start to my career I had dreamt of and I was very close to giving up on what I had worked so hard to achieve. I am now passionate about ensuring new graduates get a much better start than I had, and there is still a lot of work to be done in the industry.

Within a couple of months, I was blessed to have an experienced vet join the practice. Dani became my mentor and very close friend, and was instrumental in supporting me in continuing in the profession. I worked closely with Dani for nine years, and in 2015, I went on to take over the practice she established in 2009.

The dive into business ownership simultaneously with motherhood has been my biggest test of resilience – and tested how I saw myself as a leader.

'Our greatest weakness lies in giving up. The most certain way to succeed is always to try just one more time.' – Thomas Edison

Both Dani and my mother, Nella, are huge influences in my life. They are the epitome of strength and resilience, even in the face of adversity, juggling careers, hobbies, ill health and multiple children, seemingly with ease.

In my mind, and to my own detriment, if they could do it all and make it look easy, so could I!

I wasn't the first working mother to feel overwhelmed, why was I complaining? I had two beautiful, healthy children, my own business and a career I had dreamt about since I was a little girl. The time was flying by, and I had become a spectator in my own life instead of actively taking charge of my future.

I had become so fixated on working hard, being busy and living up to what I thought was expected of me that I didn't have the capacity to just enjoy my blessings and be grateful.

It was time to set boundaries.

'Love yourself enough to set boundaries. Your time and energy are precious. You get to choose how you use it. You teach people how to treat you by deciding what you will and won't accept.' – Anna Taylor

So, what next?

I had to let go of the idea that being busy equalled success. It's difficult to stop doing things when they have become routine, even if they no longer serve you or you no longer enjoy doing them.

For years I had committed to a weekend horse racing contract. In the beginning I had enjoyed it, as my family had been involved in the racing industry since I was a baby. As the years went on, I continued to do it because I didn't want to let anybody down, especially a club that held so many fond memories for me.

At one particular Sunday race meet, just before the last race was about to jump, I was asked a question. My children were one and two at the time and I'd already worked long hours the six days prior.

'Is this the only day off you would have had with your children this week?'

When I hesitantly replied yes, I was then asked, 'Well why don't you just say no? They'll find someone else'.

At that moment, I realised I could just stop. A huge weight lifted from my shoulders.

To everyone, except my children, I was replaceable. It was a light-bulb moment. I could just say no! It was really that simple, and now, I have gotten really good at setting boundaries and saying no.

It was okay to be selfish, because by being selfish, I was able to take back control and be a better version of myself for my children and my business.

WOMEN LEADING THE WAY

As I began to prioritise myself and work on my self-worth, I knew I deserved better in life and wanted more for my children. I felt a deep responsibility to teach my children how they should be treated. In doing so, I became a single mum of two kids under the age of two.

A whole new set of challenges were presented to me as I navigated co-parenting, but I was happier than I'd been in years. You deserve to be happy, treat yourself like you treat those you love the most.

Scheduling some time for myself gave me space to breathe and work my way through the fog.

'She stood in the storm and when the wind did not blow her way, she adjusted her sails.' – Elizabeth Edwards

I now had to get clear on where I wanted to go and my reason for doing so – my why. If you don't know exactly what it is that you want, it can be easier to write down everything you don't want and reverse-engineer your vision from there.

It felt silly at the time, but I sat down and wrote out my perfect day with extreme clarity and detail. I needed to change my story and believe I was going to create the changes I needed to live the life I was yearning for.

If you have no idea where you are going, you're guaranteed to not get there.

'The only thing worse than being blind is having sight but no vision.' – Helen Keller

Part of creating your vision with clarity involves working out your why. If your vision and why aren't strong and clear enough, then it's easy to lose focus.

Why are you in business? Why are you embarking on this adventure? Why do you want to make changes? Why do you want to be a leader?

My beautiful children, Archer and Freya, are my two biggest whys. I know the life and experiences I want to provide and the future I want to enjoy with them.

I had to return to work when my first baby, Archer, was just nine days old. It was heartbreaking, but as the only vet in my practice and the sole financial provider for my family, I felt I had no choice.

I sacrificed so much time when they were babies, so as mundane and boring as this sounds, part of my vision was to be able to drop them off and pick them up from school. I know this is something many parents take for granted.

They say what you focus on expands – so make sure you are focusing on the right things!

My goals were clear, and I had to step up as a leader to put plans in place, leveraging my staff and making my business work for me.

The crazy thing that happens when you create your vision is that the universe begins to align to deliver what you have manifested.

Scientifically speaking, your reticular activating system (RAS) is switched on to subconsciously alert you to situations and opportunities that align with your vision, which may have previously been filtered out. Your RAS is the part of the brain that filters all the incoming noise, pulling out the parts it thinks may be of interest.

When I look back on the story I wrote, I'm amazed how much I have achieved with pinpoint accuracy. I encourage everyone to write down a highly detailed vision. You will surprise yourself with what you can manifest.

I went into business ownership without a single clue about what I was doing.

I was a vet. I could diagnose and treat animals, but payroll, marketing, budgets and HR were completely foreign to me. In theory, the idea of being a business owner was exciting, but the reality of owning and running a business was challenging and very lonely. None of my friends were in business, and I felt silly not knowing the basics.

There is a very strong stubborn gene that runs in my dad's side of the family, and it was definitely passed on to me. Whilst there have been many times my stubbornness has served me well, this wasn't one of them!

It took me far too long to reach out for help to support me and grow my business in a way that would reduce the overwhelm I felt.

It was right around the time when I had raised the white flag to my GP that I also surrendered to the idea of engaging a business coach specific to the veterinary industry. I had previously been to a boot camp style conference, and the concepts intrigued me, but the financial and time investment had put me off.

Once I had reached crisis point, I was willing to do whatever it took to pull myself out of the trenches. My ego had taken a beating, but I had to accept the way I had been doing things had led me to physical and mental burnout. To add insult to injury, despite my relentless hours, my business still wasn't operating anywhere near its full potential.

'None of us is as smart as all of us.' – Ken Blanchard

Having a mentor to bounce ideas off, provide guidance and help me to set goals has been life-changing both personally and professionally. It has allowed me to implement new ideas with confidence and accountability, without becoming complacent or too comfortable. I am continually challenged and no longer feel so alone in the world of business thanks to the like-minded network I have established.

Living and working regionally is physically isolating, but we are so fortunate to be able to connect with training, mentorship and industry groups online. It's never been easier to reach out and get help; there is so much wisdom out there.

Fast-forward to my current reality:

I have taken control and led myself to a place where I am now able to confidently lead others.

I've had to accept multiple 'failures' as feedback and continue to adapt in an ever-changing world.

I am no longer stuck on the hamster wheel suffering from complete mental burnout. I have taken ownership of my life and have hope, clarity and a rock-solid vision! There was a time where I could not see the light at the end of the tunnel, but I've stepped out into the sun and am incredibly grateful for the lessons along the way.

To me, leadership is the ability to set boundaries, create space for yourself, curate your vision and inspire others to do the same.

'If your actions inspire others to dream more, learn more, do more and become more, you are a leader.' – John Quincy Adams

DR EMMA BARRETT

Dr Emma Barrett is a mother, veterinarian, acupuncturist, investor and practice owner of Coral Coast Veterinary Hospital. Coral Coast Vets is a mixed practice veterinary hospital in the North West of Western Australia – a vast and isolated regional area at the gateway to the Ningaloo Reef.

Her vocation was set at an early age by a very determined and headstrong four-year-old Emma, who would bring many stray animals home to care for on the family's banana plantation.

There is something to be said for the power of cultivating your vision from a young age!

After completing her degree in veterinary science at Murdoch University in 2006, Emma returned to her hometown of Carnarvon to begin her career. Emma gained years of experience working across a number of veterinary practices in the Gascoyne and Pilbara regions.

Emma's own experience as a new grad vet and mental health impacts within the vet industry has driven a passion for supporting graduates entering the profession. Mentorship and support, whilst allowing a new

DR EMMA BARRETT

graduate to develop with confidence, is her mission as a business leader.

When the opportunity arose to purchase Coral Coast Veterinary Hospital in 2015, Emma decided to take the scary and exciting leap into business ownership.

Within three years, Emma welcomed a son, Archer, and daughter, Freya, who continue to be the driving force behind her life work.

Juggling a young family and a full-time business as a solo vet and single parent presented Emma with numerous hurdles to navigate and overcome.

With a 'fear-free' policy and a philosophy that all animals deserve an exceptional life, Emma leads a thriving award-winning business and proudly serves her local community.

She is grateful for the ongoing support of her family and community.

If you are a vet or know of a vet looking for a sea change where mental health is valued and full support is provided, Dr Emma would love to hear from you!

Website: coralcoastvet.com.au
Linked In: linkedin.com/in/emma-barrett-a5a13b22
Email: emma@coralcoastvet.com.au
Facebook: facebook.com/coralcoastvet.com.au
Instagram: instagram.com/dr.emmabarrett

LEADERSHIP IN STEM
FIONA HOLMSTROM

Leadership encompasses many things. Skills are certainly a huge part of being a leader, demonstrated knowledge in the field is another, but similarly patience and the ability to listen and act on what's important to your team members is just as vital as the knowledge itself. In STEM, we understand that skills are just one part of the puzzle. STEM is a mindset, not just a subject learnt at school. Apart from technical skills, twenty-first-century skills are just as important for the jobs of the future. Leaders understand that to develop future talent, we need a cross-section of skills and abilities to fuel the pipeline of jobs available in the future.

We are facing an unprecedented skills shortage and talent gap across many industries, but particularly in STEM fields. When 85% of the jobs that will exist in 2030 don't exist now, leaders understand they have to start engaging with their future workforce now. This means, to support this monumental task, it starts with the education of children (especially girls) in STEM at a young age in schools. Yet STEM isn't a pathway that girls often choose. Over 75% of students in school today will end up in careers that don't exist yet, and most of those careers will involve technology and digital skills. It's imperative all children, not just boys, are given an opportunity to be exposed to these future career paths. The role

of leaders who create awareness and opportunities in STEM, can inspire girls to choose a career path in this field, by:
- Busting the stereotypes around women leaders in STEM.
- Being leaders and mentors for girls and young women.
- Providing opportunities to a new generation of female leaders in STEM.

Of the 85% of the jobs that will exist in the year 2030 which haven't been invented yet, many of those jobs will require skills such as data science, robotics, analytics and AI. These skills will be required in the biggest industries worldwide – agriculture, resources, manufacturing, construction, defence, space and even tourism. STEM is critical to the future of industry because it fosters a whole new generation of innovators and makes sure talent is preserved.

But there is a great divide between what is taught in schools and what is needed in industry. Degrees may become obsolete before the student even graduates. Technology is moving so rapidly, it is hard for curriculums to keep up. It's easy to point fingers at a broken system and say situations or policies are no good, but it's a lot harder to be a leader and contribute to the solution by providing equity and equality in education and inspiring the next generation of leaders with a mindset based on innovation, creativity and entrepreneurship.

STEM education should be available to everyone through immersive, relevant and accessible STEM programs. My own personal mission is to see more girls enter STEM fields. Studies have shown that by educating girls, in particular, in lower socio-economic demographics, their families and their communities also benefit and prosper. This has a flow-on effect of helping families to flourish as well as boosting communities and regions. If we do not invest in these communities, however, the ripple effect is alarming, with impacts on wellbeing and economies.

Why aren't there more women in STEM? is a question that demands answers. But the answer is not straightforward. The complexities lie in the myriad of barriers to entry that exist for girls and women, particularly those who are under-represented or marginalised.

For starters, the stigmas that surround what a scientist looks like. When children in the 1950s were asked to draw a scientist, over 90% drew a male. These perceptions run deep and are difficult to dispel even now. Over seventy years later, there still exists a gender bias.

Girls are more able to see themselves in leadership positions when they watch other women in these roles. At a university level, research shows girls are more likely to aspire roles in STEM when their lecturers are female instead of male.

In the Fourth Industrial Revolution, soft skills, sometimes known as human skills or twenty-first-century skills, will be just as important as qualifications in the jobs of the future:

- Connection.
- Communication.
- Collaboration.
- Creativity.
- Critical thinking.
- Empathy.
- Problem-solving.

These twenty-first-century skills that children learn equip them with knowledge where they can recognise the global impact on decisions and solutions. It allows for a problem-solving process where diversity, intersectionality, culture and equal opportunity are key drivers for value creation. People with skills to problem solve and think critically will always be in demand.

Leaders who enable positive change will create widespread awareness and create relatable pathways for children to pursue in STEM. This provides a long-term and sustainable platform to build skills and enable increased STEM leadership in government, research, industry and even small business.

MENTORS AND ROLE MODELS

If you have a successful mentor in your life, thank them. Mentors are selfless and selfish. They should be interested in mentoring you for selfless reasons, i.e. to develop your potential, hone your skills and see you succeed. If a 'mentor' is in your life to make money off your success and only for this, get rid of them, pronto. Be able to see the difference between selfless and selfish mentors. Ask what's in it for them? If the answer is nothing except seeing you succeed, then you've got a good one. NOTE: this is very different to a business coach or life coach who you're paying for a service – these coaches can be invaluable in the growth they bring to a person or business.

If you have a young girl in your life, be it a daughter, niece, granddaughter, student, relative, neighbour – anyone! – chances are, you're already a role model to them. As girls, we naturally look up to women around us, starting as babies gazing up to our mothers, and as we grow, we look at teachers, lecturers, bosses or women we admire on TV or connect with on social media. Encourage the girls in your life to seek out role models (it could be you!), to ask questions about their jobs, career paths, fields of study or research and how they manage a household and family, as this is a sure way to not only get girls interested in their futures, but to see the path blazed before them and realise what's possible. In the work I do now, we engage NASA astronauts to work at our space education events, and I asked one of the female astronauts how she became interested in the field. She said she told her mom she wanted to be an astronaut one day, and her mom replied, 'Go for it!' She was never told, 'No you can't be that,' or 'That's going to be really hard.' (At that point there had only ever been male astronauts.) She said, 'It was as simple as that.' She was supported and encouraged by a parent to do it. Someone didn't discourage her, they actively and vocally supported her to pursue it.

WOMEN LEADING THE WAY

The next generation will be tomorrow's problem-solvers. If there is a young woman in your life, don't ask her what she wants to be when she grows up or what she wants to do. Instead, ask her what problem she wants to solve. Generation Y and Z are more astute at the challenges facing humanity and are the likely saviours of our planet. If that young girl in your life says, 'I want to solve global warming,' or, 'I want to reduce hunger or poverty or war or carbon emissions,' respond positively and supportively. Encourage them to find a mentor, look up someone who is on that path, emulate the path of someone who's been there or is going there, start a support group, write to their local member, ask their closest university faculty, enrol in a course, learn about the industry and upskill accordingly. The list is endless. The stewardship the next generation receives will largely determine not only their own personal success, but that of the planet. We're all responsible to ensure we leave the planet in better shape than we inherited it, which demonstrates real leadership – because leaders shape future leaders.

I remember my school days and wondering what my future would look like. Every year a thin printed booklet called a Careers Guide would be released and we would all leaf through it looking at different jobs, their descriptions and what we'd need to study to do that job. When I was six, my family had immigrated to Australia from a small working-class town in rural Scotland, described in Wikipedia as a 'tired post-industrial place and commuter town for Glasgow'. I was familiar with trains, as my dad worked for British Rail, but I had never seen a plane, certainly not a jumbo jet.

So, when we arrived at Heathrow to take our flight to Australia, I was struck by the majesty of a Boeing 747, resplendent in its retro, orange-striped livery, replete with angular 'flying kangaroo' on the tail. Wondering how on earth something that large could get into the sky, and stay in the sky, all the way from Heathrow to Sydney, fascinated me. Even then, as the crew arrived and the pilots took their places in the cockpit, I couldn't comprehend how this magnificent beast, with these crisp-suited, capped pilots I watched through the small window, would take us across the globe. I was mesmerised. Some ten years later at school, I flipped through the pages of the careers guide and spoke to the careers advisor at school about my ambitions and interest in flying. I was recommended to visit the upcoming 'careers expo' to find out more. As I spied the booth with Become a Pilot signage emblazoned across the top, I held back. The group of crisp-suited, capped crew at the booth were all men. There were no women pilots at the expo. In my shy state, I withdrew, intimidated, not wanting to ask questions and look silly in front of a group of young men. It's hard to be what you cannot see. I didn't feel like I could do that job or be in that uniform. The only pilots I had ever seen were all men. So, I often wonder if the trajectory of my life would have been different had I had a female role model to approach at that expo. Maybe I would have become a pilot? Marian Wright Edelman, American child rights activist, famously declared, 'You can't be what you can't see.' Research shows that women need role models more than men.

Female role models inspire girls to see what's possible, to reach for the stars and to follow a path. 60% of women working in STEM say they have been inspired by a role model, compared to 46% of men.

Growing up in Brisbane suburbia in the eighties, none of my family had a tertiary education. I was the only one in my family to go to uni, and I'd rarely met a businesswoman or female business owner while I was at school. Certainly not someone to look up to. The only aspirational person in my sphere was the headmistress of my primary school in Scotland, who I wrote letters to after I left the UK (and still do to this day!). If anyone in my life could be considered a role model, she is the one. I would write letters of teenage angst and she would respond with robust faith in my ability and encouragement to achieve. At one point she told me, upon professing my love of writing, that I could be a foreign correspondent for the BBC. To this day, I still hold that praise close to my heart. The power of a positive statement like that can stay with an impressionable young person forever.

INSPIRING YOUR TEAM TO FAIL: THE ENTREPRENEURIAL MINDSET

Modern society inflicts a school system where it's either pass or fail. We're conditioned to believe that failing is bad and is not conducive to success. I believe the opposite to be true, even though failure as adults can be a tough concept to stomach. If we think back to our schooling days, what was the system setting us up for success? It was a pass/fail world really, and being taught that concept from a young age can have a damaging effect on how we face failure as adults. Failure can be such an effective tool for growth. In fact, it is an essential tool for growth, as we learn nothing without failure. Remember the saying, 'If at first you don't succeed, try again'? True innovation comes from failure. Repetitive, iterative failure.

There are glamorised views of leadership and romanticised notions of entrepreneurship. There is more to entrepreneurship than wearing black T-shirts and jeans, building the next big app and making millions. Becoming, and being, an entrepreneur is hard work, and a lot of it has to do with embracing failure as the catalyst for success. (One of my most loathed lines in business is 'the overnight success'.) The world is full of ideas. What is lacking is a mindset of innovation, creativity and entrepreneurship to turn these ideas into value for society.

Inspiring a team to succeed through failure is actually the highway to self-belief and achievement. By overcoming blockers to innovation and enabling a future-centric mindset, a new generation of innovators, solving tomorrow's problems today can be inspired. Throughout our programs and the interaction with schools across the world, we actively promote this mindset. This can be a quite challenging exercise, especially for straight-A students or overachieving adults who always strive for a pass or for perfection. What can help in this process is the application of 'design thinking' which enforces the need for rapid prototyping and evaluation of ideas. The key to success is not measured on perfection, but rather how fast you can fail to reach a suitable solution for your target audience. Although failure is a daunting emotion, by using techniques like 'design thinking', it becomes part of a process and an acceptable part in the innovation process.

History shows that some of the biggest breakthroughs have come after tremendous failure. We only have to look at Michael Jordan, Albert Einstein or Walt Disney as examples of this. Yet, we don't look at these people as failures, but rather admire their achievements and tell ourselves how amazing these people are. Don't be afraid to try and fail. Fail fast, fail frequently, fail forward, or in other words: iterate, iterate, iterate. Thomas Edison's light bulb invention went through over nine thousand failures, or iterations, before it was a success.

Our childhood and schooling sets us up to believe that failure is bad, when in fact, it's quite the opposite. The more we embrace failure, the faster we succeed. There are plenty of books and podcasts to read and listen to, which are great resources for those looking for advice and leadership tips. The other way is to look for a mentor. It could be someone you'll likely never meet, or someone you already know. Tap into what they do well and emulate their methodologies. Get out of your comfort zone. Absolutely arm yourself with as much knowledge as you can. Whether it's self-development or an actual course or qualification, the more knowledge you can have is never a bad thing. The future workforce depends on it.

FIONA HOLMSTROM

Fiona Holmstrom believes STEM education should be accessible for everyone, and believes helping children develop skills in the fields of science, technology, engineering and mathematics will prepare them for a future where they can make a difference.

STEM Punks' mission is to 'inspire tomorrow's innovators' and teach children about twenty-first century skills by enabling a mindset of creativity, innovation and entrepreneurship.

Fiona publishes Future Learning magazine for STEM each month which goes into over five thousand schools around Australia and overseas. Her customer-centric focus enables her to run STEM Punks by keeping children at the heart of every business decision made, and ensuring children everywhere are inspired to solve tomorrow's world problems today.

AWARDS:
- Queensland Women in STEM Prize.
- Big Innovation Award.
- APAC Stevie Awards.

FIONA HOLMSTROM

- Telstra Business Award.
- National Mumpreneur Award.

DEAR GEORGIA ...
GEORGIA GRAHAM

*'I am not a victim of my life
what I went through pulled a warrior out of me
and it is my greatest honour to be her.'*
— *Rupi Kaur*

Georgia, the next ten years will be difficult. You will hurt, you will grieve, you will have a long journey to find acceptance. You will grieve the years you think you have wasted. You will grieve the experiences that do not play out the way you had always imagined. You will feel defenceless and angry as you tell your story, only to be shamed and minimised. You will punish yourself for not having the strength and the courage to fight for your worth and to protect your unborn son. You will feel angry for having let yourself become an unrecognisable shadow of who you truly are. You didn't leave when you should have, you didn't fight for yourself, you let yourself down in so many ways. You prioritised protecting your appearance over your health and your safety. You will spend time believing you are a victim of your life and allowing this to consume you.

My promise to you, with hindsight, is that you will wake every day knowing your strength. You will find ways to earn back your power. You will see your courage and your bravery will arise. You will learn not to embody the shame, but instead, the lessons – and there will be many. You will make so many mistakes. You will become a great mother. You will find your purpose. You will learn how to live a connected and rich life. Your idea of 'happily ever after' bears no risk, and risk is exciting. Take the leap, trust your instincts and ride the peaks and troughs of your journey.

What you need to understand is that to achieve this, you must learn to be vulnerable. You must stop finding joy in being needed and accepted. The expectations you put on yourself will cause more damage than good. Perfection is completely unattainable, and you know that. You must embody this, so you don't pass your fears onto your children. It is okay to struggle, it is okay to ask for help, it is okay to need a break and to prioritise yourself. Open yourself up to the pain. Feel it all, process it and use it as motivation. You will find love, and the more you love, the easier it will become to live with the world. You're going to own your mistakes. You will help so many women and you will build a great life.

Georgia's checklist:
- Achieve an ATAR result in the nineties ✓
- Scholarship to university ✓
- Graduate with distinction ✓
- Meet the perfect man
- Build a successful career ✓
- Buy a house ✓
- Get married ✓
- Have two children
- Live happily ever after?

I spent my teenage years and early twenties believing that life was a series of boxes I must tick. I must excel at school; I must compete at the highest level in all extracurricular activities; I must make myself desirable enough that someone would fall in love with me; I must find the perfect career, the perfect job; marry and have children. My path was set based on what I assumed would impress others and I wouldn't dare deviate from this. I convinced myself the ultimate failure was for someone to look at me and think I was achieving merely what was expected. I had to exceed expectations. Maybe it was because I grew up in a family of quiet over-achievers, a family of incredibly intelligent and generous people who had attained wealth and thereby met my distorted definition of success. I became so hungry for the kind of praise that only came when people were genuinely shocked by my abilities and achievements.

It seemed like this hunger for external validation was the perfect fuel for my determination. I completed high school with an ATAR score in the high nineties. This led to me being awarded a scholarship to complete a commerce degree at a top Melbourne university, where I would study to become an accountant and follow in the footsteps of both my father and my mother.

I was in my first year of university, a few weeks after my eighteenth birthday, when I met someone who would check the next box. He was a few years older than me, a defence force recruit with a steady income. He was good looking, and best of all, he deemed me worthy of attention. When I was with him, I felt as if others looked at me like I was worth knowing. He was charming and charismatic, and I was the lucky girl he chose to date. After three weeks of dating, he told me he loved me in the back of his twenty-year-old Ford Falcon. It wasn't romantic and it certainly wasn't sincere, but to me, that meant I owed him, and I committed myself to him unwaveringly. Within six months he had been given an interstate posting and I was planning to move to live with him as soon as I finished my degree.

At the end of 2014, when I was twenty years old, I completed my university degree graduating with distinction – check. I was lucky enough to be given a graduate job at a top-tier commercial real estate company in their finance department. The job was in Sydney, Australia, meaning I could move to live with my partner, and the offices were in beautiful Circular Quay. Life was picture perfect.

GEORGIA GRAHAM

I packed up my childhood room, put my Suzuki Swift on the back of a trailer and moved to Sydney, needing to believe I was the envy of every one of my high school friends. I moved into defence share housing with my partner for a few weeks before we secured a rental of our own on the stunning eastern beaches. I was so excited the day we moved into our very own apartment. Another one of my boxes was checked. However, with the move came the downfall of my carefully planned and executed picture-perfect life.

The first day, while unpacking boxes, my partner and I had an argument. We were exhausted and overwhelmed, and we were disagreeing on where something should be put in the apartment. Somehow, the argument escalated so quickly and so suddenly. He became completely unable to control his anger as he verbally abused me. He then grabbed the first hard object at hand and threw it at my head. That was day one of what ended up being an eight-year-long abusive relationship. I choose not to give any power to the abuse I endured other than to say it was humiliating, degrading and destroyed my already delicate sense of self-worth.

That day I made a choice to stay in the relationship. I chose to protect the opinion other people had of me, of my partner and of my perfect life. I have forgiven myself for that choice, but by sharing my story, I hope to empower other women to make a different one.

Two years later, we moved home to Melbourne. We bought a house, got engaged and then married. Two years after that I fell pregnant. From the outside, my life was following my carefully prepared checklist – from the inside it was miserable. I convinced myself that if I could just give my husband the son he so desperately wanted, he would change. That was a delusion. While I was pregnant, the abuse escalated. I had no true friends as I was not honest with any of them. My husband had convinced me my family didn't want anything to do with me. I felt truly alone, and by this point, like I genuinely no longer had the option to leave.

'Don't ask me why I didn't leave,

WOMEN LEADING THE WAY

he made my world so small I couldn't see the exit.
I'm surprised I got out at all.'
– Rupi Kaur

On an apparently ordinary Thursday in 2019, I was twenty weeks pregnant and my life as I knew it ended. My husband was arrested and charged with a multitude of criminal charges. I was caught completely off guard. I felt shame and disgust about what he had done within the four walls of our home, all while successfully hiding the truth from me for years. I was shaken, sickened and forced out of my home as the police released him there on bail. In hindsight, and although it has taken me a long time to admit, this was the only way I was going to escape, as I don't believe I would have had the courage to leave. It meant I could finally stop pretending life was perfect and I could finally speak the truth.

So, what does my story have to do with leadership? What do I want you to gain from what I have shared?

I was chasing perfection, and just when I thought people would believe I had reached it, the game changed.

Perfection is an unattainable lie. As women, we grow up with an impression of what our life should look like, and it very closely mirrors the checklist I shared earlier. Be ambitious, but don't look like you're trying too hard. Be beautiful, but it must be effortless. Follow the path that has been walked by so many women before, and don't you dare deviate. Deviation equals failure. This constant striving for perfection becomes another stick to beat ourselves with. Happily ever after is the ultimate goal, but in truth, a fairytale ending is uninspiring.

I spent so many years putting an unending amount of pressure on myself to be perfect. It led me to become competitive, jealous, insecure and someone who sought connection as a means of fulfilling my need for external validation. Chasing perfection is like climbing a ladder where the top is constantly just out of reach. You never feel truly fulfilled or satisfied. By trying to be perfect I was attempting to protect myself from rejection, and in doing so, I had completely rejected myself. At what point did I deem myself to be not enough? Check in with yourself and see if you feel the same.

In truth, I still fight this battle every day as I am sure most of us do, but I am striving for acceptance. It is so important to me that I don't pass my perfectionist traits on to my children. I don't want them to feel that pressure. The ultimate goal is to live and lead authentically, to show people who we truly are, our unvarnished selves, and to connect vulnerably.

Connection to self is the most important form of connection.

I lived my life connecting with others from a place of lack and scarcity. I needed external validation to feel worthy, and in the process, I lost sight of my authenticity. It is very easy to become disconnected from both our internal and external worlds when we aren't living authentically.

My journey to reconnecting with myself has been long and hard. It is hard to accept your imperfections. It is hard to accept that other people might view you as 'not enough'. However, you need to see yourself as worthy and as an equal to truly connect. If you're connecting from a place of equality and not a place of lack, then you have found true connection.

I have spent the last three years relearning who I truly am. I often say to people that when I look back at the Georgia of three years ago, she is completely unrecognisable. I was a shell of myself. Everything I did and said was carefully designed to protect people's opinion of me. I had concealed all the things that truly make me who I am. I am funny, I am a smart alec, I thrive off true connection and find purpose in helping others. It is so exciting to admit I love these things about myself. What are the things you love most about yourself?

From a business sense, truly connecting to myself has helped me find purpose and build a business designed to help others. Through my business, I connect with other women who I get to teach and empower. Once I accepted who I was, it is absurd how quickly I found clarity and how quickly my business grew.

Someone once told me I wasn't enough.

I will be honest and say it has taken me a very long time to detach from the shame I felt about my husband's actions. I was not able to admit to anyone, other than my immediate family, what had really happened. It has been a very long journey, and the day my husband was arrested did not end up being the hardest day I have faced in the last few years. Imagine waking up one morning to find your most shameful secret, something you have tried to keep hidden, has been printed on the front of a national newspaper. That was a truly brutal day.

Ultimately, my son is why I survived. He gave me the courage I needed to fight. I knew I had a duty to him, as I was the only one who could protect him and raise him the way he needed. The day he was born, I truly understood the importance of connection. I had an incredibly empowering experience birthing him and the physical and emotional connection I felt was incredible. Every day I get to wake up and be his mum, and every day I work to be the absolute best version of myself for him. Though some days he does test my patience, I am proud to be his mum and I am proud of what an incredible little man he is.

I am now lucky enough to have found an incredible partner who has an amazing daughter. My son now gets to experience having a father in his life and a big sister who loves him so completely, although he does test her patience some days as well. Our life is not perfect, but it is fulfilling, and I am grateful every day for what we have built together. There are, of course, still days when I find myself comparing my journey to others. I question who I am and revert to the victim mentality. On those days, I commit to honest self-reflection, try to remember that I am a flawed human and rely on the close connections I have with those in my life to get me through.

Reflecting on that ordinary Thursday in 2019, at twenty weeks pregnant, after just learning my husband had been arrested, I took my wedding ring off, left it on the bathroom bench and as I did so I detached myself from his story. I was off to write my own.

GEORGIA GRAHAM

Georgia Graham is the director and owner of Empowering Financial Solutions, a boutique bookkeeping and advisory firm specialising in small business bookkeeping, improving financial literacy and business development. The idea for the business was borne from her personal journey to find connection and to empower other women to lead with authenticity. Georgia found true connection within an incredible community of like-minded women who have given her the confidence to develop into an authentic leader.

Georgia is a CPA accountant and registered BAS agent who loves partnering with entrepreneurs and small business owners to empower them to truly understand their finances and grow their businesses. She finds great purpose in helping female entrepreneurs gain financial confidence and loves working with other finance professionals to provide a full financial support offering to small businesses.

Georgia also finds purpose through her advocacy efforts, having worked closely with PartnerSpeak Australia participating in university run research studies, as well as training programs for Australian law enforcement designed to improve education around non-offending victims. Georgia is driven to enact change within the family court system of Australia and to spread awareness of the challenges faced by families impacted by family and domestic abuse.

Website: empoweringfinancialsolutions.com.au

DON'T BE DEFINED BY YOUR OWN STORY. WRITE YOUR OWN

HELEN WHAIT

From a childhood charactertised by emotional abuse to becoming a nun and then launching an Australian-first business, Helen Whait's journey to leadership has been anything but ordinary.

A brief glance at my LinkedIn profile shows all the markers of someone who has been 'conventionally' successful – a fast-growing business, awards, PR coverage, a great team and plenty of reasons to be proud. If you were to meet me at an event, you'd find me confident and calm. But beneath the surface there's much more to the story – my story.

You see, there was a time when I didn't have any of those markers of success. A time when years of abuse had me feeling broken. Where loneliness was the norm and insecurities were my closest confidante.

Until now, I've kept this story deeply private. However, I'm finally ready to share it.

For most of my life, I have been subject to emotional abuse and a highly dysfunctional family environment.

I was born into a family of immigrants as the youngest of four children. My parents both came from abusive, dysfunctional families themselves.

My father, a textbook narcissist, made my childhood a living hell. A devout Catholic, he professed to be a 'good' Christian man, but in the confines of my home, I experienced his double standards. He was controlling, manipulative and incapable of showing love. He was domineering, dictatorial and could never admit fault or wrongdoing. He consistently put me down, called me dumb, fat and ugly, belittled and bullied my siblings, and was deeply unsupportive of anything outside his own narrow view of the world.

As for my mother, she was complicit in his actions, constantly enabling his behaviour.

There was no one incident that led to my suffering; it was a slow, insidious process of abuse. Each little moment of cruelty by my father, and each little moment of enabling by my mother, became a part of the fabric I was woven with.

In many ways, it was a childhood characterised by poverty, both financial and emotional. Financially, we walked a tightrope, struggling to get through each day. Emotionally, our home was a prison, and our family dynamic was one of emotional withdrawal, not connection.

As kids, we weren't allowed to have friends because friends meant social support. Playing sport was a big no-no because it took me out of our family dynamic and exposed me to healthier alternatives. No-one came to the house; no-one was allowed to call.

There was sexual abuse too. One incident will forever haunt me. I remember, at around seven years of age, getting in the car with my mother's father – my grandfather – to go buy a lotto ticket. When we stopped to park, he turned to look at me. I remember clearly the look of perverse pleasure on my grandfather's face as he put his hands on me and leant over to kiss me. Every bone in my body screamed at me to get out of the car, but I didn't have a choice. 'Adults must always be respected and their orders followed,' was what I'd been told.

I wish this was an isolated incident. He was always coming up behind his granddaughters, squeezing our breasts, pinching our bums and even licking our ears. The day my sister mustered the courage to tell my mother what was going on, unbelievably, she was mad at my sister. Even writing this today, my blood boils. I felt violated and powerless.

There were less abhorrent instances of physical abuse too. My father made us do physical work beyond what a child should be asked to do. 'If your brother can do it, so can you,' my dad would often say. But his motivation was less about empowering young women and more about hard labour.

He had very strict ideas about how we should behave and dress. The truth is, when you are in an abusive environment with narcissistic parents, there is no room for your own subjectivity. They strip you of your self-worth and iron out your identity and individuality, until a shell of a person remains.

Expressing myself was forbidden, even in the smallest of ways. No make-up and no jewellery. Putting my hair up in a ponytail was out of the question. And if I dared to challenge the rules, I was met with emotional withdrawal, verbal abuse and criticism.

Living in an environment like this can be extremely damaging. You are constantly made to feel you're not good enough and that *everything* about you needs to be fixed for it to meet your parents' standards.

As a result, you never learn to set your own boundaries, either, because you have to filter your actions through your parents' reactions. It's a controlling, manipulative and oppressive cycle which makes you feel completely helpless. Eventually, you become so used to the cycle you don't even know how to break free.

It's innate in all humans to want validation and acceptance from our parents. But the moment I realised I was never going to get it, no matter how hard I tried, is when everything changed. I understood the problem was with them, not with me.

That's when I started to establish my boundaries and reclaim my power, slowly but surely. Picking up the crumbled pieces of myself that were left behind in the wreckage, I moved out of the childhood prison my parents had so ignominiously built up and started to rebuild.

University was my first opportunity to discover a new world free of criticism; a place where I could be whoever I wanted to be, without the fear of being judged. I enrolled to study occupational therapy, not because of some long-held dream, but because I drew the course out of a hat.

You see, when your childhood is devoid of dreams and subjectivity, you don't finish school with a grand plan. You finish school without a clue of who you are and what to do with your life. As it happened, the course was perfect for me. I soon found that helping people was my way of finding purpose and healing from my traumatic childhood.

Still, I felt broken from my childhood. I wanted to know there was good in the world, that light existed and people could be kind. So, I decided to join the convent and become a nun.

To anyone unfamiliar with my family, becoming a nun may sound like a plot twist. But to me it seemed like the obvious choice. There was more freedom in the convent than I ever had at home.

Coming from a practising Catholic family, I knew that joining a religious order would give me the family I had lacked. I needed peace and a place of safety and security. I wanted a better life, where values were upheld and people were good. The fact I had left my oppressive family to then join another oppressive system is not lost on me, but it felt like the right thing to do at the time.

At first, the convent was pleasant enough, if rigorous in its structure and strictures. However, I was lonely. I was the only young person and was kept at arm's length in order to 'detach from the world'. The ever-positive nature in me meant I kept telling myself it would get better. I was a candidate; it would be better when I was a postulant. When I was a postulant, I told myself it would be better when I was a novice, and then I convinced myself all would be fine once I took my vows. Before long, the cracks started to appear. Despite the outward appearance of a holy and peaceful place, there was a troubling undercurrent of mismanagement.

So, I wrote a letter to the Mother General of the order I had joined, outlining all the problems I saw within the convent in Adelaide. I was ordered under my vow of Holy Obedience to fax it to her. In less than a week, I was transferred to a convent in upstate New York. While my time in Castleton on Hudson was an improvement over the convent in Adelaide, I soon realised deep down this wasn't what I wanted long-term. I couldn't escape my past. So, when my vows expired, I left and returned to Australia and began working as an occupational therapist.

Life has been a roller-coaster since then, filled with both highs and lows. I married the first man who professed his love for me. After all, when you feel loved for perhaps the first time in your life, it can be hard to resist.

We brought three beautiful sons into the world while I juggled my career, but after sixteen years of marriage, the same narcissistic traits displayed by my father were evident in my husband. I supported him financially with career changes, study ambitions and showered him in love and attention, yet nothing had seemed to be enough.

The same cycle of emotional abuse was repeating itself, only this time I wasn't a powerless child, I was an adult with choices and agency. And this time, it wasn't just me; I had three children who were being disrespected too. So, I chose to end the marriage despite the 'Catholic guilt'. It took me years to break free from the cycle of abuse and months to get him out of the house, but eventually I did.

The bottom line is this: never get between a mama and her cubs. But in all seriousness, I would do whatever it takes to protect my sons and teach them the strong values of self-respect, respect for others and kindness that had been so lacking in my own upbringing. The cycle of abuse had to end with me, and it did.

Just prior to ending my marriage came my biggest breakthrough of all. In 2012, I founded Australia's first and only occupational therapy franchise business – ActivOT – which invests in health professionals and turns them into successful business owners.

Back then, franchising in allied health was virtually unheard of. Come to think of it, it still is! But I was convinced it was the answer. Not only could it provide much-needed support for occupational therapists, but it could deliver better outcomes for our clients. Ten years later, I'm proud to say ActivOT has over fifty franchisees and is growing rapidly around Australia.

Disrupting an industry is no easy feat, particularly in health care, but it can be done. And nothing seems impossible once you've been through some of the crap I have!

Leaving my husband, single-handedly raising my boys and scaling a successful franchise business hasn't been without its challenges. In fact, my health has seriously suffered. I've even come close to death from idiopathic thrombocytopenia and other autoimmune health issues.

Yet despite the challenges, I still find strength in my core belief that life is too short not to live your best one. In spite of it all, or perhaps because of it, I have emerged stronger than ever, knowing that anything is possible.

This story needs to be told not just for me, but also for other women facing immense challenges. There are lessons to be learned and inspiration to be gained from my story, and here they are.

WRITE YOUR OWN STORY

Emotional abuse is where my narrative began, but it was up to me to define how it would end. I could have allowed myself to be limited by the familiar patterns of behaviour endemic in my family, but instead I chose to create my own narrative. I chose to break the cycle of negativity that had defined my family for generations.

The real story of my life is not a story of debilitating emotional abuse, but a story of resilience, courage and self-belief. It's the story of how I chose to take all the lessons from my past and use them as stepping stones towards creating a brighter future.

DON'T INTERNALISE WHAT'S HAPPENED TO YOU OR ALLOW YOURSELF TO BE DEFINED BY IT

You don't need to internalise what's happened to you, no matter how traumatic or damaging it might be. Self-reflection is key, as is finding trusted, professional help to navigate the darkest parts of your childhood.

KNOW THAT YOUR BIGGEST CHALLENGE IS ALSO YOUR SUPERPOWER

Your biggest challenge can become your greatest superpower if you choose to see it that way. I chose to reframe the abuse I experienced, as an opportunity to build resilience, empathy and a deep sense of social justice. It was through those experiences I was able to disrupt an entire industry. I realise now it's my biggest demons that have allowed me to become the leader I am today – a leader driven by 'doing what's right'.

BOUNDARIES SET YOU FREE

One of the biggest lessons from my childhood is the power of setting boundaries. When we set boundaries, it helps us to feel safe and in control of our lives. It's the ultimate act of self-kindness. But we must get much better at communicating our boundaries if we want them to be respected. Women, in particular, have to learn to assert our boundaries and to not be scared of the opinions of others. In fact, it's important that people don't feel comfortable crossing our boundaries. So, expect a little discomfort, and remember, you can be assertive without being aggressive.

MAKE IT ABOUT MORE THAN JUST YOU

It's not always about you. Sometimes, it's about the people around us and the generational pain that's been passed down. If it is about you, remember the power of kindness and compassion. Remember you have the power to change the course of your future, no matter what your circumstances might be.

BELIEVE THAT YOU CAN RISE FROM ALMOST ANYTHING

With the right determination and support, it is possible to rise from almost anything. I'm proof of this. Helen today is a far cry from the little girl she used to be, yet she remains my driving force, always reminding me of my value and pushing me to do better. My difficult childhood has made me battle-hardened, strong-willed and unafraid to tackle any challenge life throws my way. This strength helped me recover when my marriage ended in divorce. It helped me speak up when I witnessed wrongdoing while working in government. And it's since helped me to build an award-winning, values-driven company.

FIND YOUR TRIBE OF WOMEN

Not all women will be your tribe, but your tribe is out there. Find them. The people I have around me now are a world apart from the people who shaped my early years. They are inspiring, kind and smart. They've helped me to believe in myself and become the successful businesswoman I am today.

REMEMBER, YOU CAN DO THIS

My story is not unique and I'm sure many of you have experienced feeling trapped, controlled and manipulated by someone in your life. If that's you, trust me when I say things will get better. You are strong, capable and worthy! It's going to be hard, and it may take some time, but you will make it through. Future generations of beautiful, strong people will thank you for your courage and strength.

HELEN WHAIT

For more than a decade, Helen Whait has been a powerful contributor and change-maker within, and for, her profession. As the founder of Australia's first occupational therapy franchise business, she's helped more than fifty occupational therapists Australia-wide build incredible businesses that provide life-changing services without sacrificing their own wellbeing.

With a proven track record, an army of happy franchisees (just ask them), and continued growth in business and referrals year after year, ActivOT is changing the face of occupational therapy in Australia – one franchise business at a time.

Helen has been widely recognised for her groundbreaking achievements. Among countless other accolades, she has been nominated for, named finalist and won several awards, including:

- Winner, OT Australia SA Williams OT Innovative Service Delivery Award 2016.
- Winner, SA Woman Awards Innovation category 2020.
- Bronze Winner, AusMumpreneur Awards, Health Services category

HELEN WHAIT

2022.
- Winner, Women in Innovation Awards, open category award 2022.
- Winner Freedom Awards community category 2022.

Helen is an active member of Occupational Therapy Australia (OTA) and the Department of Veteran Affairs National Reference Group. Through this role, Helen aims to have a positive impact on government policy development.

Being involved at the grassroots level of occupational therapy service provision, Helen is able to provide insight into government programs and how they work for clients (or fail, as the case may be). She's written and contributed to numerous submissions and discussion papers as well as policy statements, particularly in relation to veteran care.

Helen is an outspoken and respected advocate for occupational therapy as a profession. Through her involvement with OTA, Helen has been an invited speaker at their inaugural private practice symposium held in 2018. Helen describes her experience as a guest speaker as 'an honour and a privilege to be able to address my industry peers and to discuss the unique business model I've developed to help OTs succeed in private practice while maintaining very high standards of service provision and remaining client centred'.

Helen is an expert contributor to publications such as Allied Health Insights, Business Chicks, Flying Solo and Business Woman Media.

Guided by her values and vision, Helen has continued to build her thriving business, creating a unique health care service model and franchise model that is vastly different from the way it's 'always been done'. She has supported occupational therapists in new ways to practise according to their core values as therapists and to deliver outstanding results.

Helen has proven that as a mother and a woman, you can have it all — that you can put your family, your health and yourself first and still have a career. She has backed herself. As a result, she has fostered a culture within her business where like-minded occupational therapists can share resources and feel supported and empowered. And through it all, she has stayed true to herself.

Website: activot.com.au

EVERYTHING IN LIFE HAPPENS FOR A REASON
IRINA CASTELLANO

Through my story, I would love for others to believe in themselves; to believe that everything in life has its purpose, if only to make us more compassionate towards others who have gone through a similar situation.

Every few years, my German family moved for my dad's work as an engineer. It's no coincidence that my sister is married to an American and I am married to an Aussie, as we have been exposed to a variety of cultures from a very young age.

Most of my parents' friends were in mixed-race marriages, and nowadays most of our friends are too.

My own family consists of our children having three different sets of parents from their individual cultural backgrounds.

AN EXPAT KID

Moving from one country to another means many things – learning new languages, learning new religious beliefs and cultural traditions, and most of all, learning how to adapt to often-changing schools. By regularly being the new kid on the block, I learnt how to act more confidently than I might have actually felt inside.

I learnt to sympathise with other kids who were new or who just didn't seem to fit in.

Being the new kid also broadens your horizons, makes you inclusive as a human being and more tolerant if things don't happen as fast or as efficiently as you have experienced in the past.

EMIRATES AIRLINE SAFETY TRAINER IN DUBAI, UAE

From the minute I stepped onto an airplane with my family for the very first time, I said to my mum, 'This is the job I want to do one day.' We travelled a lot, and each year for holidays, we flew back to Germany to see our family and friends, but my mum made sure we always stopped over in another country on our way home as well. Those were the days when kids could visit the cockpit and even sit there for landing!

After growing up in Germany, Turkey and the USA, I completed my year twelve early, at the age of sixteen (lucky enough to skip two grades).

My father was a frequent traveller with Lufthansa, so for me there was only ONE airline to apply for.

The minimum age was eighteen at the time, so I went to France as an au pair to learn another language with the hope I would increase my chances for an interview.

At eighteen years old, I was ready to apply but realised they had recently raised the minimum age to twenty-one.

Though I was of course disappointed, my motto has always been 'everything happens for a reason'. France had made me more independent, and whatever else I was going to do now would improve my chances of doing a better job in my new dream role with all the experiences I had gained.

Adding hospitality experience seemed the most appropriate for the airline industry, so I applied at the most prestigious hotel in our small town of Darmstadt and started as a receptionist. They had accepted me because of the languages I spoke, though everyone else had completed a three-year hotel course.

From there, I applied closer to the airport by working at the information counter, as well as a check-in agent for the airport handling agent. Eventually, I made it to the check-in counters for Lufthansa airlines.

Every single job I took taught me so much about working under pressure (over-booked flights/weather delays/visa issues/upset customers), about the connection between the work one does at the check-in counter and then up in the air (passengers would complain about not sitting together and I would have to tell them they unfortunately checked in late. I could tell from just looking at the boarding pass). By learning so many invaluable skills, before even taking on my dream job, I continued to believe that 'everything happens for a reason'.

I always aim to see the positive in things; it is much less stressful, and in the long run, there always is a silver lining to everything.

It was hard to see one though when I finally did turn twenty-one years of age, and on applying for my dream job as a flight attendant, they didn't accept me for the role.

I had loved all the other jobs, but I wanted to travel to exotic places and see the world.

I was stunned. I didn't see it coming. I spoke several languages and had so much airline experience, but it was a NO from them.

Immediately, I didn't dwell on it and applied for Emirates airlines, Qatar Airways and a few others.

Emirates was the first to answer and they immediately offered me a job.

When I resigned at Lufthansa ground services they were stunned and didn't understand why no-one had even checked with them on how much they valued me. Reluctantly, they let me go but said that they would keep my role open if I didn't like Dubai!

Soon after, I realised that Emirates was going to offer me much more than Lufthansa could have ever done.

I spent eight years living and working in Dubai, UAE. It was an incredible adventure. It was always warm (I don't mind a bit of heat!), with free accommodation (at the Hilton Apartments initially with beach club access!), free pick-up services to and from work and free uniform dry cleaning, as well as a tax-free income.

The layovers were brilliant, as Emirates was still a young airline in 1990. When a route started to a new city, they would only fly there once or twice a week, therefore the layovers were rather long. We had twenty-one days in Bangkok, just doing a weekly shuttle to Manila!

I was also on monthly trips home to Germany, since I was only one of the four German speakers who had joined Emirates airlines by then.

Living in Turkey for four years made it easy for me to adjust to the Muslim lifestyle. My dresses have always been floor-length and I never needed alcohol in my life. Though since we could go to the duty-free shops before every flight, it was easily accessible and no big deal if we wanted it. Alcohol was otherwise only available in hotels or bars, or you had to have a liquor licence for special booze shops as a resident.

The expat community was rather small in the 1990s and women worked as doctors, nurses, teachers and maids, or in hospitality and the aviation industry.

Expat males worked in the construction industry, IT, shipping, doctors, nurses or in other roles in offices. Everyone met at the same three clubs/pubs, and it was a great community. As EK flight attendants, we had many perks in Dubai. I remained throughout the Gulf War and since then Dubai has come onto the map and grown tremendously. Since then, traffic has definitely become much worse.

When I eventually returned to Germany, I was finally accepted into

Lufthansa airlines (though with hiccups as well!), but service was rated so much higher at Emirates – we offered a hot meal on a flight to Bandar Abbas in Iran, which is twenty-one minutes! I was so incredibly grateful for having had the chance to learn from the best.

Emirates airlines (EK) had been voted best airline several years in a row and on each flight with seventeen crew, we had fifteen different nationalities. It was heaps of fun, diverse and so much more rewarding.

I must admit though that Lufthansa airlines (LH) provided me with new routes like Mexico City, Bogotá and European cities, which were not on Emirates' routes at the time, so I got to see more of the world still. They also promoted me quickly and I was able to represent LH on 'mystery flights', which were sold to the public without knowing the destination (usually used as check flights to train pilots in the last stages before going on Lufthansa routes). I would look after passengers while in those cities, like Dublin, Ireland. I became a bit of a tour guide for these guests, as I had also done that type of work for the EK Tours (a subsidy of EK airlines) in my spare time for German tourists in Dubai.

As a matter of fact, all this travelling and learning languages had opened many doors for me and lucrative incomes, as I helped out at fairs in Dubai, as well as in Frankfurt, Germany, throughout my years there.

During my time in Dubai, I was also chosen to work for the private flights for the royal family of Dubai, the Al-Maktoum family. That was another brilliant experience; 'Everything does happen for a reason.'

FOSTER MUM/IVF/ADOPTION

While in Turkey, at the age of twelve, I started babysitting among the expat community as I loved spending time with children.

At the age of fifteen, while living in the USA with my family, I read a book about a child being abused by his mum and how he ended up in foster care.

WOMEN LEADING THE WAY

It blew my mind, as I had never heard anything like it. I decided then and there I would have my own kids one day, foster kids and possibly even adopt a child.

I finished school, worked in hospitality and the aviation industry, and when I finally met my future husband and moved to Australia, I wasn't allowed to work for a few years until the spouse visa turned into citizenship.

In every local paper I could see ads for foster carers, and as I had too much time on my hands and David travelled two hundred days a year, I had to tell him over the phone that it had been my wish to do this for so many years – and the time seemed right.

David was a bit apprehensive as he only ever thought of us having our own kids, but he did it to please me, as he knew I needed something meaningful to do.

We started fostering a few kids, then tried IVF, moved to China for a couple of years, Singapore for five years and ended up fostering there as well. When a child needed a permanent home, we adopted our first daughter in 2004. She was one year old at the time, but had been living with us since she was five months old, after we had met her at two and a half months when she'd been placed with another foster family.

Another few IVF cycles followed, which produced a miscarriage, a stillborn, and finally, our son in 2006.

We continued to foster in Singapore, as well as in Sydney when we returned in 2008.

In 2009, a little girl came into our care for three months, and we ended up adopting her as well.

Everything is meant to be, and it happens for a reason.

If we could have had three biological kids, naturally, soon into our marriage, we probably would have never looked into fostering to begin with, but we always said we wanted three kids.

We have now been fostering for over twenty-three years and it has changed our lives in so many ways.

Our kids have learned compassion and empathy through the stories these kids have shared with them.

They have seen what domestic violence does to a family, what it means to grow up without both parents and what drugs or alcohol can do to a child's development.

There are different types of care provided for vulnerable children, and in 2023, we need four thousand homes for children who need support, boundaries, guidance and family unity.

The types of care we provide are:
- Respite – giving support to current foster carers for a limited time like a weekend here and there, you get a beginning and an end date.
- Restoration care – up to two years until the child can be restored with their own birth family or the child goes into permanent care.
- Permanent care – meaning the child will remain with you until the age of eighteen and hopefully beyond, depending on your relationship with your foster child.
- Emergency care – usually the after-office-hour service. If a child is removed from their home, they call carers on the emergency care list which is held by the government department as they are the ones removing the children from unsafe environments. They then ask if they can take the child immediately. This might mean the child comes into your care within the hour with often just the clothes on their back; they might stay for a night or a few weeks/months until a new home is found, if you don't want to do restoration or permanent care.

We have done all types of care over the years.

My life has been rather unusual, and I have continued to learn more about how to help these kids.

I have obtained a Diploma of Community Services and I teach students at diploma level. I have attended over a hundred courses on topics like trauma-informed care practices, FASD, ADHD, autism and more.

I am a facilitator of the nationally accredited workshop for potential foster carers and adoptive parents, as well as an independent panel member to authorise foster carers and adoptive parents.

Currently I am enrolled to complete the Graduate Certificate in Developmental Trauma and I have completed my coaching certification to help and guide others to become carers or adoptive parents, as well as those who would like to find purpose in life after hitting middle crisis point or becoming empty-nesters; in fact, anyone willing to find their passion in life.

It is not a coincidence that a large majority of expat kids end up in social jobs, teaching, medicine or coaching. These are all jobs with the aim to guide and support others, as we have seen so much in this world in terms of poverty and inequality. We are strong advocates for the needs of others.

CONCLUSION

I have found my passion, and it works wonders if you go through life by just having an inner peace and believing that EVERYTHING HAS IT'S PURPOSE.

Somehow, I have come full circle in my life.

I don't need to prove myself to anyone. I am finally able to help others when I want and how I want.

I am at peace. I am incredibly grateful to have met David and to have had him on my journey.

Living in eight countries has made me appreciative of other cultures and languages, and it has made me more non-judgemental and inclusive.

I could not work in an environment made up of only one culture. I would struggle as I feel it is so much more interesting to get different perspectives on things, especially from different beliefs and viewpoints.

IRINA CASTELLANO

Irina has lived and worked in eight countries.

From being an expat child, she became an expat worker and expat spouse.

By learning more about how the brain heals from trauma, as a neuro change practitioner, she has started her coaching business to guide others on their journey to find their purpose in life.

Irina has found hers by being the coach and the foster parent (together with hubby and kids) to over seventy-five kids along the way.

Her purpose is to find more safe homes for the many kids in need in Australia and anywhere else in this world.

She offers professional one-on-one support, as well as training and guidance to potential and current carers and adoptive parents.

Irina has a Diploma of Community Services and is currently completing a Graduate Certificate in Developmental Trauma.

She has been featured on a dozen radio shows (*The Meaningful Monday Show, SBS German*, Tom Reaoch, Michael McDonnell etc.) and is keen to speak at any event possible to raise awareness for the need of foster homes.

Irina runs the nationally accredited workshop for foster carers and open adoption seminars.

Her FREE ebook on the topic of fostering is available by contacting her and she offers a thirty-minute free chat to see if fostering is for you.

Her upcoming memoir will cover the joys and challenges she has experienced on her foster and adoptive journey.

Irina lives in Sydney with her husband, son, two daughters, dog, lizard and a frog.

Website: irinacastellano.com.au
LinkedIn: linkedin.com/in/irinacastellano
Podcast: elevatebooks.com/category/podcast
Facebook: facebook.com/irina.castellano.fostering

MORE THAN SKIN-DEEP
JUDY CHEUNG-WOOD

Today, I am considered an industry expert – a pioneer who is changing the industry with a highly efficacious specialist skincare range.

But as a little girl growing up with her toes in the sands of the Solomon Islands, I had no idea that finding business success would require a journey of personal discovery, challenges and courage. It would require the discovery of my purpose.

ENTREPRENEURIAL DNA

I was born in Hong Kong, however, my childhood home will always be the Solomon Islands. When I was three years old, my entire family moved to the tiny island nation, including my maternal grandparents.

My mother was very close to her father, my 'Gung Gung' or grandfather in Cantonese. He was a serial entrepreneur, and my mother was his right hand.

I grew up listening to them talking about the businesses my grandfather had built and how my mother was his trusted 'gofer'. He manufactured toys, skincare products, ran a grocery store, an advertising agency and restaurant.

As a qualified chemist, my Gung Gung developed his own products.

I remember sitting with him and watching him mixing ingredient after ingredient before finally declaring: 'This is how you make glue.' The glue was for framing his own watercolour paintings; he was an artist and poet too.

I witnessed their dedication to the integrity of their products, and I could never have counted the number of times they spoke to me about focusing on the long-term, not to be lured by short-term gains.

FALLING THROUGH THE FLOOR

At eight years of age, my world came crashing down. My parents lost all their businesses due to my father's high-risk deals. While they were dealing with that highly tense situation, my sister and I were sent to boarding school in Macau.

Eighteen months later, rather than returning to the Solomon Islands that I had always known, my family moved to Hong Kong. I struggled to connect with my new home and find an emotional fit with my peers as my upbringing had been so different.

Then, when I was eleven years old, my father simply left our home and didn't return. I only found out later he was running away from shady loan sharks he'd borrowed money from to fund his secret gambling addiction.

There was a darkness to our life then. It made me ask myself some big questions about why I was here, who I was and what was the point. All questions I didn't have answers for.

Around the same time, I developed persistent acne, which further battered my already low confidence.

I put my head down and focused on my studies, developing a love for chemistry and biology which was reflected in my top grades.

Around the age of sixteen, my mother offered me an opportunity I couldn't refuse, 'Do you want to go overseas and study?'

My response was an immediate, 'Yes!'

The idea of leaving Hong Kong offered me a glimmer of hope but I knew the flame of that candle had a wick which ran right through the foundation of my family.

My mother, like other Asian parents of her time, viewed her children as an extension of herself. I knew my new-found freedom was not just an opportunity to secure my future, but an expectation, a duty, to do the same for my family.

DUTY AND FEAR

I was staying at my uncle's house in Sydney the summer that I finished high school. My results showed just how hard I worked. First family duty – achieved.

I sat completing my application for tertiary education. I knew I had scored high enough to gain a place in my first choice of degree, a bachelor of biochemistry, and I filled out my paperwork to apply.

But just before the deadline, I got cold feet. I realised the chosen degree would likely lead me to a role as a researcher, which didn't really appeal to me.

I got the courage to confide in my uncle.

'Well, what do you want to do?' he asked me.

'I don't know.' My voice was only just loud enough for him to hear.

He then suggested a few typical options. 'Accounting? Law? Engineering?'

'I love business and commerce, maybe marketing too?' But even as I said it, I knew it was an industry in which gaining employment would be very challenging as an international student. *Think of the long-term, Judy!*

My uncle was a drafter and suggested a Bachelor of Urban Planning. After thumbing through the curriculum, I decided it looked interesting enough and was the type of professional degree that would offer stability and a certain new life; exactly what my mother wanted me to achieve from studying abroad.

It was the first time I allowed my fear to make me compromise a decision. Looking back, it felt as if I'd given away a little piece of myself.

I completed a Bachelor of Urban Planning in four years. Family duty number two – done.

I landed an enviable graduate position at a top global engineering firm, Woodward Clyde. When I told my mother, she was so proud of me.

Throughout university and the early years of employment, I continued to get pimples.

Even as a student with limited resources, I would spend money on expensive Dermalogica and Clinique creams thinking, *Surely these expensive ones would work better than the cheap supermarket products.*

And when they inevitably didn't, I moved onto the next cream. Each time the experience ate away at my self-esteem.

LOSING MYSELF

A few years later my partner decided to take an attractive job in Sacramento, California. I agreed to follow, even though it meant quitting my job and feeling my mother's disappointment.

With no working rights and more spare time than I'd ever had before, the first six months felt stress free.

Each morning I would walk to a nearby Borders bookstore and read books, with my Starbucks latte and maple walnut scone. They were not books on planning or architecture.

My enforced unemployment had given me the permission, time and mental space to explore other areas that interested me.

I devoured endless books on alternative health, holistic medicine, vitamins, skin health and various areas of marketing, like 'how to build your own website'.

I had no product idea or even a vague concept of entering into the skincare industry, but looking back, I felt the universe was preparing me to do so.

My skin was the best it had ever looked, which was due to both my research and the lack of stress in my work-free life.

But the clock on my expatriate honeymoon was up. I became more and more restless and resented the loss of my career, my independence and my social circle.

I began job hunting and was offered multiple roles, but as soon as employers heard they would have to sponsor me, the offers were revoked. It was crushing.

I eventually gained sponsorship and a position with a private town planning consultancy and spent four years in the United States.

GAS TO A FLAME

When I moved back to Australia, I accepted a role with a highly respected specialist urban planning company, founded by a prominent female town planner.

She was a very tough boss, but also sharp, smart and fair. I relished the opportunity to work with her, other influential businesses and high-profile development projects throughout Sydney. I worked hard, achieved great results and was nicely renumerated.

Family duty number three – done.

My job was incredibly demanding, but I put my head down and kept going.

One day, a very good friend of mine at work asked me, 'Are you okay?'

I looked at her, confused by her question and replied, 'I'm fine. Why do you ask?'

'Well, you've been a bit teary lately and you're not your usual upbeat self.'

I was shell-shocked. It was almost like she was shaking me or waking me up from a dream.

It brought me back to the time my father had left, and I began to ask myself the same questions about purpose and meaning.

At the same time, my skin was going crazy.

It really started to bother me. I spent so much time covering up and trying out every new acne cream, but the results were always the same. Nothing worked. In fact, some of them made things worse.

My life was in a state of turmoil and my skin was a visual representation of that.

Then one day, a friend of mine who had suffered with acne in the past told me to investigate vitamin B5.

It immediately piqued my interest, and I began googling. It led me to a medical paper on a hypothesis about the biochemistry of B5 in the body and how it could resolve acne.

The paper described an experiment where subjects taking a high dose of vitamin B5 had incredible results.

I needed to try it for myself but every vitamin store or pharmacy I tried didn't stock it. I found some online but couldn't get past the feeling that they 'looked dodgy'. Still, I never stopped looking.

One day, I found myself in the vitamin section of a GNC store near the Pitt Street Mall in Sydney. I found a whole shelf of vitamin B5 and took it all to the checkout counter.

'Wow! You know about vitamin B5 too?' The attendant seemed impressed.

'I bet you're not using it for what I plan to use it for.'

'I use it to help me workout. It gives me more energy and stamina. What are you using it for?'

'To clear up my skin.'

I started taking vitamin B5 at the dosage described in the medical paper, which meant taking twenty capsules a day. In two months my skin was clear and glowing.

My friends and family started to notice and asked me what I was doing differently. My experiment and the reaction to it caused me to have an epiphany. My candle turned into a bonfire.

I must bring this to the world and help other acne sufferers.

For the first time, I had a purpose that truly spoke to me. But I also had a list of hurdles blocking my way:

I needed to find a way to reduce the dosage with the same or better results.

I was going to take on a large, highly competitive industry completely dominated by giant multinationals.

I didn't have enough money to start such an ambitious business idea.

I knew I was going to disappoint my mother.

I embarked on intensive research, identifying synergistic nutrients which worked together with vitamin B5, and came up with the first formula.

I partnered with a friend. We knew all our competitors were focusing on treating the symptoms while our product went straight to the cause. We were pioneers. Our product worked. We could change the world.

When I wasn't working in my full-time urban planner job, I devoured resources about writing business plans, marketing plans and preparing financial projections.

We wrote our first business plan and reached out to dozens of Venture Capitalists around Sydney, only to be told we had to prove ourselves by making a couple of million dollars first.

We turned our focus on finding an angel investor. We received a few enquiries, but the most interesting was from an owner of a medical centre with a strong interest in alternative holistic health.

We chose a fancy restaurant in Sydney's Darlinghurst area to impress our potential investor and sat, full of nerves, as we waited for his arrival.

When he did arrive, we hit it off right away. And then he said, 'I would be interested in investing in your idea, but I won't be able to offer you a million dollars. If you can make $100,000 work to launch your idea, I'm in!'

Of course, we said, 'Yes!'

When I told my mother I was resigning from my professional urban planner job to start my own skincare business, she didn't say much over the long-distance call, but I could feel her confusion and deep disappointment.

But I was on a mission to launch this new business, and no-one could persuade me to do otherwise.

We changed our business plan to an online ecommerce model to fit our new budget, came up with a simple brand and we were off.

Right from the beginning, we knew our brand would be global because there was nothing else like it – not outside of Australia either. So, we began by speaking to the Australian Trade Commission.

They were in the process of putting together an exposition of Australian natural health products to showcase at Cosmoprof Hong Kong, the world's largest cosmetics skincare expo. And they wanted us.

There was just one problem, we hadn't made any products yet.

We allocated a large chunk of money to make our first batch of product, just in time for Cosmoprof. We came out of the event with our first export customers from the Philippines and Singapore.

I then moved to Melbourne to be closer to my business partner and we built our website. As the day the site went live approached, I was racked with doubts.

What if no-one wants to buy our products? Why would they try an unknown brand?

But launch day arrived. Our marketing focused on reaching potential clients through acne forums and search engine optimisation and orders started coming in.

I couldn't believe it. People from across the world were ordering our product. But then I realised that, like me, there were people out there suffering acne breakouts who were desperate for relief.

With our online operation running smoothly, we worked with a business strategy consultant and made a play for the retail market via the health food channel. It worked. We got our first Australian distributor.

NO MORE COMPROMISE

Issues started brewing under the surface with my business partner.

We began to disagree on more and more elements of the business, and I started to realise we had very different value systems.

The lessons I had learned in life and business meant I was no longer willing to compromise on my purpose.

As disharmony grew, we both started to pursue other projects, giving our business just enough to barely survive.

Again, I found myself in a dark place. I had given up everything for the business and I knew it could be a huge success, but I could feel it slipping away.

One day I was reading customer letters. There was letter after letter filled with heartfelt gratitude and praise. Each one telling me how our product had 'changed their life' or 'given them the confidence to face the world'.

I became emotional every time I read a letter and every day I would read another, saying to myself, *You can do it. Believe in yourself. Don't give up.*

One evening, I shared a particularly poignant letter to my husband. Of course, he knew of the troubles I was having with my partner. He looked at me and said, 'Why don't we buy the partners out so you can be your own captain and build your vision?'

It made me excited but also overwhelmed, 'How is that possible?'

He simply said, 'We'll figure it out together.'

From that moment, I set my intention.

TRUE BELIEVERS

Today, I've built a noteworthy challenger brand as the sole owner and director of my business. I have a team of true believers who have faith in my cause, support me and don't take no for an answer.

I used the concept of believing and trusting our product to build our business by offering team members of pharmacies who declined to stock our products the opportunity to try them for themselves free of charge.

They are now not only stockists but passionate advocates.

To this day, when times get tough, my go-to reminder to not give up and keep fighting for my vision is still the steady stream of emotional letters and emails we get from our customers.

My business is entering a new growth phase and I have support from the very top of an industry that once told us we didn't have a place in it.

I live my life with purpose. I build my business with purpose. And through my work I help people regain their self-confidence so they can flourish and pursue their own purpose, free of skin worries.

Life took me on a journey to find my purpose. But because I did, my business is so much more than skin deep.

JUDY CHEUNG-WOOD

Multi-award-winning entrepreneur Judy Cheung-Wood's vision is to support people to feel confident and well with acne-free skin. She founded SkinB5, a global brand that offers effective, holistic, everyday skincare treatments for healthy skin and acne control.

Knowing what it's like to suffer the pain of teenage and early adulthood acne, Judy's quest to create a highly effective treatment, based on a revolutionary, patented vitamin B5 formulation, has seen SkinB5 rapidly grow to become a thriving global brand.

SkinB5 is a combination of highly effective, proprietary nutritional supplement formulations and healing skincare products that treat acne as naturally as possible, with zero nasties and without side effects.

SkinB5 is trusted by an increasing number of health professionals as a workable alternative to prescription acne medication.

Unlike other mainstream acne products, SkinB5 addresses underlying nutritional deficiencies and targets the root causes to stop acne before it starts – from within the body first. Thousands of acne sufferers have been successfully treated in this way since 2006.

WOMEN LEADING THE WAY

Customer feedback is strong. Many report that SkinB5 products are game changers because they heal both the skin *and* the crushing isolation that acne sufferers often feel.

Judy's maternal grandfather was a chemist and manufacturer of natural skincare products. Inheriting his expertise and passion for traditional, nutritional medicine and his ability to create effective natural skincare products, Judy began her quest to find the solution to her own acne challenges as a young adult. Supported by her grandfather's extensive knowledge and wisdom, she emulated his ways by starting to care for the whole body from the inside first.

Today Judy continues her grandfather's legacy. She's here to make a real difference, by helping acne sufferers to heal and flourish. The very heart of the SkinB5 brand is to make effective, natural skincare available, to help users believe in themselves more and confidently present their full face and vision to the world.

SkinB5 is now a successful global company because of Judy's initial courage to hold her vision and move beyond all doubt. When asked to reflect upon her powerful inner drive to help others, Judy credited it to her unusual upbringing and the difficult experiences and relationship she had with her father.

Judy is an author in two anthologies by Oprah's all-time favourite guest and renowned international humanitarian, Dr Tererai Trent, *Sacred Promise* and *Ubuntu*.

Born in Hong Kong, Judy spent her early childhood in Honiara, Solomon Islands. An international student in New Zealand and Australia during her teenage years, Judy then lived and worked in California for four and a half years, before returning to Sydney. Judy currently resides in Melbourne, Australia with her funny, kind and supportive husband Jason, who is also a devoted father to their daughter Jasmine.

Her rich life experience was the foundation for her exceptional open-mindedness, visionary nature, and ability to adapt, see and do

JUDY CHEUNG-WOOD

new and 'different' things and create the global success story that is SkinB5.

Website: skinb5.com
Instagram: instagram.com/skinb5/
Facebook: facebook.com/SkinB5
YouTube: youtube.com/user/skinb5video
LinkedIn: linkedin.com/company/skinb5-pty-ltd & linkedin.com/in/judycheungwood
TikTok: tiktok.com/@skinb5

TAKE TWO – RESETTING HISTORY
JULIE OKELY

PRESENT DAY

History itself can be a journey of discovery, reading and remembering events that happened in the past, events that changed our lives and influenced them to evolve to the lives as we know them today.

It can be exciting or heartbreaking – depending on the historical event being studied.

The imagination is a key influence in taking us back to the events that changed nations – the moon landing, the assassination of JFK, the crash of Wall Street and the long-awaited construction of a global landmark.

Beyond that, imagine if it was possible to travel back in time and become a cowboy in the Wild West, a dancer in Paris during World War I or witness Einstein create an invention?

The opportunity to travel back in time is certainly one of the greatest adventures anyone could hope for in their lifetime – I would assume.

A time machine would be intriguing. To slip in and out of our own current reality, to discover the planet and life as it was back then.

Although with the limited technology available to the average person, how do we do it?

In most cases, when we sit to watch a movie, a story, set in a particular time, the studio can show us a different lifetime and take us, as the audience, on a journey of epic proportions. In my life, through the amazing skills of the cinema, I have been able to explore outer space, journey though the African kaleidoscope and witness the world in 3025, where robots have taken over as domestic goddesses, whilst family members fly off in the family sky car – no roads or tyres needed.

History has exposed us to language, customs, traditions and mysterious architectural wonders from every part of the world. We may subconsciously not even remember the experience, until one day, in a highly active conversation with friends at a local restaurant, our eyes light up – because we remember.

Whether we remember. It is with a sense of emotion or trepidation. We find a common bond with the storyteller, and soon we are drawn into their world where we wait, with bated breath, to hear their animated views on the topic at hand, all the time highlighting their perspectives and opinions on how they believe the events were told.

Was the delivery accurate?

Was the narrator able to capture them and recreate the event or plot correctly?

And was it 'remember-able'?

Was it possible to deposit a little of the storyline or facts – in our already over saturated brains?

PAST HISTORY

There is a saying called *sliding doors*. The term, based around a sliding doors moment, became a term popularised in the late 20th-century meaning seemingly inconsequential moments that nonetheless alter the trajectory of future events[1].

It was a popular saying that originated around the movie of the same

---

[1] en.m.wikipedia.org/wiki/Sliding_doors_moment

title with Hollywood actress Gwyneth Paltrow, and it stuck, becoming part of universal language culture that explains it as: when life can change in a precise moment, and completely redirect the pathway you thought was to be your chosen journey, a new path awaits!

So, coming back to the time travel conversation, what if it was possible to go back and re-enact historical decisions, and change the course of historical wars, financial disasters or diseases that elevated into global pandemics?

Food for thought.

So, let's try this. Imagine a part of history you would change if you had the chance.

What part of our planet's lifetime would you change?

Has there been an event or a government decision you would rather have seen never exist?

Would you have stopped the extinction of the dinosaurs?

Would you stop a war?

Or would you alter the way the event actually occurred in history?

One of my greatest dreams would be to be present in the crowd during AD 27-29 when Jesus was delivering his message to the masses. That would be special, right?

It's okay – we are allowed to think big here. It's our imaginational playground and we can push past the boundaries of reality.

If I had to ask myself *what I would change?* automatically my thoughts become small and focus on specific events that impacted me; the memories that have altered my life from what I believed was my safe predictable pathway.

I would have to choose an event that happened when I was a child. I was the youngest of four siblings and had just witnessed one of my parents being driven away in an ambulance. I was never to see her alive again. She was thirty-nine years old, and her life was over. The memories were still there, as best as they could be remembered from the perspective of a nine-year-old child.

There is a lot of history and storytelling that dissolves when a parent is lost. It leaves an assortment of questions a young child should never have to think of and opens a conversation of complex discussions around the child's future, and which direction is best for them. No longer is the future opening to what the child thought it *was* going to be.

It becomes a *sliding doors moment.*

So, my choice would be to travel back in time to see her again, have a conversation and reprint her image into my eyes, to rejuvenate the memory of her voice and to hear her laughter. She loved to laugh.

A loved one is the more likely choice in most cases when people are asked the question about time travel. Time is the one thing that cannot be changed, rewound or altered in our existence, yet it is the main element we, as human beings, strive to control.

It seems to be the automatic response trigger from the brain, when we ask ourselves the question of change. We begin with memory recall, and it flows freely, showing us images of our past experiences, automatically filing them into the chronological order. We then consider what the events trigger in us, from an emotional perspective, and why it left a memory scar, how big that memory scar is, and where were we at the time it happened. For some of us, it will be simpler to focus on a little event that is more of a curious choice, than a subconscious one.

Are we nervous about the emotional trauma and residual hurt still surrounding certain events, and is it easier to attempt this exercise in jest, rather than truly digging deep to grab that one moment that truly changed our direction in life?

HIERARCHY

At the very core of every historical event within history sits a human being, and the decisions of that one individual, or group of individuals,

WOMEN LEADING THE WAY

to determine the outcome of where our race is taken into the next generation.

Living in a mostly democratic process, we look to put our trust, our lives and our futures into the people who make up our political bodies, elected to rule our separate societies.

Within the action of governing those societies, we place a vast amount of responsibility into the capacity and skills of those elected parties.

Mostly, the most common way to control a society or affect change within that community is to use a technique called Maslow's hierarchy of needs[2]. It is an idea explained within human psychology, describing the stages of growth in humans, based on a theory of human motivation and where it focuses. It is based on how humans are engaged by using behavioural motivations, supplied by others or themselves.

It is broken into eight different stages. Maslow used the terms *psychological, safety, belonging and love, esteem, cognitive, aesthetic, self-actualisation* and *transcendence*.

Termed as *a hierarchy*, each of these individual levels contain a certain amount of internal sensation that must be met in a specific order for an individual to complete their hierarchy and reach the stage of self-actualisation.

It is also possible for the stages to merge in some situations.

Now, I am aware this is a lot to take in, but if you have read to this part, this is where it gets interesting – and I am going to introduce you to something even more intriguing.

NEEDS
- Psychological – food, water, warmth and rest.
- Safety – security, safety.
- Belongingness and love – intimate relationships and friends.
- Esteem – prestige and feelings of accomplishment.
- Self-actualisation – achieving one's true potential, including creative

[2] en.m.wikipedia.org/wiki/Maslow's_hierarchy_of_needs

activities.

Maslow's hierarchy of needs is usually presented graphically as a pyramid, which is easier for the brain to process when we talk about the different needs of human beings.

The most fundamental four layers of the pyramid are termed as the 'deficiency needs (d-needs)' which are esteem, friendship and love, security, and physical needs.

So, a question. At any time have you felt that your basic d-needs have been threatened or challenged? Or has there been a moment in time when there was a situation where your d-needs were slipping away? Did you feel a physical or psychological reaction to that situation?

It's possible that by being deprived of one of the d-needs, you felt a sense of deficiency, which in turn motivates us to strive to find the one thing we are being held away from?

If we are found to never progress past the four fundamental layers, and these most basic needs are never met, in most cases, it is near impossible to redirect and become motivated towards the next levels or to higher-level needs.

This can be seen in many of our fellow humans. When motivation is lost, and they seem to almost give up on life itself, they stay on what we call the hamster wheel, and just *exist* in life – not live fully immersed in it, with all that life can offer.

It is here where we separate the leaders from the followers, the ones who want to strive for a higher purpose, and those who have a 'meta motivation' – the people who strive for what is beyond the most basic of needs. These people are known as the 'go-getters'; the ones who personally want to make a difference in the world and leave a legacy for the next generation.

In wanting to control a society, create a following and gain supporters and influence the way people think, this is the strategy used in most instances.

Think of the politicians, the child who wants to be team captain and the co-worker who desires to be part of the management team. In what way can they influence their successful outcome, and sway the voting power of their specific audience, to go their way – and win?

How did Gandhi protest without violence, weapons or death? Yet Hitler dictated through violence, weapons and death. Both achieved a certain level of control, but in two completely different ways. One positive and one negative; yet they both had supporters to their specific causes.

In history, we find there have been many ways individuals are able to control the planned outcome of events, and as we learn more about the past, we are able to understand the ways this manipulation was achieved. With or without weaponry, there is the initial buy-in from the core participants, while the many objectors are usually sidelined and their voice made irrelevant.

Manipulation is achieved in history by applying pressure through techniques that affect our four fundamental needs. When any of our d-needs are threatened, it is easier for humans to be controlled and redirected in our thought process to believe in what the manipulator is striving to achieve.

OUR PAST

Now let's apply our thoughts of history and focus on the discovery, or invasion, of Australia and its original custodians – the Indigenous habitants; a First Nations population who had successfully lived and been custodians of the land for over sixty thousand years.

It is a long time – think about it. How much has your world changed in just your lifetime?

What significant events could the First Nations Indigenous population have witnessed during those generations, and what knowledge was inherited through them, living amongst the natural resources provided to them by their ancient Elders, sharing their heritage and cultural intellectual property?

To understand the events that occurred during that time in history, we need to come back to what drives a person to become so focused and obsessed with the need to change the natural order of the world to their advantage, and see them apply enough pressure, to apply a time line shift by manipulation of critical circumstances.

Here is where we start to revisit the concept of time travel, the land of imagination and the theory of time travel.

Through the magic of storytelling, I am going to take you on a journey back to the 1700s where a First Nations warrior is standing at the edge of the water, looking out towards the vast ocean's horizon. Still and patient, he watches as a large water creature grows larger as it swims closer.

The area where he stands has had its name for thousands of years. It is proudly known as the land of the Eora Nation – its First Nations custodians, a name given with the colonisation of the earliest European settlers.

The area where Pemulwuy lived during his lifetime was rich in resources that provided food, shelter and nature's gifts. He is thankful. The abundant lands had always provided life for his village and community, allowing them to thrive and grow.

In today's terms, many would call it a paradise, a Garden of Eden.

He stands alert with his spear, standing tall and proud, holding it firm in his right hand. A protector of his people, watching the scenery change in front of him.

The warrior, Pemulwuy, is unaware he is witnessing his first contact with the colonists, and he stands, unknowing he will soon be a casualty, a part of the beginning of colonisation. The *invasion* of the white man.

Brave but cautious, the warrior sees the visitors. He has never seen a pale-skinned man before, and he is confused, watching through narrowed eyes.

There have been mob wars and conflicts over the past generations, so he has learned the exceptional skills to become a practiced warrior, a leader to his people.

The large water creatures give birth to many small canoes, and the visitors paddle the oars towards the white sands – towards the perfect sands his ancestors have tasked him to protect.

What was unfolding in front of him was alien, something he'd never witnessed in his lifetime, nor throughout the ancestorial Dreamtime stories. The unfamiliar way these strange-looking beings were clothed and moved was confronting to him, and he felt the ancient spirit inside of him begin to ignite.

It was his cultural land, and it was his spirit journey to protect it.

Hopefully, I have taken you on a journey back to see our First Nations peoples.

A vital part of my history. A vital part of your history. The ancient history, and the Dreamtime stories of the First Nations peoples, lives through the sliding doors moments, through the pain, the loss and the trauma, through the past to this time line, calling for answers, understanding and to be heard and acknowledged.

JULIE OKELY

I am a proud Kamilaroi woman, born in Coonabarabran NSW. I called Sydney, Kenebri and Baradine home during my childhood.

I commuted a lot as a child between Sydney (the big smoke) and Kenebri and Baradine – which is located just outside Coonabarabran (the bush).

I grew up in a fractured family, with my mother and father separating during my childhood and our house having a strong presence of domestic violence and alcohol. As a result of this, my mother Jean, at thirty-five years old, relocated to Sydney in an effort to start a new life as a single mother to my three siblings and myself.

Upon settling on the Northern Beaches of Sydney, tragedy struck our family and she passed away at thirty-nine years old.

Our Indigenous heritage vanished with her, and our lives changed.

Since my sister and I were very young, we were taken to live on a small family farmhouse with my paternal non-Indigenous grandmother. It was located in a tiny country town called Kenebri, located halfway between Gwabegar and Baradine. From memory, it had, at best, twenty houses in the town with a few scattered properties on the outskirts and a railway track running parallel to the main road. The town itself had very little in the way of infrastructure, as there was one communal one-stop-shop as a general store/beer garden/petrol pump as its only commercial building.

I caught the bus to and from school every day, the only way in and out of town for the school children to Baradine, a town thirty minutes away. It became a very isolating way of life. I learnt to grow veggies, play with the farm dogs, and climb trees among other farm activities to keep myself busy.

I moved to Sydney when I was seventeen, as I was struggling with my education, after beginning year eleven at Coonabarabran High School. I began to look for employment in the hairdressing industry, as I knew it was something I had enjoyed during past work experience opportunities.

I have had some highs and lows in my working life. I suppose my worst job was a window cleaner, which didn't pay very much. I remember walking around suburban Sydney for hours and looking for customers that needed their windows cleaned. It didn't take long for the enthusiasm to fade away with that one.

It was during the holidays between year eleven and twelve, I began meeting salon owners with the hope to become employed.

My first job was as an apprentice studying hairdressing at Bankstown. I was seventeen. I won the job by default and only because my boss knew of someone and the fact that I was a country girl helped too. It was difficult in the eighties to find an apprenticeship, as hairdressing was a favoured career at the time.

Since that time, I found the mentoring of younger hairdressers very rewarding.

Throughout my hairdressing career, I have been able to deliver the creative and necessary technical skills to educate hairdressing apprentices. I have also been able to encourage students to diversify within their career, whilst developing their own portfolio of hairdressing skills and gain experience in other areas.

I have opened several salons successfully – four which are still operating today with the new owners, and I have been able to train over 150 staff in the necessary skills that are required when operating a business and keeping it successful. I encourage staff to grow their skills to further their abilities to become leaders themselves.

I lead with respect and understanding, with the ability to communicate and educate, and keep students engaged and willing to learn.

I have learnt resilience and the ability to reassess and accept situations or directions that may have not always been the pathway I had originally chosen.

I have since enjoyed a successful career in hairdressing, having educated and trained over one hundred apprentices, school-based apprentices (ASBA) and casual employees during my career as a hairdressing manager/owner, technical advisor, and product developer.

I believe the purchase of every new business is a milestone. I have owned several salons during my hairdressing life and each one was important in its day.

Realising at forty that I have an Indigenous heritage, I felt the need to identify and develop an understanding for culture.

Therefore, in my business, the most significant change was when I decided to rename my business. Once I had embraced my Indigenous heritage, I realized I needed to make changes within my business. I changed the trading name to Dilkara Hair. I then spent time understanding the meaning of the Kamilaroi and Aboriginal languages and I decided on Dilkara. This held many meanings relevant to my business from a colour, physical and spiritual level. Dilkara is an Aboriginal word meaning 'rainbow'. It's fitting because of the colours within the range of hair. I also believe Dilkara represents the different skin tones that are found within our Aboriginal and Torres Strait Islander peoples.

WOMEN LEADING THE WAY

This has been embraced with positive energy from clients, mentors and corporations whilst providing them with an understanding of what the Indigenous language is.

The then development of the Dilkara Essence of Australia hair care range has been a notable milestone for me. Being able to use native Australian Bush ingredients as the formulation base for the hair care products, is really exciting.

I love the Indigenous influences and the bush blends that create such gorgeous results.

I love contributing to the sustainability of Indigenous communities.

I love the feedback that we receive on a daily basis, and the smiles of the customers that have given us the most amazing stories of their personal experiences.

I am now facilitating the global exportation market with this product.

I am passionate about using Dilkara to make a difference towards reconciliation. I believe understanding Aboriginal and Torres Strait Islander heritage and culture and taking it to another level is a key element to reconciliation.

My products use specific bush botanical blends once and currently sourced by Indigenous communities. It's exciting to be able to share this ancient knowledge and carry it into modern industry, keeping cultural education current in the eyes of all. I believe in bringing together Aboriginal and Torres Strait Islander peoples and non-Indigenous Australians, as we all deserve equal value, quality, and education.

Dilkara Essence Of Australia was born from me recognising the need to create a pure organic line that utilises the Australian Bush Botanicals and brings the awareness of our Indigenous community's knowledge to the global community with a core presence in the hairdressing industry.

This uniquely niche market and the idea to create my own hair care and body care products, led to the creation of Dilkara which has been asked to participate in editorial shoots that are featured in global magazines. A core part of the business is to also offer consultancy services to global companies to further develop their products and services. This supports the Closing the Gap initiatives that the Australian Government oversees. There are eighteen products in the range, which utilises my connection of Indigenous raw ingredients with Indigenous Australia. My aim is to have Dilkara Essence of Australia in hotels, day spas and salons around the world showcasing what Australia's Indigenous community can accomplish.

The reason I'm so passionate about my brand is that it not only provides a unique product for Australia but also an opportunity for Indigenous communities to sustain a better way of life. Dilkara Essence of Australia has also been a product of choice from the Qantas InSky shopping catalogue, something that I'm very proud of. That is the reason that keeps me going.

I also went on to study again at CIT to increase my qualification level. I now hold the highest qualification in Australian hairdressing. I am proud to be gaining further education in knowledge and skills that I can pass onto others to help them grow and further the potential of Indigenous individuals.

I have enjoyed a satisfying career within hairdressing doing many roles.

I always feel the need to be constantly challenged, and that's something hairdressing, mentoring and business provides.

I use my business wherever I can to create opportunities for others and empower and excite Indigenous females by creating career pathways and opportunities for them.

I often engage in editorial work and create amazing images of hair for photographers and with international and national magazines including Italian Vogue.

I am devoted to the ever-changing opportunities Indigenous females are given, so it is a privilege to be able to use my career and my goals to effectively reach out to others in many ways, above all by teaching Aboriginal and Torres Strait Islander students, participants in workshops and helping them gain sustainability in their own economic futures.

I approach all challenges within my business with positive perspectives and assess the alignment of my values with the task at hand. I always look at the bigger picture and look to solve the problem with multiple solutions.

I have several mentors that I turn to that assist with me with valid solutions, and they allow a valuable sounding board to bounce my ideas off them when needed.

Two examples within our manufacturing business were when we were sourcing the raw ingredients from Australian suppliers. Rather than go through the generic pathway, we have chosen a select group of suppliers that provide better financial returns to the Indigenous communities. This provides an on-flow effect to create sustainability to communities within their own familiar environment.

The second example was when I began formulating the hair and body products that would become the DEOA range, it was important to have a transparent supply chain with Indigenous values within the range. The importance of having all botanical ingredients come from the Australian bush through Indigenous communities was vital.

During manufacturing, I had instances where the incorrect essential oils such as vanilla and Japanese flowers were added by the biochemist. I made it adamant that the need to reformulate and focus on the key botanicals harvested through these Indigenous communities was quintessential to the values behind Dilkara. I believe, to be pure and honest and to upkeep the values of my brand helps me to be a role model for all customers, affiliates, and industry collaborators.

Therefore, through Dilkara, I have engaged authentic raw suppliers that have been approved by Indigenous communities. This is an important part of our ethical practices and we market this transparency as part of

JULIE OKELY

our supply chain campaign. I have a strong social media presence that we utilize to promote the Australian botanicals used within our brand. We have established a social media platform to facilitate consumer engagement to share our message and we look to nurture these connections to showcase our Indigenous business.

This year we have sponsored Indigenous sporting teams and donated products to charities, fundraisers, and Indigenous functions.

I endeavour to make decisions based on the impact that I have on future generations of the people around me. If I can have a positive impact and create sustainable income streams for Indigenous peoples, businesses, and communities, this aligns with my company's values and core mission statements. I choose organic, paraben free, sodium laureth sulphate free components that are used within the Dilkara formulations. I will not support any nasty chemicals or carcinogenic ingredients that are health impacting and those ingredients that create skin reactions and irritations. I will not support animal testing or anything that creates a negative impact on our environment. I choose recyclable packaging and refillable options that prevent excess landfill and wastage.

Now I often meet with companies like EY, KPMG, Woolworths, Coles, Aldi, IGA, BP Australia, Qantas, Supply Nation, and The Indigenous Defence Consortium headed by Adam Goodes and Michael McLeod.

My proudest achievements are when I was awarded the Supply Nation Indigenous Businesswoman of the Year 2017 and ACT Indigenous Business of the Year 2015.

After the loss of my mother, my heritage went with her and I was disconnected from my Indigenous community, until many years later, after doing my family history and later identifying as an Indigenous person – a proud Kamilaroi woman. To achieve this award was beyond explanation. I felt complete within my heritage, I finally felt accepted by my peers and fellow community members, and I had proven myself within that network. From that award, I felt a deep satisfaction of total acceptance and achievement.

Through all of this, I learnt that life's accomplishments are a journey and to never give up on who I was born to be.

I also became a published author, with the book already optioned for a TV series. This was something I had wanted to do for many years, and now I have achieved it. This suits me, as I love pushing the boundaries and pioneering new ideas often.

Currently I am working to bring the community together with the automated web platform All First Nations, where it will bring all First Nations peoples together. This will also host the Our Sistahood e-commerce education modules, where female Indigenous members can find free resources to help them gain knowledge in several areas.

I stand for strong independent Indigenous businesswomen. I embrace opportunity and aim to be the best that I can be. My goal is to inform and educate the world about the value of Indigenous business, services, and cultural heritage. To assist in the understanding of the culture and capabilities of our organisation, we write vision and mission statements, engage in cultural educators and we introduce all these components to all new employees.

Being a proud Kamilaroi woman, I believe in the respect of culture and heritage of all our Indigenous communities.

My immediate family understands our culture, supports me in helping to raise awareness for the education of Indigenous female Australians, and know it is very important to me. I feel that even the smallest progress and positive influence is better than staying stagnant, and the ability to think broadly and influence others to achieve their goals is very important.

I am involved in supporting the community through mentoring, sponsorship, motivational talks, and fundraising initiatives.

My hairdressing salon in Canberra, Dilkara Hair, offers mentorship to local Indigenous and non-Indigenous female youth who want to pursue hairdressing as a career.

I've also given talks locally and interstate encouraging Indigenous youth to create their best future.

My businesses have sponsored local Indigenous football teams such as Indigenous Tag20 and the Deadly Sisters tag team.

I've also coordinated a remote fundraiser to assist in repairing inoperable water bores at Utopia on the Northern Territory, saving the community approximately $2,000,000. Involving the NT Government, Coca Cola, ABC Radio, and the community made it possible.

THE ROLE OF WOMEN IN MODERN LEADERSHIP
KAREN WEAVER

Now more than ever, women are leading the way in this new era of leadership; leading with their hearts and less from a competitive perspective. Leadership is definitely going through a period of transition. No longer do men in suits sit in big corner offices and dictate orders to employees. That's not 'progressional', and I'm relieved that leadership looks so different in this era. Women who are stepping into leadership positions are showing how it's done.

People are now thinking for themselves and seeing the possibilities that open up when they step outside of the box. Women are leading the way forward and making a real difference in our world, both economically and in the quality of life we are choosing.

No longer is this kind of leadership just 'talked about', these days it's being shown in positive action. I call it *inspired leadership*, when a woman steps in and shows the way. I believe it's the only way forward. The dictatorship of the former days of leadership, of 'being told what to do', is not sustainable. People are now thinking more for themselves and thinking outside of the box to see possibilities opening up their hearts and minds to higher purposes.

And those calls to action are fuelled by women who are stepping up, showing up and showing how it's done.

And it's making a real difference in our world economically, and also in the quality of life we're choosing. We have transitioned from the linear thinking of women staying at home to raise the children and the men going out to work. We now have a lot of women leaders working from home, still wanting to run their households and raise their children. They want it all; the best of both worlds. But it can be tough.

It's a tough way to *do life*, but it's also the most fulfilling. You don't miss out on anything. You can still be an independent woman and business leader as well as be a hands-on mum. As a mum of six children, running several successful businesses, I understand how this works and the challenges we all face. I financially sustain myself and my family, as well as living my purpose. I'm very ambitious – and there's nothing wrong with that!

But I also understand the three key things that I need to do, and which work for me, to enable me to continue to be a mum first, and also a business leader.

Number one is to never compromise my values. I need to know myself and what my core values are. I know what is the essence of me, and these days, I never compromise that, because I've experienced a couple of times when I did allow myself to compromise my values, and I can tell you, no success is ever worth the compromise.

Next is self-care; I must be doing something that fills my cup. That's why I created a job for myself that lights me up every day. I can keep my cup full, which means I can give my best to others. And I open my arms wide to earn an income doing what I love.

It's not a hobby. And it's not something that 'just keeps me occupied', it's important work and it pays well.

Number three is to understand that I'm not here to *control* my kids. I'm here to guide them, to allow them to grow into themselves and to support them to discover their own passions and purpose.

Yes, it will usually be a juggle and I often feel a lot is happening in my life, but that's not going to be forever, because as any parent will tell you, kids grow up so fast.

It doesn't matter whether a woman has children or not, women are leading the way forward with passion and compassion. Children or not, but more obviously for women with children, there is still plenty of discrimination around women in leadership and this must be eradicated.

A woman with children can show you how to treasure your life, as well as treasuring the balance of what you take for yourself, along with how much you can give.

A woman with children who steps into leadership will show you how you can achieve great success with minimal time and resources.

Women are changing the face of leadership and that's why it's so important for women to continue to step up and lead the way. Women of all ages, colours and cultures are stepping up, connecting into their highest purpose and showing up for that. Yes, there will be adversity; there will always be challenges on any journey. In fact, any journey worth having will come with adversity, but the challenges are not there to block you and stop you. The challenges are there to evolve you into becoming a new person, and your greatest goal will feel like the very next step.

That's how we change future generations. That's how we make a difference. One of the important things I talk about is when a woman has a higher calling other than motherhood. Again, we can be a great mother, but we can still have ambitions, goals and dreams. If we sacrifice those dreams just to become a mother, there's a good chance we're not going to be happy.

And our kids are going to see that. Our kids will see us sacrificing ourselves through motherhood. What are they going to learn from that sacrifice? What will that teach them other than how to sacrifice themselves for others? As much as I think it's amazing that we support and assist others, is the only way through sacrificing ourselves? No, we can show our children how we help others through our work, through our passion and through our purpose. When we set goals and intentions, and stay focused on them, we always bring other people along for the ride, and that will always lift them up and support them in a far greater way.

So, let's pick other people up as we are on our journey and keep moving forward together, not deviating off the track. Move forward together with focus and confidence, along with purpose and passion for the greater good. This allows everyone to benefit – especially our children. They will see that hard work pays off. They'll see you successfully navigate challenges and how you grow through adversity. They'll see that dreams can become reality, and that will encourage them to experience life to their highest potential.

When your children see you shine through your passion, they will have a totally different belief system than what many of us grew up with. Most of us were brought up with our parents' beliefs and as we have journeyed through life, we have had to 'unlearn' those beliefs. If we can guide rather than control our children, they won't have so much to unpack, or so much to 'unlearn'.

So, *Women Leading The Way* is an important conversation to have. We are powerful and we are important. Eleanor Roosevelt said that 'behind every great man is a greater woman' but we are not just here to support men. There is nothing wrong with supporting the men in our lives, of course, but more importantly we must support ourselves and champion other women, lifting each other up and making a difference for the future. Because when women lead the way, good things happen. When women are independently financially, it can only lead to a better world, because women have a tendency to build businesses that are purpose-driven and built for the greater good.

So, let's support all women; ourselves and each other. Encourage our girls to step into the light, growing forward into their passion, and help our boys to learn the importance of supporting inspired female leaders in their classrooms.

WOMEN LEADING THE WAY

We all deserve to be heard. We all deserve to have everything we value and want in life. And we can be the difference for the next generation. We need to lead the way and show how it's done.

Women have come a very long way, not just in the past century, but in a few short decades. They have gone from being expected to stay at home and raise children while men went out to work, to having the ability to have both a career and a family. It is a tough balancing act, but it is also the most fulfilling way to live life. Women can be independent while being hands-on mums. They can financially sustain themselves and their families, while living their purpose and being ambitious.

Here's a reminder of the three key things you can do to enable you to continue to pursue your dreams and goals:

1. Never compromise your values. Know yourself and what your core values are. No success is worth it if it means compromising who you are.
2. Self-care. Do something every day that fills your cup – something that lights you up. Only by having a full cup, can you give your best to others. Open your arms wide to earning an income through important work that speaks to your passion and purpose.
3. Understand that you are not here to control your children. You are here to guide them, to allow them to grow into themselves and discover their passions and purpose.

In conclusion, women of all ages and cultures are leading the way forward in modern leadership. They are showing us all how to lead in a way that is sustainable and fulfilling, passionate and caring.

The importance of having a higher calling other than motherhood cannot be overstated. While women can be great mothers, they can also have ambitions, goals and dreams, and this will encourage our children to live a life of their highest purpose too.

And women leaders are showing that when they support each other, everyone benefits, especially our children.

KAREN WEAVER

Women must continue to step up and connect with their highest purpose, if we want to make a difference in the future of our world.

KAREN WEAVER

Karen is an award-winning publisher, author, TEDx Speaker and advanced law of attraction practitioner.

Author of numerous books across many genres – fiction, motivational, children's and journals – she chooses to lead the way in her authorship generously sharing her philosophies through her writing.

Karen is also a sought-after speaker who shares her knowledge and wisdom on building publishing empires, establishing yourself as a successful author-publisher and book writing.

Having built a highly successful publishing business from scratch, signing major authors, writing over thirty books herself and establishing her own credible brand in the market, Karen has developed strategies and techniques based on tapping into the power of knowing to create your dreams.

Karen is a gifted teacher who inspires others to make magic happen in their lives through her seven life principles that have been integral in her success.

When time and circumstance align, magic happens.

KAREN WEAVER

Website: serenitypress.org
kmdbooks.com
mmhpress.com

NATURAL-BORN LEADER
LISA WALKER

From as early as age six or seven, I recall regularly being called bossy, dominating and a 'big personality'. These were all words used with negative connotations and hurtful inferences, but seriously, who was going to organise my Barbies and keep my brothers in line? Being the middle child in a migrant family, with an older and younger brother, these particular traits were not seen as pleasant or palatable for a young lady, but I didn't care. My voice was just as important as the boys', and I knew I could yell even louder – so yell I did!

Whether it was being the goalie on my junior soccer team, organising everyone in front of me, literally catching what was thrown (or kicked) at me as the last line of defence, or as the leader in my Girl Guide group and leading the way through a forest in the rain to make camp for the night, I have always had a natural knack of taking the lead, getting on with the task and taking my crew with me for the journey.

Throughout my journey, I've had some amazing leaders and mentors – let's call them the 'Simons'. Yes, three of my biggest career influences were all named Simon. All three of them taught me incredible skills in leadership and finance – and all taught me some things I definitely never wanted to do as a leader.

Here are my top five leadership lessons from my last twenty-plus years of leadership experience – gee, that's gone quickly. Take what you will, whatever resonates or makes you laugh. Learn from my crazy experiences and be your most authentic, real leader that you know you are.

LESSON 1: MANAGEMENT VS LEADERSHIP

This leadership ride isn't always easy. There is a massive difference between leadership and management, so often discussed, yet still so badly delivered, by far too many managers.

I had my first real 'management' role at age twenty, with a team of four – all older, and with way more workplace experience than this young whippersnapper. I was taught you had to be tough and hard as a manager. I went in all guns blazing, trying to rule with an iron fist. I wanted to be the 'boss', assert my authority and make them listen to me – oh, the arrogance of a twenty-year-old.

Imagine my frustration when they didn't want a bar of it. Why wouldn't they do the things I was asking them to? Why wouldn't they go the extra mile and want to do a good job? These people were horrible and trying to make me look bad in front of my boss – surely. The audacity of them. How the heck was I going to turn it around and meet our goals and targets?

I had to put my thinking cap on, as back in the early 2000s there was no Google or YouTube tutorials to help guide me. I watched other managers in my organisation and other organisations (literally the Coles manager at our local shops), listened to my friend's stories from her job at Maccas and also continued working in my family business, taking tips and tricks from them all.

It felt so unnatural to me, and I soon came to realise it wasn't as necessary to rule with an iron fist as it was to lead with a golden heart. *Leadership lesson one.*

I quickly learnt that if your people can see the bigger vision, the strategy and their part or purpose to get to the outcome, they will be onboard and want to do a good job for themselves and their team. That's just human nature. Take them on the journey with you and don't micromanage. Give them direction but allow their thoughts and ideas to help shape the outcome. Two heads, or more, are always better than one.

Bingo – all of a sudden the team were coming to me with thoughts and ideas and better ways of doing things. We were mind-mapping and brainstorming and collaborating on every idea, and soon, our little team was the top income earner in our firm. This felt right, how it should be, and we thrived. Never have I made that mistake again.

This now seems like such common sense, a real no-brainer, an absolute given, right? Yet this is the most common mistake of all management roles, a serious fail, and often, the number-one reason why people leave an organisation. Give your team value and purpose and they will reward you with hard work and loyalty. This is a key principle as to how I operate my five businesses today and will always continue to do so.

LESSON 2: YOU DON'T HAVE TO BE FRIENDS WITH YOUR WHOLE TEAM TO LEAD THEM

I was never popular at school or in my former careers, and this previously bothered me – horribly. I have always worked hard with honesty and integrity. I always do what I feel is right, even if I can be over the top, so why don't they like me? I'm a good person. I work hard. I granted their leave, gave them an extension on their work, allowed them a longer lunchbreak or to leave early when they needed to, so why am I not in the 'in crowd', 'inner circle' or part of the 'cool kids'? It was so perplexing. Surely, I am good enough?

After returning from my second maternity leave in as many years, I felt I needed to prove myself, and that it would be easier to do all the work myself, until 3am each morning. I thought it would ensure the whole team 'liked' me and we got praise from the bosses for an amazing *team* effort. But I had actually done the work myself, while the rest of the team took longer lunchbreaks and had days off ... again. With two young children under fifteen months old and my husband often travelling internationally for his job, this was not sustainable and certainly not fair – so stuff that!

My team were not respecting me or my role. They were walking all over me, and my family needed me more than my team did. When it came to the crunch, I had to choose my mental health and family's welfare over being 'liked' by my team. In fact, people came to respect me for this decision, and even – gasp – admire me, as I set the lead for our whole division. I changed the dynamic and spun it on its head. I stopped pandering to their requests, didn't care any longer about who liked me or not, cut the gossip, cut the cliques and made each team member accountable for their tasks. This took time, a huge brave face and lots of resilience, but I managed to change the culture, in a productive, conducive way. *Leadership lesson two.*

I don't need to be friends with my team to get the job done, I just need to show up consistently and show that I have the determination and grit to get it done, while providing them with leadership on the journey. Amicable yes, pleasant and empathetic, sure, people may not like you or want to be your friend, but they will respect that you can get the job done. And that is perfectly okay. Oh, and if you do become friends, it can be a bonus.

Being authentic and your real self to lead your crew is the best way to be. They will see how you lead and want to match your values. I also came to realise that I'm not for everyone – for access to me, I need to like you too.

LESSON 3: BE REAL – PLAN FOR THE WORST, HOPE FOR THE BEST

The best-laid plans of mice and men ... you know how the story goes. As a leader, the best-laid plans can come unstuck and unravel far quicker than they get planned in the first place. Always have a backup plan, a contingency, a redundancy – always. *Leadership lesson three.*

As the world is ever changing, and especially in the health care field, which is my main business space, we always need to have some kind of redundancy built in. The businesses we operate are often everyone else's backup plan, so who or what would be ours? Thinking caps back on …

After my paternal grandmother, Lisa (yep, my namesake), passed away in my arms in late 2014, six months after I had taken over failing health care businesses, I knew we had to do things better for every 'Lisa' out there.

From fifteen years of business and government experience, I came up with some core values and principles these businesses still use eight years later. The values and principles have helped set up our team culture and philosophies, which we have become known for in the sector. We have never had to advertise for clients and rarely advertise for staff, as our reputation precedes us.

Our values and principles have, literally, become our backup plan. No matter who we hire, they simply must meet our criteria, and this is then a fail-safe for the quality of our team. We only hire people who want to be here, who want to be a part of something amazing and those who can see the vision for our business. We take them onboard and help them with their career in response to their commitment.

Our clients are also all hand-picked and we need to be satisfied we are happy for our amazing team to work with *them*. We will not tolerate disrespect or our team to be treated badly. We do our best to place the best-fit team member for each client so it is a mutually beneficial relationship. Simple, yet extremely effective.

We position ourselves with like-minded partners: our solicitors, our employment advisers, our accountants, our insurance broker, our uniform supplier. They are all like-minded individuals who have common values and goals for their businesses. This is not a coincidence. Every single one is hand-picked to be a partner, and we regularly review these relationships to make sure they are mutually beneficial, which means our clients and ultimately our team get the best also.

These considered relationships, team, clients and partners, sets up our fail-safe, our redundancy, to manage whatever is thrown our way.

LESSON 4: KNOW YOUR SUPERPOWERS AND THOSE OF YOUR TEAM

One of the things the 'Simons' taught me was to use your superpowers to do the things you can do and surround yourself with skilful people who can do the bits you can't or aren't your strength. Empowering my people and utilising their skills makes for a great team, and every team still needs a captain to steer the ship. *Leadership lesson four.*

When I first took over management, and then bought, two failing businesses, I soon realised I was only as good as my team who was delivering the service. While I have great sales skills (thanks to the Simons) and can literally sell sand at the beach, this just gets us through the door to *deliver* our services, it is my team who have to show up and be amazing to keep us there, giving us the opportunity to be the provider of choice which, unsurprisingly, has worked.

I had a few amazing team members who I inherited with the business and am so grateful I did. Two of them are still with me today, both with more than ten years of service. This is absolutely unheard of in the casual workforce. Both have furthered their careers and transitioned through different stages of life, while I have had the absolute privilege of watching them from the sidelines, helping and supporting where I can.

Over time, I also learned that to lead you have to listen first. I always make a point of seeking feedback from my team, listening to their responses and empowering them to ensure they feel valued, seen, and most importantly, heard. This means you will know your people and their skills, and make sure everyone is useful and has purpose in the team. One of my core beliefs is that in any organisation, your team is always your most valuable asset. So often, managers forget this simple concept, while leaders help build 'future leaders' in their teams.

LESSON 5: BUILD THE NEXT LEADERS

One of my greatest joys is not always leading, but being a cheerleader, a supporter, a wing-woman and a right-hand person, allowing others the space to grow and develop as new leaders. I've sometimes done this without even realising I'd been doing it.

I've had the absolute pleasure of watching my crew grow, both personally and professionally, and this is one of my greatest achievements to date; seeing them step up into their own leadership roles. There are a number of amazing people I have worked with numerous times throughout my career, in various roles at different organisations, and the ongoing respect we have for each other has shaped our professional lives. For this, I am extremely grateful. I'm always so excited for their next steps and continue to cheer them on.

The third amazing team member I inherited with the business is now my business partner, best friend and one of the best humans I've ever had the privilege of knowing. I took a massive chance offering her a partnership into a crazy life-changing business, and she took an even bigger chance accepting it. There are ups and downs, sideways and rockets, but I don't think we would have it any other way. Knowing she didn't have any business experience, I was acutely aware I needed to step up and lead us both forward, including helping her grow and develop as a businessperson. It has been an honour to watch this growth and development from the front seat over the last seven years, and I am so proud of her and every one of her achievements.

What you give out comes back. I was recently announced as a finalist in four categories for a prestigious business award. When my team posted this to our social media, the comments from my team members in each and every one of my previous and current careers, was overwhelming and humbling. What I thought was a small thing I had said or done, had been a turning point, sliding door moment or life-changing conversation for these team members. You never know who you impact, or how, by being your authentic self. *Leadership lesson five.*

I am absolutely honoured to be a part of the 'new breed' of female leaders, empowering women and taking them upwards and onwards. This is something I have found extremely underdone in my previous careers; no-one would take you under their wing or teach you what they knew in case they became irrelevant or you got a better promotion.

Women don't need to compete. We need to collaborate with a like-minded community and that's when the best will always come.

LISA WALKER

Firstly, I am a bit crazy, a bit cooky, a bit extra, I like to think outside the box, but I have a huge heart! I've had a varied career in many sectors including government, accounting, retail and now agriculture and health care, yet I still don't know what I want to be when I grow up! I completed my Bachelor of Commerce Accounting in 2002 and my certified practising accountant qualification in 2007. I was honoured to be awarded a Fellowship of the CPA in 2022. I am the mum of two – Mason, eleven, and Serena, thirteen, as well as my spoilt fur babies. My husband, Matt, and I have a number of businesses we have established or rebuilt together including two health care businesses we rebuilt and two new ones we co-own which we are so passionate about. With the rest of our time (!!) we are working in our Truffiere with the first truffles hopefully coming in 2023!

DARE TO BECOME MORE THAN MEDIOCRE
MEGAN HARRISON

Do you remember the first time you ever *felt* success? It was year eight for me. I had joined an intensive program with the Western Australia Institute of Sport for sprint kayaking in which we trained eight times per week and competed at various national championships. In other words: a *big* commitment of time, energy and spirit for a young teenager. No doubt, my squad worked *hard* – harder than I'd reckon most eighth-graders are interested in! It took heaps of sacrifice and focused determination, but when I won my first competition … *whoa!* That moment, my first rush of winning, felt *so* good – especially after training so hard for it. In fact, it had felt better than anything I had yet felt before.

And the thrill of winning didn't stop at the finish line. Success, I quickly learned, is the gift that keeps on giving. After that first win, my dad was so proud of me, he took me to the surf shop to buy me a new outfit, and all my friends and family wanted to talk to me about *the big victory*. Seemingly overnight, people thought I was *interesting*. And I *liked* that! My first slice of success was so intoxicating I was instantly hooked on it. I knew then that I wanted 'that winning feeling' as much as humanly possible, and I knew I'd do whatever it took in my life to achieve it. If success in life was a race, I was ready to train – and train hard.

At a similar time to this first taste of success, I started to become increasingly close with my Auntie Jennifer, a wildly eccentric woman with an outrageously bold personality and outfits to match. Due to her unorthodox manner, none of the other young nieces and nephews found a strong bond with her. But me? I flocked to her. Beyond the unconventional exterior, I saw she was a highly successful, academically bright, well-travelled woman who was supported everywhere she turned by robust and meaningful friendships. *Hello* – who doesn't want that? I craved being around her as much as possible because I knew I wanted to be like her. I saw in her life all the things I wanted for mine: confidence, success, wealth, a purpose, a supportive community, a legacy. Others saw her as too 'out there', but I knew there was *something* about her ways that I needed to learn.

Ralph Waldo Emerson said that 'our chief want in life is somebody who shall make us do what we can'. Every truly effective leader has had at least one person in their life who modelled to them the art of excellence, success and leadership – a mentor. And though I didn't fully comprehend it at the time, I now see that Auntie Jennifer was mine. As a commissioner, she was always up to something amazing and travelling to unique places, and she often included me. Considering her high-level job, she hung out in circles of incredibly influential women who were doing out-of-the-box things. *Interesting things.* They were all women who were in some sort of significant leadership role, and they were all actively making a tangible difference in the world. This group of women stood out to me because the things they were doing and discussing were not 'normal', and I was extremely drawn to that.

Even from a young age, I knew I didn't want the 'normal' life I saw people settling for everywhere I looked. And my auntie and her pals definitely did not lead a normal life! Luckily for me, she loved to bring me around her friends often, and the thing which sticks out most strongly in my mind about spending time with that group of women in my youth is that they *never* wanted to talk about themselves. Never. They always wanted to know what *I* was up to, what was new with *my* family, how *my* classes and sports were going. I would walk away from spending time with them and think, *Wow, why are they so interested in* me? As a teenage girl at the time, I didn't think I was anything special, but they sure made me *feel* special, and that had a huge effect on my life. Because they took the time to get to know me, listening to what I had to say as if it was truly important to them, they were able to draw out all kinds of beautiful passions and dreams in me, which planted seeds of confidence for success in my future.

I learned from this group of mentors that listening is one of the most powerful tools a leader can possess. Letting others know you value what they have to say builds rapport, trust and confidence. And not only does it empower those you lead, but it informs your own leadership decisions. As Woodrow Wilson put it: 'The ear of the leader must ring with the voice of the people.' And when I look back on my time with my auntie and her friends, I understand that they weren't just there to support my growth, but I was there to help inform *their* choices as well, even if in some minor way. They were the voice of the people, and that included the youth (me). I looked up to my Auntie Jennifer so much because, despite her high social status and success, she never acted higher-than-thou. She valued the voices of others. Today I strive to carry that torch in all of my interactions, both professional and personal, because I learned rule number one to becoming a better leader is that you must speak less and listen more.

Building upon what my early mentors taught me and actively listening to others throughout my own leadership journey since, here are my top five tips on how to become more than mediocre – because you can't expect to do what everyone else does and achieve excellence.

WOMEN LEADING THE WAY

Surround yourself with people you can learn from. What do you do when you want to become something? You do whatever you can to learn from those who have already become that something. I wanted to be a winner, so I did whatever I could to learn from winners. Auntie Jennifer was my first mentor, but I have sought out many more since, and it has always led to improvements in my life.

I once asked the general manager of the Australian Sports Commission to be my mentor after meeting her one time at a conference. *Who does that?* People who are serious about success, that's who! She said yes, and years down the track she offered to be my person of reference at a job I applied for at the Australian Sports Commission. With my qualifications and her reference, I was a shoo-in for the position, and it all happened because I had the outrageous confidence to take a chance and ask to learn from her. A good leader will almost always say yes to a bold mentee request like that, so I encourage you to find someone you really want to learn from, muster up your confidence and shoot your shot.

You've probably heard that if you're the smartest person in the room, you're in the wrong room. So, unless you're already a sensei, go find rooms of successful people you can learn from. Leaders don't do normal, and that includes the company they keep.

Strive to be a hard-ass with a soft heart. When I worked at a mine site as a young adult, I had a boss named Bill. He was ex-Navy and smoked, drank and swore like a sailor. He was my first real boss, and though I was a bit intimidated at first, he turned out to be a damn terrific one. He was such a hard-ass, holding us all very accountable for what we did or didn't do, yet he also had a healthy soft side. He took time to get to know us somewhat on a personal level – but not *too* much. Just enough to know what was important to us and what made us tick, which then allowed him to tailor his leadership style to each of our unique personalities. Because of that, despite him having extremely high work expectations of us, we all fucking loved him! (Pardon my French, but I say it in homage to Bill.)

Whether you're leading a Fortune 500 business or a high school sports squad, building a close-knit team culture is extremely important to success. Bill taught me that, as a leader, finding the balance between friendship and authority is key to gaining people's trust, fostering mutual respect, and drawing out the best work you possibly can from them.

Be different and be confident in that difference. Drawing from the excellence I saw my auntie model, I knew I could not be excellent myself if I was ever content with mediocrity. So, I vowed to do things differently – to go big or go home – whenever I could. This meant I nailed my first job interview after university by bringing props and a presentation, which impressed the employers as they'd never seen anyone do this before for an entry-level job. I bought my first home when I was twenty-one and owned six properties by the time I was thirty. I worked and excelled in the male-dominated mining industry on a health and safety team in my young twenties. I became a multimillionaire in less than a year after starting my own business – in the middle of a pandemic!

The point is, I *chose* to be different and took the risks required to do so. What I've learned is that you have to be confident in those risky decisions to be different. And frankly, that's a difficult task because very few people are going to back you up for choosing to do things beyond the status quo – you have to be brave enough to back yourself. Doing so is the most important thing that distinguishes the average from the excellent.

Intend to bring others up with you. Authoritarian leadership is a relic of the past. Good leaders help others achieve their goals while on the journey to achieving their own. They foster an environment where individual *and* collective success are both important. They encourage success in the people they lead. They work for a cause, not applause. At the core, this leadership trait requires humility, and it's an extremely attractive and effective characteristic for a leader to learn.

In my business, I strive to build a team I can bring with me – and *wants* to come with me. Old-school leaders who place a high importance on themselves and their authority eventually fall – hard and alone. Modern leaders, on the other hand, understand it's much wiser to have people *with* you than *under* you. As theorist Simon Sinek argues, 'The best leaders don't derive their standing from official lines of authority. We follow them, not because we *have* to, but because we *want* to.'

Bring people up with you by inspiring them through the demonstration of your interest in their ideas, passions and opinions and by creating leadership pathways for them. This is particularly relevant in this day and age when discussing females in leadership. Some might say women have a tendency to be catty or competitive with one another, but the real flex is when women commit to lifting each other up. We need more females who are willing to do that. In a world in crisis on many levels, it's not just about 'me-me-me' anymore. As they say, a rising tide lifts all boats.

Allow your leadership style to evolve. 'Consistency,' Oscar Wilde declared, 'is the hallmark of the unimaginative.' And when 'unimaginativeness' takes hold, it will certainly be the death of a leader. The ability to adapt is the cornerstone of leadership, and this includes allowing your leadership style to evolve. What you knew yesterday is not what you know today and none of it will be what you know tomorrow.

A perk of the art of listening is that the more you absorb from other people, the more you will distil your leadership style over time. Always keep an open mind and be willing to refine your style. Style isn't meant to be forever. Allow yourself the grace to continually change, because the bottom line is, people who don't allow change are the people who think they know everything – and those are often the people who actually don't know much.

Rewinding back to the first time I ever *felt* success, today I can say with pride that my continual 'training' has brought forth many wins in my life. What I've learned since is that this training is, at the core, a training in confidence. And a leader is merely someone who has mastered the craft. My time with my auntie helped instil confidence in me at a young age, which I continued to slowly build on throughout my life. She and her friends took time to plant those seeds of confidence in me because they knew, if I wanted to be like them one day, I would have to tend to that one very important skill.

Like my Auntie Jennifer, and like every effective leader I've ever known, being a leader means you will have to learn to be confident enough to stand on your own, despite what the mainstream hive mind has to say about you. It means you will have to be okay with being seen as a little 'out there' in the eyes of the masses. It means you have to be outrageously bold – *wild*, some might say. After all, as Robert Green Ingersoll dramatically put it, 'In the republic of mediocrity, genius is dangerous.' But the simple fact is, you can't do what everyone else is doing and expect to be different – it doesn't work like that. You have to be different to be different. You have to dare to become more than mediocre.

MEGAN HARRISON

Entrepreneurial powerhouse Megan Harrison brings more than fifteen years' experience in the health, safety and sanitisation industry, both as former health and hygiene advisor in the mining industry and founding director of WA's leading sanitisation company, SanSafe. With a bachelor's degree in sports science and nutrition, a postgraduate diploma in health promotion and a masters of occupational hygiene and toxicology, Megan's involvement in public health initiatives is substantial, including advisory services on developing and delivering complex industrial training and assessment programs, as well as designing protocols, policies and budgets.

Though she is educated in, experienced with and passionate about hygiene, at the core, Megan is truly an innovator. Brené Brown says, 'There's no innovation and creativity without failure. Period.' And Megan is a shining example of the reward that taking risks, braving setbacks and being persistent can bring to life and business. Understanding that failure is a defining feature of the landscape of success, Megan's commitment to perseverance despite the odds is the foundation of her massive success in an extremely short period of time.

MEGAN HARRISON

In 2017, Megan debuted her entrepreneurial spirit and founded FlashMop, an Uber-style, industry-disrupting app that seamlessly connects residential and commercial cleaners with clients. While FlashMop was by all means considered triumphant, Megan was hungry for something more, and when COVID-19 suddenly flooded the world with uncertainty, Megan knew it was time to take a leap. While much of the world panicked and froze, she went into action mode, strategising to bring a new business idea into fruition in an extremely short period of time and in a business landscape that was becoming increasingly chaotic due to the pandemic.

What emerged was SanSafe, a disinfection and sanitisation company that successfully answered one of the biggest public-health problems our world has ever seen. This brave pivot moment turned out to be a move that changed her life, making her a millionaire nearly overnight. Having been quickly awarded contracts for the sanitisation of COVID-19 quarantine hotels, FMG and Newcrest Mining, as well as for WA's shipping and airline industries, Megan took SanSafe from a startup to a million-dollar business within a span of only twelve months.

Today, SanSafe remains operating as a proactive solution to modern-day health challenges, and is supported and managed by a team of qualified, experienced and professional administrative, organisational and operational staff. Despite having certainly achieved that 'something more' she was after with SanSafe, Megan is never prepared to rest on her success.

A serial entrepreneur with a 'go big or go home' mentality, she is always looking for new creative ideas and prepping to launch the next thing. Recently, she has launched *For My Sisters*, a company on a mission to end 'period panic' at schools, workplaces and beyond by making period products reliably available where they are needed most — for free.

Megan is walking proof that success isn't just about an idea, but a mindset. Living in Perth, Western Australia, with her husband and four children, she is driven to leave a legacy for her family, inspiring her children and generations to come that *anything* is possible when you put your mind and heart to it.

Website: sansafe.com.au & formysisters.com.au

JOURNEY OF AN AIRLINE PILOT TURNED CLIMATE TECH FOUNDER

CAPTAIN MOLLY FULLEE

I wasn't fulfilled anymore with just staying on autopilot, pun intended! After a twenty-year career as an airline pilot, I wanted something more to challenge myself beyond my comfort zone. From soaring through the skies to soaring towards a new venture, I landed in the world of climate tech, determined to make a difference in the world. I have always been an adventurous soul, so being born on the tiny island of Mauritius felt like destiny. I grew up exploring my small island with great curiosity, dreaming of one day travelling to places beyond my own horizon.

As a little girl, I was fascinated by the sky. My gaze was always skyward, literally walking the ground whilst looking up. Whether it was an airplane doing a slow island tour or staring at the magnificent starry nights, my eyes were glued to the sky. Deep inside me, I knew I was an explorer, here to discover the world and immerse myself in different countries and cultures. In typical island fashion, going to the airport to drop off or pick up someone was a family affair. Watching the airplanes up close at the airport was the ultimate joy as a kid. Little did I know that, at some point, I would become a captain on one of those airline jets!

It was a dream come true in the year 2000, when I experienced my first flight as a passenger, aged fifteen, leaving Mauritius to come to Australia. Taking off over the turquoise beach and climbing over the deep blue sea felt like flying through heaven! The big white clouds looked like giant marshmallows that the plane swallowed as it climbed higher and higher. Seeing the island get smaller and the vast horizon ahead felt like a big wide world was waiting to be explored. When I landed in Sydney, I was spellbound by the sight of the iconic Harbour Bridge and Opera House, and I knew then that anything was possible. The next ten years were filled with hard work, perseverance and endless hours of study. Being enrolled at university and learning how to fly was exhilarating, satisfying and hugely rewarding. After successfully getting all my licences, I decided to become a flying instructor. It was the ultimate way to give back and help other aspiring pilots, like me, soar through the skies. Having built up thousands of hours of flying experience, I was selected to join as a first officer at a major domestic airline in Australia.

What began with just a dream had now turned into an amazing journey, filled with passion and determination, flying around the world. Proving once again that anything is possible if you set your heart on achieving your dreams, I worked relentlessly towards my command upgrade.

Becoming one of the youngest female captains of a jet airliner in Australia is a huge highlight in my life. To think, a little islander girl from Mauritius who dreamt of becoming a pilot was now the captain of a multimillion-dollar jet airliner – the pinnacle of the dream come true!

What followed for the next ten years was a fun-filled life exploring the world, making new friends and discovering new cultures. I was living my dream every day, enjoying the diverse crew I flew with, and I was proud of achieving my goals.

However, a series of life-changing events that unfolded shook me to the core. Although I loved the sensation of soaring through the clouds, I felt like something was missing from my life – a sense of purpose that could not be found in an airliner cockpit.

The death of my father taught me that life is too short to not pursue my true purpose. I wanted to make a difference in the world and leave a positive impact for future generations. That's when I dived into climate tech and co-founded my startup. Overcoming the grief made me realise how high my pain threshold was and to never let fear stop me in my endeavours.

PAIN THRESHOLD

Mauritius is often referred to as Paradise Island. The year-round sunshine, soft sandy beaches and warm lagoons make it an idyllic place to grow up. The beauty of the island with tall mountains in the centre wrapped around turquoise blue water is unlike any other. Life was simple growing up, with a self-sufficient way of living.

Every few years on the paradise island, we get severe cyclones that ravage the entire island. Weeks of no electricity, running water and living on rations are life lessons that broaden your pain threshold. Having survived a few deadly cyclones through my childhood gave me a different perspective of how to deal with life when the gale-force winds are ripping buildings apart and the torrential rain is flooding the surrounding area.

Rebuilding after such catastrophic cyclones brings a unique gift called resilience. The sun does shine again after the storm. A brand-new beginning awaits the brave. Helping the community rebuild again and again after cyclones equipped me with the tools to help communities rebuild. Having a high pain threshold also means you don't let the little things in life bring you down.

Every storm that comes through your life allows you to rebuild. Rebuilding anew allows you to grow stronger and more beautiful.

THE REINVENTION JOURNEY

It was a moment of clarity that changed my course. After a lot of soul-searching and trying to discover my true purpose in life, I felt a pull towards ocean conservation and decarbonising mobility.

The beach has always been my happy place. Sitting on the white sand and looking at the amazing palette of blue in front of me is so calming. Time seems to stand still and somehow all the other weights of the world seem to vanish.

But in 2020, everything changed. After seeing the devastating effect of the oil tanker spill on the beaches of Mauritius, I couldn't help but feeling part of my soul crushing inside.

There is nothing worse than feeling helpless when a devastating event occurs. As I watched for days on end how the whole event unfolded, I was disappointed and frustrated that the aftermath was so poorly handled.

With the world grinding to a halt, it was time to rebuild. With new-found grit and passion, I decided to leave aviation behind and venture into uncharted territory: climate technology.

Drawing on all our experiences from flying around the world, together with my husband, we launched our startup dedicated to making a positive change in the world through smart battery charging technologies. I was amazed to find out that two-wheeled electric vehicles displace five times more oil than passenger car electric vehicles. One of the solutions to decarbonise mobility is to make it easier for people to adopt e-bikes, which are cleaner and easier to scale globally.

Electric bikes are both great for the people and the planet, but charging batteries is a pain point for owners. Slow charge times, frequent costly battery replacement and the fire hazard of charging in homes are all reducing the uptake of this impactful technology for daily transportation.

To address these challenges, we developed Impulse – a smart battery charger for e-bikes that extends the life of your battery by as much as five times and monitors the entire charging process. It disconnects if a hazard occurs to prevent fires, giving hassle-free charging and peace of mind to e-bike owners.

We discovered that it's possible to increase a battery's lifespan by slowing down its deterioration. This in turn helps reduce both environmental and ownership costs. The advanced charging algorithms get the best out of your battery. With AI and pulse charging, it shortens charge time and extends battery life by reducing lithium degradation.

We are driven by a passion for innovation and a commitment to making a positive impact on the world. Despite facing countless challenges along the way, we worked tirelessly day and night until finally launching the business globally.

Drawing on my experience as an airline captain, I knew I had the skills to make this venture successful. My strong communication skills, problem-solving abilities, analytical thinking and a knowledge of global operations proved invaluable when dealing with clients and deadlines. Also, having grown accustomed to making split-second decisions while in high-alert situations gave me the confidence to negotiate contracts or develop strategies for success.

Our vision was quickly recognised, and we were selected to participate in a global accelerator program. It was a dream come true to present our product to a major energy company in America. We are now on a mission to provide sustainable solutions that benefit not only the environment, but also the lives of people around the world.

My reinvention journey is not just a glimpse of passion and grit, but also one of hope and possibility.

GOING GLOBAL

When the opportunity came knocking to participate in a global energy accelerator, the decision was simple. We had to go all-in! Seizing this opportunity and jumping on the ride was daunting, yet exciting. After months of online meetings, the date finally arrived to make our way to San Francisco and Texas.

There were so many reservations about how we would accomplish travelling with the whole family, minus the kitchen sink. There were moments of deep uncertainty and doubt.

The power to keep going came from the tremendous support and encouragement from our new-found friendships. At times when nothing seemed to go our way, there were tears and tantrums, but we were determined to make it work.

Arriving in San Francisco, the tech capital of the world, was so enthralling. Seeing places we'd only dreamt of visiting and walking the grounds of so many inspirational geniuses, fuelled our souls and gave us a huge boost of motivation to keep pushing on with our journey. We were surrounded by doers and shakers, people who were eager to help us achieve our goals. A city where dreams come true every day.

I was blown away at the hospitality of the people. Spending time with like-minded people who believed in our mission and were willing to come on the journey with us was gratifying. As we travelled across the USA, we found fast friends and very supportive crowds.

Being in Texas, the energy capital of the world, was exhilarating. Seeing cars literally 'fly' along thirteen lanes of the highway, with the overpass stacked four roads high, was mind-blowing! Watching NASA launch rockets from the pad felt as if nothing was impossible. Having breakfast with an astronaut reinforced that if you have a dream and work at it every day, the impossible starts to look possible.

Looking back and reflecting on our journey of how we overcame our fears, insecurities and doubts gave us a renewed boost in our determination and confidence.

Climate tech is taking the world by storm, and for good reason. With rising temperatures, natural disasters and melting polar ice caps on our doorstep, it's never been more important to make sure we have solutions in place to combat global warming. That's why so many communities are now turning towards climate technology as their go-to solution.

Climate tech connects nations and people around the world to come together for a bigger cause. Feeling more like a global citizen, I have a renewed desire to keep expanding our reach and collaborate with nations around the world. Together, we can create solutions to combat global warming and build a brighter, more sustainable future for all.

The five mottos I have used while leading the way are:

I AM THE LEAD ROLE IN MY LIFE.

As a child, the magic of imaginary play allows you to be whoever you want to be on the day; living life like it's your stage and you are the director of this amazing movie called *My Life*. This helped me perform in the most daunting moments by not taking myself too seriously and making sure my cast members, in a particular scene, were having fun. It really changed the outcome of how the play or showcase of events rolled.

As we grow older, it is important to realise that we haven't achieved our full potential yet. Putting yourself in uncomfortable situations is hard and dealing with the imposter syndrome makes you nervous, however, when you surround yourself with friends and family who are constantly cheering you on and are proud of your achievements is the ultimate fuel that lights up the rocket inside your soul to make you reach for the stars.

So, let's take a moment to embrace the magic of childhood and use it to propel us forward into the amazing story that is our lives.

LEAD WITH BELIEF

I believe you have in you *everything* it takes to achieve success. I know it's not always easy, and sometimes it feels like success is out of reach, but trust me when I say that every little win counts. Celebrating every little win and giving yourself a high five when things are going your way clears your path to even more success. They say success breeds success! Now, when you add to this mix your support community of friends and family, fulfilment and contentment come along your journey. The ultimate combination of success and fulfilment is what makes your soul jump for joy and empowers you to tackle any adversity head-on.

You have the power to overcome any obstacle that comes your way. Keep pushing to be the best version of yourself. You've got this.

LEAD WITH YOUR SUPERPOWER

We all have our own talents. I've had to do a lot of soul-searching as to who I am and what I want to be when I grow up! Finding the things that gave me joy fuelled my soul. Knowing what you are good at also means knowing what you suck at. Making peace with my shortcomings and not dwelling on them gave my character strength. I really had to be honest with myself and focus on the things I excelled at. Doing more of the things I was good at led to more success along the way. The universe has an amazing compounding effect which puts you on a roll with the success that's being produced. All this culminating into winning a community award, was the cherry on top for all the hard work put in so far.

One of my greatest joys is infusing a bit of island vibe into my interactions with others. After speaking with me, I want people to feel rejuvenated, like they've just returned from an amazing tropical getaway. And helping others to lighten their load and find strength within themselves is an incredible power I hold dear. It's a fulfilling feeling, and one that I treasure deeply.

LEAD THROUGH FAILURE

Imagine a world where failure didn't mean you were ashamed of the outcome, but instead you were praised for giving it a go. Where you weren't depressed when you got knocked back, but instead lifted for showing up.

When a baby falls over when learning to walk, the world is quick to give a hand to get the baby back up and is cheered vehemently to try again. So why did we stop doing that when someone is learning to run a business or writing a book?

Failure is part of growing up. Yet we fear it and are unable to properly deal with it. What if it was normalised as part of the journey?

Personally, I know that dealing with failure is hard. To realise all your efforts, together with the blood, sweat and tears you invested, didn't pay off is heart breaking. You start with the best intention of winning and when things start to get off track, it is you who has to pick up the pieces and keep going.

No-one gets taught how to handle failure. There were always hurdles that needed to be jumped. Some of them, I jumped really high and kept running, while others, I fell flat on my face. The hardest part when life knocks you down is how you are going to get back up.

The art of dusting yourself off and gathering your strength to keep going is a part of what makes the journey rewarding. So, let's change the narrative and celebrate the efforts made, even if it doesn't result in immediate success. Let's normalise failure as part of the process and lift each other up when we fall. Because it's through our failures that we can find the courage to lead towards success

LEAD WITH LIGHT

My purpose in life is clear to me: to spread light wherever I go. I know every person I meet is struggling with their own battles, and I strive to be the beacon of hope they need. There is a certain energy within me that draws people towards me, and I use it to make everyone feel valued and special. When I see someone struggling, I make sure to offer a kind word or a helping hand. Seeing their face light up with joy and relief is the greatest reward of all. Through my actions, I have formed deep and meaningful connections with people from all corners of the world. I feel so blessed to have been able to touch many lives with my light. It gives me a sense of purpose and fulfilment that cannot be matched. Every day, I wake up with the intention of spreading even more light and positivity to the world around me.

Ultimately, The transition from the cockpit to climate tech was a thrilling adventure I never could have predicted. But that's the beauty of life – sometimes the unexpected paths lead us to the most incredible destinations.

My journey was far from easy, but with hard work, determination and a willingness to learn, I was able to soar to new heights. It was a challenge to adapt to a new industry, but by combining my old and new skills, I was able to create a successful path forward.

Through the ups and downs, I never lost sight of my passions and dreams. I used every obstacle as fuel to propel me towards success. And now, as I reflect on my journey, I am filled with pride and fulfilment.

So, to all the women out there, never stop chasing your dreams. Believe in yourself, work hard and never give up. Who knows where your path will take you – it could be the ride of a lifetime.

CAPTAIN MOLLY FULLEE

In the tropical paradise of Mauritius, Molly's adventurous spirit and unyielding determination were born. With a heart set on taking flight, she embarked on a journey to Australia to pursue her dream of becoming a pilot. Molly soared to the top, earning her wings as one of the youngest female captains at a major Australian airline. Her mastery of the skies took her to the four corners of the world, navigating her way through both clear skies and turbulence with grace and confidence.

However, Molly's passions soon led her beyond the cockpit. From her bird's-eye view as a pilot, she witnessed the world changing before her eyes – floods, bushfires, storms and heatwaves becoming more frequent and intense. As an open-water diver, she also witnessed the destruction of coral reefs across the globe. Fuelled by a fierce desire to create positive change, Molly took to the world of entrepreneurship and founded Fulle – a climate technology startup that produces smart EV battery chargers for two-wheeled vehicles.

With unwavering dedication and innovative thinking, Molly's vision came to life. Fulle quickly gained international recognition for its sustainable solutions, and Molly earned accolades for her role as a leading female entrepreneur in the climate tech space. She has become a beacon of hope and inspiration, proving that with passion and commitment, anything is possible. Today, Molly's mission continues as she leads the way towards a brighter, more sustainable future for us all.

Molly's journey began in the turquoise lagoons and sandy beaches of Mauritius, where she developed a deep love for the ocean and its inhabitants. It was this passion that inspired her to take action to protect our planet, and ultimately led her to co-found Fulle, a company that produces smart EV battery chargers for two-wheeled vehicles.

Achievements:

- Finalist at Startup Victoria Climate Tech pitch night.
- International Women's Day Scholarship Winner at Stone & Chalk Innovation Hub.
- One of three companies selected in Studio X elite Accelerator Program.
- Verge2022 participant, biggest climate tech conference in San Francisco.
- Fundraising tour in USA, Houston and Austin.
- Austin Startup Week showcase.
- Winner of 2022 Climate Salad Climate Tech Award.

GETTING UNSTUCK

A JOURNEY BACK TO SELF
NITI NADARAJAH

Just outside my study window is a beautiful pomegranate tree with lush green leaves branching outwards and upwards in every direction and a multitude of bright crimson flowers welcoming the summer sunshine.

Every year, I would watch those delicate red flowers blossom and wonder whether this would be the year I would finally see a little pomegranate. Every year, I was left disappointed as the flowers came and went without the appearance of any fruit. By 2021, I had given up all hope that the tree would ever produce any and had come to accept it as a pretty, flowering tree and nothing more.

Imagine my surprise then, when one morning in early 2022, I went out into my backyard with my son to see, not one, but many, little pomegranates growing on that very tree! As we now head into another summer, I am overjoyed to see the flowers have multiplied in number, promising an even more bountiful supply of pomegranates in the months to come.

My journey over the last twenty years has been like that pomegranate tree – stagnant for many years, then bursting into an explosion of colour and abundance of fruit, bringing with it immense joy, the likes of which I have never experienced before.

THE ROOTS

Growing up in Australia, as the child of first-generation immigrants from India, my sister and I were acutely aware of the emphasis the South Asian community places on education, career and financial success. As a high achiever, getting good grades was never an issue, but when people asked me what I wanted to do when I left school, I would shrug my shoulders and tell them I didn't know.

Consequently, when I was choosing what degree(s) I wanted to do at university, I used a process of elimination, finally deciding upon a double degree in law and commerce, as it had a higher entry score and wasn't on my list of 'definitely not' degrees, as well as a diploma in French as a nod to my passion for learning languages.

Luckily, I really enjoyed studying Law, particularly those subjects relating to human rights and international law. My dad had taught us to treat people with kindness and fairness, no matter their skin colour, political or religious beliefs or personal circumstances, and we would often discuss, with disbelief, social injustices around the world and the prejudices others held. I decided I wanted to work in international law, but when I was researching how to enter that field after graduation, it became apparent there was no straightforward pathway. Instead, others advised me to do an articled clerkship at a major law firm, get a few years of private practice under my belt and *then* make the move into international law.

STAGNATION

Within weeks of starting my articles, I knew I didn't want to be a private practice lawyer, but life had other plans in store for me and so, despite my unhappiness, I continued to progress my law firm career for the next decade, every so often wistfully researching how to transition to a human rights legal career and thinking to myself, *Perhaps one day, I'll be courageous enough to follow my heart.* Finally, after one too many times of sacrificing my personal life, health and wellbeing to my job, I decided to leave private practice, but by this stage I had given up on my dreams to become a human rights lawyer and so I became a corporate in-house lawyer instead.

Life improved. I was intellectually stimulated and satisfied and working with some great people. I had more balance in my life, was able to nurture my relationships with friends and family and spend more time looking after my own health, which had suffered tremendously during my last few years in private practice.

Somehow though, it wasn't enough. Work satisfied me, but it didn't fulfil me or make me want to leap out of bed in the morning. I felt like I was on a treadmill – walking mindlessly through my career, without an understanding of why and without a destination in mind. I knew something was missing.

But whenever I thought about doing something else, I told myself it was too late to change careers – that ship had well and truly sailed. I told myself I didn't have any other skills or options, and I needed the financial security and safety that an in-house legal job provided. I told myself that, perhaps, I just needed a change of scenery – to change jobs. If it wasn't for the pandemic and more importantly, the resulting shift in my perspectives on life, I would have done just that. And one day in the future, I would have retired after a successful, yet personally unfulfilling, career as a general counsel.

An Explosion of Colour!

Having given birth to my second child in 2019, I was getting ready to return to work in March 2020, just as the world was starting to wake up to the dangers COVID-19 presented. Having not seen my colleagues or team members much during my parental leave, I found myself desperately searching for a way to maintain connection – to share my experiences and stories and to hear those of others I knew. Prior to the pandemic, I had dabbled in writing on LinkedIn, and I found myself returning to the platform – a place I, oddly, found safe and comfortable. My musings became my journal, albeit a very public one.

At first, I shared my experiences as a senior female manager and mother during COVID-19. I spoke about the challenges of working from home with two young children, one of whom was doing remote learning. I shared the joy of having a window into the personal lives of the people I worked with, at seeing people drop their professional personas and become real, multidimensional human beings. I even discussed my own mental health challenges and learnings relating to self-care.

Soon, I started to receive messages, often from other women, telling me that my stories had resonated with them. My stories had made them feel less alone in their struggles and I had helped them. The first time I received one of those messages, my heart swelled with pride and joy – with contentment.

As I found my voice and others found me, I became braver in what I shared. I started talking about gender and racial bias; about the challenges women face in the workplace when they become mothers; about the identity crisis children of first-generation immigrants face. Until finally, one day, I sat down with my laptop, took a deep breath and started to write a story I had written in my head and spoken out loud in the shower countless times before: the story of my pregnancy losses and resulting mental health challenges. It was a story I had long wanted to share as I had felt the impact of my losses and resulting loneliness and isolation all too keenly. I wished for a world where loneliness wasn't the norm; a world where we talked about pregnancy loss, infertility and stillbirth more openly; a world where we held space for each other's grief and pain.

Pressing the ENTER button on my keyboard that day was a turning point, as I laid myself bare and shared my emotions in a way I had never before had the courage to do. With one flick of a finger, I embraced a vulnerable side that had been buried beneath layers of armour since my childhood, and with it, the deeper sense of purpose that drove the telling of my story.

As the messages came flooding in from far and wide in response to my story, I felt my heart expand. I realised then that this feeling of profound fulfilment and purpose was what I'd been missing throughout my career. Having now experienced that feeling, I knew I could never go back to a life without it. But with the realisation came confusion. Apart from sharing my stories, how could I truly embrace this feeling and make it a bigger part of my life? Could I turn it into a career or perhaps even a business? What would that look like and how could it be financially viable?

Luckily, I received some timely and invaluable advice just as I was starting to spiral out of control in my mind. One woman I spoke to expressed her admiration for what I was sharing and the personal revelations I was experiencing. She advised me to spend some time reflecting on my personal values and strengths; to focus on understanding who I am at a deeper level, what I desire and what I bring to the world. Someone else told me to stop worrying about the future; to let the opportunities present themselves to me and the path to my ultimate destination would illuminate itself in time.

Reflecting on my personal values was a harder task than I thought it would be. As I contemplated the events of my life that had shaped me into the person I now was and my related values, I started to experience the external world differently. I became more aware of the daily happenings in my life and started to be a more present parent with my children, noticing things I would have otherwise missed in the rushed chaos and routine that often accompanies parenting. I also began to make a link between my personal values and emotions, triggered by different people and/or events in my life. It also became easier to recognise the areas of my life where things were not harmonious with my values. Consequently, I started to create firmer non-negotiable boundaries and with them, a stronger, more aligned sense of self.

Concurrently, the opportunities began to flood in. I started to write articles for various publications and to appear on several podcasts, sharing my story and talking about issues I felt passionate about. Feeling a strong pull to do more in the racial equity space because of my own privileges, namely my Australian accent and education, I reached out to women working in that area to see how I could contribute my time and effort to their causes. I also started mentoring other women and volunteering my time with a pregnancy loss support organisation to satisfy an intense need to help women who were suffering in silence. And importantly, I continued to share my stories on LinkedIn, my voice getting louder and more unapologetic with each story I told, building a community of inspiring individuals from all over the world who shared my passion and vision.

My eyes were now wide open to *possibility*. And with greater clarity on who I was and what I had to offer to others, it had become clear to me that my purpose lay in empowering other women and in doing my part to help create a more equitable future for the little girls of tomorrow, like my daughter.

Even so, a little voice inside my head told me I didn't have the credentials; that perhaps I needed to wait a year or two before I could start something new; that I couldn't make a living from doing this work; that perhaps I might fail. And so, I stalled and remained stuck, straddling two worlds but not fully committed to either.

AND FINALLY, FRUIT!

That all changed when, one day, I read an article about legal freelancing.

An idea started to take shape in my mind. Perhaps I could meet my need for financial security and stability through freelancing, while also having the time and financial freedom to pursue my passion and purpose.

With this thought taking root inside my mind, I finally made the decision to leave full-time employment and become a solopreneur in early 2022. Handing in my personal belongings and key card to my employer, I felt an immense weight lifting from my shoulders and my soul; the weight of internalised expectations of who I should be and what I should do as an adult; the weight of having fallen into a career I enjoyed but did not love; the weight of feeling unfulfilled and letting fear control me; the weight of unhappiness and resignation to a life half-lived; the weight of not realising the full potential of ME.

Nearly one year has passed since that day and I have grown exponentially since that time. I no longer wake up in the morning, sighing because it's a workday. I no longer feel something is missing or ask, 'Is this all there is to my life?' Instead, I wake up knowing I am making a difference, that I am helping other women to be their most empowered selves, and in doing so, I am realising my deeper purpose.

It hasn't all been plain sailing though and I've had to rethink my relationship with stability, money and promoting self. I have experienced times of great discomfort and self-doubt. But to quote Susan David PhD (a Harvard Medical School psychologist who delivered the widely watched TED talk, *The Gift and Power of Emotional Courage*), 'Discomfort is the price of admission to a meaningful life.' I would experience all that discomfort time and time again in exchange for the puzzle pieces of my life finally coming together to form the picture they were always intended to create.

You may ask, though, is purpose and meaning really all that important? Do we all need it? Should we all be pursuing purpose? Is that even realistic?

First and foremost, I believe our focus should be on understanding who we are, whether through self-reflection or through conversation with others – reflecting on our values, strengths, skills, passions, achievements and struggles. When we understand who we are, purpose becomes self-evident. Importantly though, purpose doesn't need to be a full-time gig. For some, it will be. But for others, that may simply be impracticable or even undesirable. Purpose can be satisfied in many ways, including through a side hustle, a portfolio career, volunteering, mentoring, a hobby or through parenting or caregiving.

What *is* important, is that when you discover the thing that lights you up and gives you a feeling of deep fulfilment, you lean into it in a way that is sustainable and feels right for you. What you will then no doubt discover is that fulfilment is self-perpetuating because it fuels your body, mind and soul to BE more, GIVE more and DEMAND more in, and from, life.

I could never go back to my life as it was before – a life where I asked, 'Surely there is more?' The explosion of colour and abundance of opportunity my journey of self-discovery has unleashed in me propels me forward, because making a difference is no longer optional. It is non-negotiable.

NITI NADARAJAH

Who am I?

Well, I could tell you a story about an intelligent, but shy, little girl who grew up in Australia with immigrant parents from India. A girl who chased the missing 2%. A girl who grew up thinking strength meant keeping things bottled up within. A girl who often felt lonely, as if she didn't belong. A girl who knew from an early age the power of *compassion*.

Or I could tell you about the young student who devoured books about people and places and saved up her student earnings to backpack around the world. A student who wanted to see, learn and experience new things and who was discovering who she was as she took in the beauty of the world around her. A student who embodied *curiosity*.

Or perhaps there's the young lawyer who experienced for the first time the challenges of workplace politics, difficult managers and a work-hard, play-hard environment that left long-lasting scars. A lawyer who learnt that sometimes, you need *grit* to survive.

I could also tell you a story about a naive, but successful lawyer who became a mother, expecting her hard work to simply speak for itself when she returned to work after parental leave. A woman who learnt that prejudice and bias are everywhere. A woman who started to veer outside her 'professional lane' to share her stories to promote belonging and *inclusion*.

Or I could tell you the story of the woman who always felt something was missing from her career. The woman who felt satisfied but unfulfilled. The woman who found her voice, and with her voice, discovered purpose and passion. A woman who had the *courage* to follow her heart to find freedom.

Compassionate.

Curious.

Gritty.

Inclusive.

Courageous.

These are the qualities I bring to everything I do and that make me who I am. These are the qualities that saw me leave a long and successful career as a corporate lawyer to start my own passion-fuelled coaching and diversity, equity and inclusion consulting business, *Coaching by Niti*.

Having discovered the life-changing essence that is *fulfilment*, I am on a mission to help women who are feeling *stuck* in their careers to connect with the reasons why they find themselves unable to move forward, whether because of having internalised the expectations of others, a deep fear of the unknown or of failure, imposter syndrome or perhaps even the impact of having experienced prejudice and bias. I believe when we connect with our own 'inner compass', we can overcome those barriers, start living our life in alignment with our deeper desires, and more easily navigate the road map to our true north.

Creating a brighter, more equal future, requires bold steps and bold women who know *who* they are and *what* they want. My goal is to help make that a reality.

NITI NADARAJAH

Niti is also a master NLP practitioner, coach and gender equality expert at Grace Papers, coach with Coaching Advocates, freelance general counsel through her business Legal by Niti, legal adviser and consultant to The Creative Co-operative, angel investor with Nobody Studios, DEI Ambassador at Human Leaders, member of the inclusion, diversity, equity and accessibility practitioners panel for NASA Astrophysics, mentor at Future Women and keynote speaker. In 2022, she was recognised as a LinkedIn Top Voice (Gender Equity).

She also volunteers as a peer support companion at The Pink Elephants Support Network and is a community partner for White Ribbon. In her spare time, she can be found reading, doing savasana, travelling, enjoying good food and wine and dancing up a storm with her two beautiful children.

LinkedIn: linkedin.com/in/niti-nadarajah
Instagram: Instagram.com/storiesbyniti

INTUITION IN LEADERSHIP

UNLEASHING THE POTENTIAL OF INTUITION IN DECISION-MAKING
DR OLIVIA ONG

I've come to understand, over time, that lots of people are 'paralysed' and living their life in an invisible wheelchair. They might be stuck in a job they hate, trapped in a loveless marriage, shackled in unfulfilling relationships that are built on the principles of people-pleasing, or any number of other situations that limit their ability to be truly happy and fulfilled.

I was completely unaware I was trapped in one of those invisible wheelchairs until I found myself having to rely on a real one. Paradoxically, it was the real wheelchair that showed me the way to free myself through self-compassion. This is how my story began ...

Wednesday 10 September 2008 should have been a great day. I got out of my car and walked through the hospital car park. It was the same path I took most days. Out of the corner of my eye, I saw an old, worn-out Toyota reversing out of the disabled parking spot. I didn't think much of it.

Then, in the blink of an eye, I was thrown up in the air and landed with a hard thud on the ground. I opened my eyes and noticed excruciating pain in my lower back.

It was one of those moments when time seems to stand still. I remember thinking I was lying in an awkward position and that the car I saw reversing must have hit me. Then I was struck by the idea that I was still alive and realised God had protected me. I thanked Him profusely for saving my life.

I then put my doctor's hat on and did a head-to-toe inventory. My thinking was intact, so I knew I didn't have a traumatic head injury. I started moving my arms and concluded I was not a quadriplegic.

Then I realised I couldn't feel my legs. That's when I panicked.

I immediately knew I had a spinal cord injury, and hoped against hope I wasn't a paraplegic.

Suddenly, I heard the words, 'Code blue in the car park. Code blue in the car park.' A group of doctors rushed towards me. I recognised them. They were the doctors I was training with at the time.

That's when I realised *I* was the code blue. The looks of concern on the faces around me were impossible to miss. My intuition told me I was in for the long haul and my life would never be the same again.

I asked Dr Robin, the senior rehab doctor on duty, whether I would be admitted to the main hospital where the accident had happened. Dr Robin avoided my gaze and told me in a soft tone that the emergency department was full. I would have to be transferred to another hospital.

The paramedics came swiftly and put me in the ambulance. The siren was on and I was on my way to Melbourne's major tertiary trauma hospital – as a patient, not as a doctor.

I realised no-one had called my husband. I felt helpless and alone and wished someone were in the ambulance with me. I waited for a long time in the hospital bay before John was finally able to come in and see me.

Dr David, the orthopaedic surgeon on duty, came and talked to me.

He had a compassionate manner; I can confirm there is no truth to the rumour that surgeons are a cold-hearted bunch with no compassion! I vowed that once all of this was over, I would emulate Dr David's approach and be a compassionate doctor like him.

Dr David organised a CT scan of my lower back. It felt weird being in the scan machine for the first time. I noticed how cold the metal surface was, as I was lying on the table, and how cold the radiology room was. Less than fifteen minutes later, the porters whisked me back to the bay in the emergency department where John was waiting for me.

It felt like an eternity, but it was probably less than an hour, before Dr David came back to fill me in. He looked sad when he arrived, and my heart sank.

He informed me I had a burst L2 vertebrae fracture with L1 and L2 dislocation in my lower lumbar spine. This meant my L2 vertebrae, one of the primary bones of my spine, broke in multiple bone fragments under intense force from the impact and the L1 and L2 vertebrae bones were forced from their normal positions.

This can't be happening, I thought to myself. I felt as if my life was ruined. John slumped in the chair, looking absolutely distraught.

We looked at each other, speechless, as Dr David told me I needed to have emergency spinal surgery that day. My hand shook uncontrollably as I signed the consent form.

My memory of being transported to the operating theatre is crystal clear. John was walking next to me as the stretcher glided along the corridor. I lost sight of him once I reached the operating theatre. In all my life, I have never been so scared and distraught. *We have never been apart before*, I thought. *What if we end up being apart forever if I don't make it out of surgery alive?*

I looked around the operating theatre with white-cold fear coursing through me. I was afraid I might die on the operating table.

Dr David and his boss, Dr Susan, came in to speak to me. Dr Susan spoke to me calmly and gently about the details of the operation. I nodded and accepted my fate.

I remember the anaesthetist, Dr Sam, putting an intravenous line in, and then I was waking up in the recovery room. I was disorientated, but alive. John was sitting in a chair, looking completely exhausted – nodding on and off to sleep. I realised that, at the very least, I was alive, and I thanked God for that.

The next two weeks were hell on earth. My lower back was excruciatingly painful, and the medication made me drowsy and disorientated.

Eventually, I improved enough to transfer to the rehabilitation hospital. I spent four months in the rehabilitation ward, learning how to live my life in a wheelchair. I learnt to use a slideboard to transfer from my bed to my wheelchair and back again. The specialist spinal nurses taught me bowel and bladder management.

I might have been making steady progress on the rehabilitation front, but the truth was, I had lost all my dignity. I was receiving great medical care, but the fact was, I had lost all hope.

A couple of months into my inpatient rehabilitation stay, I was eating lunch in the dining room with Gerry, a fellow spinal cord patient. We were talking about the movie dates with our partners that were scheduled to happen over the weekend; a trial run to see how ready we were to cope with going back into the community in our wheelchairs.

Suddenly, another patient, Rick, came into the dining room with an air of excitement. He started telling me about Project Walk, a rehabilitation centre in San Diego in the USA that helps people with spinal cord injuries to walk again.

I got a bit excited myself. My intuition told me to pack my bags and head to Project Walk right then and there. But overnight, I chose to ignore my intuition and went back to doing what I was told to do by the rehab team. I ignored my intuition for a very long time, but what I'd learned about Project Walk ensured I never gave up hope of walking again.

WOMEN LEADING THE WAY

Let me turn the lens away from me and onto you for a moment. Have you ever heard your intuition telling you to follow your heart and pursue your dreams, and then had 'logic' kick in, telling you that you weren't good enough or worthy enough? What did you do? Did you give up on your dreams?

Intuition, also known as 'gut feeling', is a vibe we get around how something should really be. Experienced doctors often get a sense when a patient's story just doesn't add up. Intuition helps us make decisions in complex medical situations. Clinical evidence can only take us so far, and for anyone who is open to it, the heart and gut does the rest. Sadly, many people are not open to it.

It took me twelve months to finally listen to my intuition. It was Christmas 2009, and I was lying on the bed with John in the supported accommodation we were renting while our house was being modified to suit my wheelchair. I suddenly got an overwhelming sense of intuition, telling me to pack my bags and leave for the Project Walk Paralysis Recovery Center in San Diego.

Fortunately, my boss was totally understanding and supportive when I told him I was planning to go away for two years. I was touched when he gave me his blessings and told me to go ahead and strive for my dream to walk again.

I was full of hope as John and I packed our bags for the long-haul flight to San Diego via Los Angeles. There was no doubt in my mind about having made the heart-centred decision, pointing me in the right direction. However, when we got to the airport the following day, I began to feel nervous. This was the first time I'd travelled internationally as a disabled person and I started thinking things like, *What if the airline damages my wheelchair during the flight?* Not only did my wheelchair arrive intact, but the same wheelchair still accompanies me on trips, both within Australia and overseas.

The Project Walk Paralysis Recovery Center in San Diego was a game changer for me. They had the latest, state-of-the-art technology for locomotion, such as exoskeletons and robotics, not to mention expert trainers, which made the idea of travelling halfway around the world a no-brainer for me. I thought these were the things that would help me, but not long after I arrived, I knew there was something much deeper going on at Project Walk.

I learned something much more powerful than how to use my legs again. I learned how to nurture myself through self-compassion, and how to use future vision and strategic intuition every day to imagine myself walking again. My imagination increased my motivation to take the actions that brought me – step by step – closer to walking again. My inner leadership skills got stronger, as I trusted my intuition more and more each day.

There were three aspects of self-compassion I needed to be able to learn to walk again. I needed to be mindful of each muscle I used with every step I took. I needed to connect with fellow spinal cord injury survivors and be buoyed by our shared bond. And most importantly, I needed to accept myself for who I was and rediscover the true meaning of self-worth.

Nothing could stop me once I reframed the situation I was in and focused on what I could do, rather than letting myself get bogged down in what I couldn't do.

I went hiking and kayaking with my trainers. I got a local discount pass that gave us entry to places like Disneyland and SeaWorld in San Diego. There was something calming and mesmerising about watching the sea animals go about their business. I was incredibly touched, and even cried, when I watched Shamu the killer whale in the live shows. Shamu was such a beautiful creature. I appreciated this soulful experience which also filled me with awe as it taught me gratitude for all that I have been blessed with thus far and inspired me during the long challenging days of intensive rehabilitation at Project Walk. This experience was a far cry from the shame and embarrassment I felt when I first ventured out in my wheelchair.

Another truly memorable experience I had involved a group of us going to Las Vegas for the Fourth of July celebrations. Two of us were paraplegics. My husband, John, was the designated driver with responsibility for getting us there in the scorching heat of Nevada in summer. The car could have broken down at any moment due to the sweltering 100°F temperature in the region, but we didn't care. This was an adventure we had been looking forward to for a long time.

John and I became even more adventurous after our jaunt to Las Vegas, and we travelled to New York City, not once, but twice. Words can't express how free I felt when I stood with my sticks – no wheelchair – at the top of the Empire State Building.

With experiences like these, I never begrudged the five gruelling hours of physical therapy every day from Monday to Friday. It taught me grit, determination and resilience, which became my strongest assets as a leader.

After three agonising and wonderful years with Project Walk, I learned to walk again. Physically, I had not totally recovered – there was still a long way to go – but emotionally, I had definitely turned the page. I was over the moon when I returned to Australia, and in August 2012, I went back to my job in Melbourne. I was happy, enthusiastic and ready to tackle new challenges when I walked back into my life as a doctor and medical leader.

A decade later, I'm now an established medical leader in the area of pain management and rehabilitation medicine, as well as an award-winning business owner of three companies. This would never have happened if I hadn't listened to my intuition to go to Project Walk.

As leaders, we must learn to hone our creative and intuitive gut instincts. I've had several instances when relying on my gut instincts would have saved the day, but because I had no relevant data or information to back up what I felt, I backed away from my intuition. Those situations always backfired. With the ever-increasing speed of information and technology, intuition has become a vital skill for leaders and business owners.

For those of us who are keyed into the workings of divine guidance, we are also able to tap into that realm of knowledge. Intuitive skills are vital in innate leadership by trusting one's inner wisdom and learnings in the personal space.

DR OLIVIA ONG

Dr Olivia Ong, known as the heart-centred doctor, is a Melbourne-based rehabilitation medicine and pain physician with fifteen years of clinical experience and an expert in resilience and burnout. After being hit by a car in 2008, Olivia was told she would never walk or practice medicine again. She spent years as a patient in hospitals and rehab facilities in Australia and the US in an attempt to regain some of the capabilities that were torn away from her. Little did she know she was going to get a whole lot more than she'd bargained for. After an intensive three-year recovery process, she walked again. Today, she shares her experience with others.

Emerging from such a dark period in her life inspired Olivia to start a business to address the unspoken toll that doctors bear when they don't find the support they need. As a high-performance leadership coach and mentor for doctors, she now runs programs helping doctors transform their lives, moving from burnout to balance.

Being able to speak from her own unique life experiences gives her presentations a deeply authentic feel, and her warm approach has made

DR OLIVIA ONG

Olivia a sought-after speaker and online educator. She is the author of *The Heart-Centred Doctor*, which features a foreword from one of her mentors, Jack Canfield, co-author of the *Chicken Soup for the Soul* series and *The Success Principles: How to Get from Where You Are to Where You Want to Be*. Olivia also collaborated with Jack Canfield on *Soul of Success Vol. 3*, which won her the Best Sellers Quilly Award from The National Academy of Best-Selling Authors in Hollywood for recognition of her authorship and thought leadership. She has also co-authored chapters in the AusMumpreuners anthology books *Goodbye Busy, Hello Happy* and *Ignite*.

As the founder and CEO of The Heart-Centred Method Institute, Olivia's vision is for the company to be the leading global personal growth and professional development company for physicians and clinicians in healthcare, so that they can be well-rounded, heart-centred health care workers.

As a physician entrepreneur, Olivia has been awarded the Disabled Business Excellence Silver Award by the founders of AusMumpreneurs, Peace Mitchell and Katy Garner, for demonstrating her leadership, resilience and business skills in establishing her company against all odds.

Olivia has been featured in and written for *Thrive Global, Yahoo! Finance, International Business Times Singapore,* and *Australian Business Journal.* Her media appearances include Sky News, Studio 10 and Ticker TV, and she regularly speaks at industry-leading events including Australasian New Zealand College of Anaesthesia and Faculty of Pain Medicine, on topics such as physician burnout and how mindfulness and self-compassion can transform chronic pain. Originally from Singapore, Olivia now resides in Melbourne with her husband John and two young children, Joe and Jacqui. Her forthcoming book *The Untethered Physician* is due to be released in August 2023.

Website: drolivialeeong.com

WE RISE BY LIFTING OTHERS
PEACE MITCHELL

As I stood before the audience, the room fell silent and I became acutely aware of the ticking clock in the distance, the gentle hum of a dishwasher and the sound of my own heart pounding in my ears.

Though I'd presented to many audiences before, none had been quite like this one – a room filled with traditional male VC investors. I felt the weight of their expectations bearing down on me, and the pressure to deliver something profound and wise, something meaningful and impactful, was greater than ever before.

Despite my experience, I had never been more nervous. The anxiety was almost unbearable, and I silently wished for it all to be over already.

And yet, I was there for a reason. I had one clear intention in mind: to share my message that investing in women is the most powerful way to change the world.

'I'm an investor, but I have a confession to make. I don't have a background in finance. I'm not an experienced venture capitalist, and twelve months ago I really didn't know much about VC investing.'

In fact, at university I trained to be a primary school teacher, not an investor. I wanted to change the world by shaping young minds. I thought I'd always spend my days looking out at children in classrooms, not adults in conference rooms.

I'm now an entrepreneur working with thousands of startups and small businesses around Australia and internationally. My primary school teaching days are long gone. I want to change the world by encouraging women to step into their power and take their place as leaders.

But I've come to realise that the qualities I had as a teacher still serve me today in the work I do with entrepreneurs.

As a teacher, I saw the unique gifts and talents in every student. I mentored them to set goals for themselves and implement strategies for growth. I provided them with the resources and support they needed to succeed and identified the high-potential ones – the ones with ambition, determination, a strong work ethic and big ideas. I was able to predict their future trajectory.

I loved teaching and was a good teacher, but even back then, I knew there was more for me to do in the world, and I was always on the lookout for the next opportunity.

Leadership for me is about seeing the potential in others. It's not about me, it's about you. How can I help you to see everything you are and everything you are capable of being? And then, how can I support you to reach that potential?

It's what I did as a teacher and it's what I do today as an entrepreneur.

As a teacher, I invested my time, ideas and energy into encouraging children to find and follow their dreams. Today, together with my sister and co-founder, Katy Garner, I invest my time, ideas and energy into encouraging women to find and follow their dreams.

I believe investing in women is the most powerful way to change the world.

I remember the pivotal moment when I found my calling. A profound and memorable conversation with Her Excellency, the former Governor of Australia, Quentin Bryce, brought about the realisation that mothers were the ones with the most influence on young children and that if mothers were well, happy and fulfilled, they were better able to look after everyone around them.

Our journey has taken us a long way since that day. We began by starting a local non-profit to support our local community in the recovery period after a natural disaster. It was hugely successful, and we hosted local events, rebuilt public spaces and ran parenting workshops to support local families.

Once the community was back on its feet, we took steps to help mothers further afield, publishing a book of advice for first-time mothers called *What I Wish I Knew Before I Became a Mother*.

We knew we could reach more women online, so we created an online community focused on supporting Australian mothers in business. Our first goal was to have three thousand followers and a bigger readership than our local paper. We'd smashed that within the first twelve months and now our community is twenty times the size of our local hometown, at 150,000 strong and growing.

Recognising there was a need within the community for more accessible business education, dedicated to women, we then created The Women's Business School – an accelerator program providing group coaching, one-on-one mentoring and a structured program. I was back teaching again, but this time with my own school.

We recognised there were barriers to women at different levels because of intersectionality, and we discovered what the implications of this were. Barriers, faced by women like us in rural and remote areas, were just one type of challenge women were facing. There were different kinds of barriers for Aboriginal women, for migrant and refugee women, for disabled women, for women with disabled children and for women escaping domestic violence or financial abuse. Listening to women has been an important part of our journey and the more we have learnt, the more we have worked to uncover our blind spots and do more to ensure we are creating an inclusive community where all women feel welcome, valued and included.

From day one, we gave back by providing full scholarships for marginalised women to have access to support and education. To date, we have provided over $1 million in scholarships and have seen many success stories of women who just needed a helping hand, encouragement and support to get their idea off the ground.

We hold educational and motivational events online and in person, providing opportunities for women's voices to be amplified, as well as a platform for ideas to be shared with thousands of people from all over Australia. Each year, we bring women together at our national conference for women in business. The connections they have formed through these events are beautiful to see.

For the past fourteen years, we've hosted a national business awards event, which receives over two thousand nominations every year. Unexpectedly, this has been an incredibly powerful way to hold a mirror to women to show them their potential, and we've been surprised by how this acknowledgement has changed the way they see themselves, while inspiring them to continue to dream bigger and strive harder for achievement for the work they are doing, particularly those in purpose-led businesses.

We publish books and amplify stories through our imprint and have published almost two hundred authors so far. For some women, sharing their story is a powerful way to take back their power, to rewrite their narrative and to show up as their most vulnerable, courageous and authentic self. We've been humbled and privileged to witness powerful transformations through this process.

We take founders on international trade missions to create global connections and new opportunities. So far, we've taken our delegates to Portugal, the UK, France, Ireland and the United States. International travel is a game changer for women in business, as it opens the door to new opportunities, experiences and connections but often also unlocks ideas, creativity, inspiration and innovation.

I'm also the Australian Ambassador of Women in Tech; a global movement dedicated to changing the status quo for women in the tech industry. A role I took on in 2019, it supports me to connect to an additional 142,000 men and women in the tech industry across the world.

I am the Australian Ambassador of Women's Entrepreneurship Day, celebrated globally on the 19 November each year in 144 countries.

And, I am the chair of Tererai Trent International, a US-based charity focused on ending child marriage for girls in rural Zimbabwe, led by Oprah Winfrey's all-time favourite guest.

And in late 2022, we launched Women Changing the World Investments, a fund dedicated to helping women to get the capital they need to get their ideas off the ground.

I'm often overwhelmed to be holding space for so many people and things but I'm also eternally grateful that I get to be a part of so many people's lives and to play a part in helping women to reach their dreams.

This is leadership to me: holding space for others, providing platforms and spaces for women to show up and shine.

When I think of great women leaders I admire, Jacinda Ardern, Dr Tererai Trent, Princess Diana, Oprah Winfrey, Mother Teresa and Michelle Obama are just some of the women who come to mind.

So, I asked myself, *What are the leadership qualities I aspire to that they all have in common?*

My favourite one would be compassion yet strength. Jacinda Ardern, the former prime minister of New Zealand, is a great example of this. She was celebrated for her ability to hold both strength and compassion, a rare skill in leadership, in which she excelled, able to both comfort grieving people whilst also taking strong and decisive action on preventing future problems.

My next would be vision. Dr Tererai Trent had a powerful vision for change in her own life. As a young girl growing up in rural Zimbabwe and married at just fourteen, although being unable to read and write, she dreamt of a better life, of getting an education, of going to America and getting her PhD. She achieved all of this and then committed to a bigger vision: to end early marriage and create generational change for the girls in her village. I'm fortunate to be able to see her leadership in action, firsthand, and to witness the power of her vision to change the lives of the girls in her village.

Lifting others up is another quality that appeals to me deeply. Princess Diana and Mother Teresa dedicated their life to service and making the world a better place through kindness to others.

Communication is an essential leadership quality, and Oprah Winfrey comes to mind, with her enthusiasm for sharing stories, her ability to deeply listen and her art of conversation. Michelle Obama, the wife of the former US president, and a powerful and accomplished woman in her own right, speaks with grace, power and conviction.

When I asked my community which leadership quality was the most important to them, what came through as the overwhelming majority choice was authenticity. The ability to be vulnerable, to be honest, to be humble, to speak your truth and take people on the journey with you.

Leadership to me is all of these things and more.

I've come back to my values and to my calling too; the call to uplift others, to celebrate women, to amplify women's voices, to create a platform where all women can be heard and to hold a mirror up for women to recognise their own magnificence. I believe that investing in women is the most powerful way to change the world.

When thinking about the essence of this book, I wanted to write an inspirational chapter about feminine leadership, about all of the beautiful leadership qualities there are, and perhaps I have. But there is also another leadership quality that keeps playing over and over in my mind. It's not glamourous or aspirational, nor extraordinary or exceptional.

Nevertheless, it's necessary – it's dedication.

You might know it as persistence, as trying again and again, as grit or determination. It's the willingness to fall and fail again, and to then get back up and keep going. It's a sacred commitment to yourself, to your cause and to your people, to never give up. To rest, but not quit. To be in it for the long haul, because often leadership is a marathon and not a sprint.

For me, commitment and dedication is essential to leadership. Anyone can talk big and say they're going to do things, but what really matters is their ability to stick with it and see it through. Not everyone can do that. Your people need to know you're not going to walk out or give up on them when it gets too hard. It's keeping your word and doing what you said you would. Leadership is working together for a common goal and taking people on the journey to a future vision that you help to keep them motivated and focused on.

The truth is, leadership is not always easy or fun. It takes difficult conversations. It sometimes means letting go of people or things that aren't right for you. It means making tough decisions and standing up for what's right. Sometimes you'll need all of your strength and courage, or you'll need to embrace resilience, because sometimes the setbacks will keep coming. But if you're prepared to stick with it, to keep going, to try one more time and then one more time – you'll get there.

Even though it's hard, having the courage to step into your leadership will be one of the most memorable and powerful things you'll ever do. There are so many benefits of embracing leadership. Leading a movement or a cause you are passionate about gives you a deep sense of purpose and fulfilment, knowing you are making a difference in an area you care deeply about. It also requires you to develop a host of new skills, learn how to communicate effectively, build new relationships and manage resources. These skills will help you grow as a person and develop professionally in a whole host of ways. By leading a movement, you can have a significant impact on your community or society as a whole. Whether it's promoting social justice, environmental sustainability or advocating for a cause you believe in, your efforts can make a real difference in the lives of others. Leading a movement can also provide you with opportunities to meet like-minded individuals who share your passion and vision. This will help you build a network of contacts and collaborators who can support you in your efforts, now and into the future too. Successfully leading a movement can provide a deep sense of accomplishment and pride, knowing you have achieved something meaningful and made a positive impact in the world is a rewarding feeling like no other.

As for me, I'm excited about what the future holds. I'm determined to continue to lead a number of movements. One of these is to open more funding opportunities for women. Women have the power to change the world. They have the ideas, the creativity, the fresh perspectives for ways to solve problems and yet for so long, their ideas have been underestimated, overlooked and dismissed. It's time to change that – to encourage women to see themselves as investors and become investors and to encourage women to believe in the power of their ideas and to ask for the funding to scale them.

I want to lead with compassion, with authenticity, with vision and with courage. I hope I have what it takes to stay committed to the vision and the determination to see it through. My hope is that I can encourage, inspire and support other women to take the lead in their own causes along the way too.

PEACE MITCHELL

Peace Mitchell is one of Australia's leading women's entrepreneurship experts. Peace believes that investing in women is the number-one way to change the world and she is passionate about supporting women to reach their full potential. Together with her business partner Katy Garner, she has helped thousands of women achieve their dream of running a successful business, with an online community of over 150,000 women.

Peace is the co-founder of The Women's Business School, AusMumpreneur and Women Changing the World Press. She is the chair of Tererai Trent International and Australian ambassador of Women in Tech and Women's Entrepreneurship Day Australia. Peace is an investor, international keynote speaker, TEDx speaker and author. She lives in North Queensland with her husband and has four children.

COPRENEURS
HOW TO JUGGLE YOUR PERSONAL LIFE AND OPERATE A BUSINESS WITH YOUR PARTNER
PETINA TIEMAN

Like many women, I spent several years being single. I was focused on building my skills and knowledge, progressing my career and juggling single motherhood, all at the same time. But my heart had a void that needed fulfilling … I wanted to share my challenges, successes and journey with someone special.

Given how busy I was, the best way for me to find someone was via online dating. To this day, some thirteen years later, I am still unsure if my online dating experience was more positive than negative. It certainly helped me define my 'checklist' of what I did and didn't want in a partner, as I vetted hundreds of potentials, the majority of who I never met in person; they simply didn't fit the checklist.

For many years, I have studied the world leaders on personal and professional development, including laws of attraction and manifestation. I figured I should 'manifest' the person I really wanted to attract into my life. You never know who's on the other end of online messages (prior to Zoom), until you met them in person. Finally, after weeks of continuous messages, I agreed to meet this one guy. I didn't want to meet him for a coffee or a dinner date, that was too 'boring', so we agreed to meet at a games arcade, spending hours being kids at heart.

The man I met is not someone I would have noticed if I was on a girl's night out, however, because we had so many easy-flowing chats online and over the phone, I knew we connected intellectually, which was important to me. I looked beyond his outfit and somewhat nerdy appearance and enjoyed the man for who he was. Thirteen years on, he is the biggest challenge of my life, given that he is a Gemini, third-generation military, stubborn, somewhat narcissistic and suffering from PTSD and chronic depression, using alcohol to cope.

However, he is also the only person who truly understands me. He empowers me to be who I am and what I want to be in life. He walks alongside me personally and in business, keeping me grounded. Yet he enables me to pursue whatever in life I want to achieve. Our life together has been the biggest adventure, experiencing more ups and downs in our journey than most people, while I coach others that it's safe to live fulfilling lives as I share our stories! He is my uniquely different happy ever after!

Over the past thirteen years, we have owned and operated several businesses, lived in many places across Queensland, travelled extensively for business (and enjoyed quality personal time amongst those trips) and been recognised with numerous awards, accolades and media articles.

In contrast, we've also lost everything and suffered dire financial ruin in partnership with a third party. We were too proud to go bankrupt, so we negotiated and paid out $700,000 of debt across twenty-three creditors over six years. We have suffered extreme health issues, including me having two major surgeries and my partner suffering two mental health breakdowns. We have rescued my daughter and grandchildren from domestic violence and helped fight their legal battles in the family law courts. I have been unlawfully arrested and locked up, having to then fight for my life in the courts because of a vindictive ex-employer with mafia connections wanting to destroy my life. And then COVID-19 crippled our businesses.

As you can see … quite a roller-coaster of a journey.

Many nights we have slept apart – angry at each other, resenting each other, needing space from each other – because we didn't prioritise the personal. We were only focusing on trying to survive and achieve new wins in business.

It's true, we have endured more than most, but what has held us together is that I was constantly changing things up to ensure we balanced our personal and business lives. That's what successful COPRENEURS are all about!

So, who are copreneurs – couples in business?

Here are some examples:

- A husband and wife running a farm.
- Two real estate agents – one in sales the other in property management.
- A builder/tradesmen or civil earthworks constructor out on the tools or plant while the wife is doing admin, marketing, financials and scheduling.
- A couple operating a retail store together or a manufacturing business.

I used to think copreneurs were only in regional, rural or remote areas, but my studies have provided evidence that there are also many couples in metropolitan areas operating businesses together, in particular in construction and trades.

Often, the wife will leave her job and/or career to have children. Rather than return to work with an employer who doesn't offer flexible working arrangements to accommodate the needs of children, the couple decide the wife can help out in the husband's business by doing the admin, marketing and bookkeeping etc.

This arrangement is great for balancing the commitments of raising children, however, it's often the case that the couple have not thought about giving the wife an identity within the business, such as a position title, a uniform or an email footer. And often, she doesn't get paid. The other issue is that she becomes home-bound for twenty hours per day; busy but bored. She has very little escape from the home-based business, blending with home duties, limiting any social interaction she has.

Subsequently, she becomes bored, withdrawn and insular; symptoms of depression can start to show. Subconsciously, she starts portraying resentment for her partner and becomes frustrated and short in her responses communicating with him. Does this sound like you?

So here is a bit more about my story and why I believe I am a woman leading the way.

Just two months into our relationship, my partner and I registered two businesses in partnership. We realised we had complementary skills and knowledge in training and consultancy, and both of us wanted more from life than working high-profile careers for someone else. Over the following years, we continued operating the hobby businesses, whilst working full-time in senior management employment roles.

As I'm such a kid at heart, socialising regularly and love being outdoors, I was able to introduce my new partner to lots of adventures including social outings, dancing, mountain biking, boating, jet skiing, kayaking, camping, sapphire and opal mining, motorbikes and 4WDs and travelling in the outback. He actually created a website showcasing our thousands of photos from our adventures and mishaps. Sadly, like most relationships, it wasn't always smooth sailing!

Common sense would have waved red flags at the start of business, as we are both very independent, strong, stubborn, knowledgeable people who like to think we know best. That resulted in us stepping on each other's toes regularly, because we never implemented any boundaries or strategies to prevent the blurring of personal versus business relationship lines.

It would be okay if we were on the jet ski or boat, or on bikes, as we couldn't have business conversations whilst hooning around. However, it's very different when you are sitting around a campfire, on a long drive to somewhere or at the dinner table, and you have things that you want to get out of your head regarding business ideas or concerns. You worry that if you don't share it now with your partner, you'll forget about it!

Given my background in coaching, communications and problem-solving, I started talking openly to my partner about how the dynamics of our relationship was changing to be primarily focused on business, because it was new and exciting and both of us loved being intellectually challenged and stimulated. However, as a woman in touch with her emotions, I felt I was missing the emotional connection, as well as the fun bond and laughter we used to share when we planned and participated in crazy adventures and activities.

Our hobby businesses were becoming successful, generating regular income to supplement the lifestyle we wanted to live, above and beyond what our careers paid us, but we were sacrificing our love life.

I knew something had to change quickly, as I felt we were both losing interest in each other. It was more important to me to nurture the personal and build business around that, to provide the additional quality of lifestyle we were seeking. But how could I change someone else's behaviours and decisions which impacted my own? He is his own person after all, and I didn't want to change 'him'. But I needed and craved to get back the attention, affection, emotion and bond we shared in our personal relationship. I had spent thirteen years single waiting to manifest and attract my 'forever' person and this is what I'd ended up with – more business than personal.

It started making me doubt what an ideal relationship should be. I had thought sex was supposed to be 'on tap' when you live with a partner and that communication should always be open, honest and free-flowing. I started believing he was only interested in being with me because of my business brain; that he wasn't really interested in me as a partner and potential wife. This raised many insecurities in me; a woman known for her strength and independence.

So, I reached out to research and study world leaders again to help me figure out if I was wrong in wanting and expecting this uniquely different happy ever after? Should I go against my beliefs and settle for less; settle for being unhappy and lonely in my personal relationship yet happy we were building successful businesses together, recognised with awards, good revenue, status and profile?

I began by talking to my partner on a different level, rather than the nagging and needy partner. My learnings studying world leaders challenged my thinking. It made me realise that as a man of his generation (born in the sixties) and third-generation military, society conditioned him not to share, or rather simply to ignore his emotions. His 'duty' was to be a tower of strength, the provider, primarily responsible for generating income.

These findings contradicted everything I had lived and breathed over past years as a single mum. I had been financially independent, 1,000% responsible for every single decision, and I never allowed myself to falter in any aspect of life, as I didn't have a support network, given I was estranged from my family.

I needed to make a choice.

Option a) Did I want to stay with this man I loved, knowing it would mean I would have to utilise many of my learnings and coaching techniques to reinvent the emotional bond and reignite our personal relationship.

Option b) Do I just let it take its own path and focus on building the businesses with him, hoping that when they were generating good money and operating stably, we would be able to pick up the pieces of our relationship and reconnect?

We didn't have children together and we didn't have a mortgage together, but I was already deeply invested emotionally and financially. I chose to invest the extra energy, time and emotion to stick with him and change MY behaviours. To create boundaries and strategies between us that would temporarily address my needs and concerns, providing me with emotional security, while giving him the strength and the relief of me no longer nagging him. It would provide both of us with some structure, direction and timelines.

I knew there was no point in giving my partner an ultimatum; to give me what I wanted and needed or end the relationship. That would only hurt me and destroy what we had built together. No, if I wanted this to work, then I had to step up and do what was required to create balance between our personal and business relationships.

My many prior years of studying, coaching and counselling had taught me that most men don't want to be involved in the researching, planning and talking about things – especially when it comes to anything that requires talking about feelings, wants and needs on a personal level. Most men prefer to simply jump in and get their hands dirty, 'doing the doing'.

I needed to give myself the role and responsibility of being the person doing the research, planning and talking to others. When I had something solid and structured, I would share it with my partner showing him what we were going to do, when, how and why. BUT … I would always make sure I had a 'Plan B' or an alternative to something he might not like or agree with.

The hardest part is teaching yourself to think and act objectively. When we are stepping into the role of thinking, planning and talking to others, we need to step outside of ourselves, remove any selfishness and think about what the both of us want together; unified as a couple. It's a fact – we really do know what our partner wants, because we have heard them say it in arguments, or in conversations with others. It might be things we don't want to hear, but if you want a future with your life partner, there needs to be compassion, empathy, negotiation and compromising, for what each other want and need.

Importantly, you need to make sure there is fun, laughter and affection along the way. Not just because you need it, but because often our partners need and want it too. Have you ever thought maybe they are reluctant to reach out to us for fear of rejection? Or because we're grumpy with them? Or because we're too tired from our day at work or looking after the kids and the home? I spent many years as a couples intimacy coach, working with couples on how to reconnect their bond, through understanding the other's reasons for lack of giving affection or having a low sex drive.

With many couples, the man also felt unloved and unwanted, as if he couldn't reach out to touch his partner. There are many reasons the women gave this impression, but my point is, although I know women in a relationship feel the affection and intimacy dies off and they are craving to get some of it back, the same feelings are often shared by the male. This creates a fear of rejection and resistance in both partners, leading to bigger walls and blockages between you, as your relationship starts sliding into the friend zone or the platonic business partners zone, and you regularly question internally, is this relationship, with lack of affection, love and sex, what I really want for the rest of my life?

At the end of 2022, my company was engaged to develop content for the Queensland Government business website, and one of the topics they required us to develop first was 'exiting a business'. It was through research and development of this project that I identified from a different perspective just how many relationship couples operate businesses together, and how many are at that point of separating, either failing in business or wanting to sell the business.

Couples primarily focus on operating and growing the business and forget to focus on their personal relationship, thinking the business comes first, hoping to pick up the pieces of their personal relationship when they get through surviving and thriving in business.

I hate to be the bearer of bad news, but for most couples, it's already too late! We must remember, we were a relationship couple first … if you didn't have the relationship, you wouldn't be in business together. So, it's only logical you should invest the time and energy into both your personal relationship and your business relationship simultaneously. And ladies … it's up to you to drive that change in your relationship, as it is women who have stronger nurturing abilities to balance multiple activities.

In closing, here are a few strategies you can implement to help get your relationship back on track while growing your business:

Have a strategic planning session – work out goals for the year ahead to make sure you are both on the same page. Where do you want the business to be in twelve months – financially, resourcing, expansion or diversification – and how will you get there?

Schedule a date with your partner once per fortnight (dinner, movies, bike ride). Dress yourself up nicely to reignite those 'date night' tingles when you first met.

Go to bed at least one night per week not wearing pyjamas – studies show wearing pyjamas to bed inhibits intimacy.

Schedule a BBQ/dinner with friends or family once per month – start committing to social interactions with others.

Join two Facebook groups outside of your immediate normal circle of connections – look for like-minded women to bounce challenges with and keep you inspired and motivated.

Write a list of hobbies and interests for you and your partner, individually, to start committing to two to three hours per week.

Get yourself out of the house on your own for thirty minutes every day. Whether it's going for a walk or sitting in a park journalling. Listen to podcasts or music.

Create an 'allowance' for you both individually – i.e. if your wages are paid into a joint bank account, pay $100-200 per week to each of you in separate individual accounts to create some financial independence, allowing the ability to purchase gifts for each other or get your hair done etc.

Implement boundaries. No talking business in the bedroom, bathroom or at the dinner table. Come up with lighthearted consequences to prevent those discussions. For example, your partner has to paint your nails, brush your hair, make you breakfast.

Set a morning briefing time at the business between you and your partner. Say 8 or 9am every morning to discuss with each other things you need to do or tasks to delegate for the day.

Set an afternoon debriefing at the business between you and your partner. Share what's happened in the day, discussing issues or priorities. This keeps business talk at the business, making it easier for no business talk at home.

Set up some rules of how you will make major business decisions moving forward to prevent the stress and tension impacting your personal relationship.

PETINA TIEMAN

Petina Tieman, founder and director of Complete Business Solutions (QLD), Australian coach and mentor, Cairns Holiday Letting, Cairns Business Hub and Indigenous Artists Hub has been recognised with multiple state and national awards, media articles and accolades for the outcomes achieved for clients across Australia and Papua New Guinea.

Petina is a serial entrepreneur who is dedicated to helping startups, micros, SMEs and Indigenous businesses thrive. Coming from a life of adversity, abuse and constant transition, she is passionate about advocating for change and driving economic development opportunities to those from disadvantaged and underprivileged backgrounds. Petina is also renowned for her counselling and empowerment work with women who have experienced domestic violence.

Mentoring startups and business owners for twenty-five years, she deeply understands the business ecosystem and what drives business success without dependency on welfare, investment or funding. She lives her life through her passion of building business, empowering people!

WOMEN LEADING THE WAY

The fundamental values across all her businesses are to build skills, capability and capacity in others through education, empowerment, collaboration and connectivity!

Facebook: facebook.com/groups/copreneursbypetina
Website: petinatieman.com.au & completebs.com.au

THE FLOWER
ROBINA SAVIDIS

Imagine you're having an average day and in comes a woman who immediately has your attention, and before you know it, she is taking you on a journey. She is telling you a story but in such a way that you feel as though you were there too, flailing arms and all. You realise she is a bit of a force to be reckoned with and so you pull yourself in a little bit closer because you know this is priceless advice you could not get anywhere else – certainly not for free. The interaction is over before you can really process what happened and all you are left with is an overwhelming sense of motivation, as though you need to do *something*. Suddenly, you are fantasising about possibilities; all the things you dreamed about achieving that seemed a little too far-fetched. Suddenly, you step into planning mode, looking at ways to take action, all while questioning what just happened.

THE SEED

This is what an interaction with Robina feels like; she is quick paced, gets right to the point and does not spend much time, if any, dwelling on what could go wrong. But you might not be able to fully appreciate an interaction like that without getting the full picture – beginning in 1980.

Iraq and Iran were engaged in open warfare, as Iraq invaded Western

Iran, which lasted eight years before troops were withdrawn. In 1985, Robina was born, and her mother quickly worked out she was different to her four children who followed her. Robina always had a genuine curiosity which dominated any fear or hesitation she may have otherwise felt. This meant she was not afraid to ask questions or approach anybody to have a conversation. Regardless of their age, she asked plenty of questions and was not afraid to disagree from time to time, or push the limits.

A TREE WITHOUT ROOTS SHALL NOT LIVE

During this time, Robina's father was drafted to war and came and went, leaving her mother to look after their children with the help of a tight-knit community of family and friends. Robina's mother recalls becoming so accustomed to the sounds of open explosions and missiles landing that she would take her children, along with other family members, to sit on the roof and watch. When she thinks back now, she feels it is strange to speak about it in such a lighthearted way, but she did not believe it would make a difference to be inside or outside in terms of safety. What was important for her was to put on a brave face for her children and to find humour and make light of even the darkest of moments. Intuitively, she knew if she was afraid, her children would also be afraid, and she would not have that. This and many other pearls of wisdom have proven to be incredible character-building qualities that helped Robina think and behave the way she does today.

NEW BRANCHES

As the war was ending, Robina's parents decided it was no longer safe for them and their children to live in the country anymore; they did not know if, or when, war would break out again. Having fled from North Iraq to South Iraq and back to North Iraq again to escape the tyranny,

Robina's family had lost all documentation and proof of existence and were no strangers to making decisions on the fly. Sometime in 1989, Robina's parents woke all their children in the middle of the night, and it was then that they embarked on their journey to the Turkish border where they believed they could seek refuge. However, this was no easy feat as many did not make it – frostbite, drowning, exhaustion, landmines or open gunfire from Iraqi snipers in the mountains all contributed to the danger. This was a risk they were willing to take – after all, what was the alternative? It took them three days, on foot, walking in single file in complete silence, moving mostly at night.

Once they reached the Turkish border, they waved their arms as a sign of surrender and were captured by the Turkish soldiers. Here they waited at the border for two weeks, awaiting their verdict, unsure as to whether they had made the right decision. To their surprise, they were taken in as refugees and resided in a refugee camp for a period of nine months before they finally made their way to Australia. A new beginning and promising opportunities awaited them.

ROOT ROT

Having escaped the nightmare of Iraq, Robina's family believed they were safe and could now begin to live their life in peace. However, the roots ran deep, and the cracks began to show. The tortures of their home country were not easy to shake and appeared to have come along with them. Between the pressures of assimilating to a culture so vastly different, trying to develop a sense of community and belonging, as well as trying to be present and heal from their past, the family struggled. This was particularly difficult for Robina's father, who developed addiction problems, which then made it difficult for her mother to look after their five children, as they lived well below the poverty line until Robina began her journey into the workforce.

In addition to this, neither of her parents understood or spoke English, which made it exceptionally difficult to navigate their new world and ensure they were providing the best opportunities for their children. Robina's mother nurtured her children and adjusted to Australia as best as she could, however, her father did not and could not adjust.

Despite all this, Robina's mother continued to put on a brave face and work with what she had to give her children the best start in life. Robina particularly remembers that her mum did not have a car to take her or her children anywhere, and through all her struggles, she never asked anybody for help with her children. If she needed to do some grocery shopping, all five kids would come along, and they would all walk there. To Robina's mother, this walk was nothing compared to the hike from Iraq to Turkey. Her mother never complained and navigated through life with courage and grace, another quality that Robina added to her character repertoire.

A TREE WITHOUT BRANCHES WILL NOT GROW

Robina took her big sister role seriously. When she saw a problem, she strived to find a solution and decided to venture out. At the age of fifteen, Robina left school to enter the workforce. She went to TAFE and began an apprenticeship as a beauty therapist at her dream salon. It was something she took pride in, often using anyone and everyone as her models and testing subjects. Robina began to put herself out there, through employment in different salons, and in the blink of an eye, she became astonishingly dexterous in her trade; she was well-known for her talents. Her humble beginnings in business commenced in her parent's garage in the suburbs of Western Sydney, New South Wales. It was Robina's hands, with their expertise, creativity and dexterity, that would wait for the smallest opportunity to turn it into a great achievement.

In the beauty industry, Robina developed various relationships and began to perfect her craft. In true Robina style, she always believed she could do more, so she did. At the age of twenty-five, she went on to open her own salon, which grew rapidly and ran successfully for a period of ten years.

FALLEN LEAVES

Whilst establishing herself in her career, Robina met the love of her life, Perry Savidis, who supported her endlessly and blessed her with three beautiful children. Robina had her eldest daughter Athena at the age of twenty-two. Athena is a wise and gentle soul that comes with a kick. She has a wicked sense of humour and is always correcting her mother, often displaying the same courageous traits and 'bitey' personality as Robina. Athena is able to bring a sense of calmness and serenity to any chaotic situation that surrounds her.

Penelope was born three years after Athena. She too was a beautiful soul with a contagious smile that could light up a whole room. She had the ability to make everyone and anyone fall in love with her. Penelope had her first seizure at eleven months old, causing Robina to feel like her heart had been ripped into a million pieces. If Robina's life had taught her anything, it was to find a way to overcome whatever is thrown her way. With Penelope's diagnosis of global developmental delay and epilepsy, Perry and Robina worked day and night to sustain Penelope's therapy and medical bills. The unconditional love and support from close friends and family members made even the toughest of moments bearable.

Eventually Penelope succumbed to her condition and entered heavens gates at the age of five, causing Robina's world to fall apart, with no sign of it ever being repaired again.

STORMS CAUSE TREES TO MAKE DEEPER ROOTS

Robina began to spiral into deep depression, turning any flame that burned bright into the ashes of the world she once knew. Love became a foreign concept. Life was just a thing she had to endure, and everything that once mattered, mattered no more. However, no matter how dark the storm, every cloud has its silver lining. For the next four years the passing of Penelope caused Robina and her family to grow a bond that was deeper and stronger than ever before. She was finally able to see how powerful and healing the love from her family members could be. Family are much like the branches of a tree, they seem to grow in different directions, but their roots all remain the same, and these roots allowed Robina and her family to stand tall and strong together.

Robina turned to God and prayed day and night for her to feel strong again, and through a tragic situation came a beautiful blessing in the form of a healthy baby boy. Harrison has enough energy to light up a whole city, which in turn ignited a spark within Robina she believed to be long gone. Harrison's charming manner and sparkling wit caused anyone who met him to burn with love and adoration. His invigorating personality is strong and grounded in his ways, displaying the strength of his mother and the intellect of his father. Robina slowly began to feel as if her life was going back on track. Every day her love began to flourish and the little flame inside her gradually grew.

SPREADING SEEDS

Robina utilised her pain as fuel, allowing her to achieve a successful career as a salon owner and an even more thriving role as a mother and wife. Her clientele began to expand which was naturally followed by a higher demand for her services, leading to an increase in staff. This provided her the ability to spend more time with her new and growing family while watching years of hard work finally paying off. This newfound freedom allowed Robina's creativity to manifest itself into the biggest turning point of her entrepreneurial career – Panemorfi. As a salon owner, Robina began to see a gap in the market for both clinical and at-home products, and after looking high and low for the right products she stopped searching and started creating. Robina has always said, 'If you want something done right, you are just going to have to do it yourself,' and after countless nights with little to no sleep, endless phone calls and driving everyone around her crazy with all the product trials, Panemorfi Skin Care was born.

The salon was at its peak and Panemorfi was the creative outlet Robina needed to occupy whatever free time she had – if she had it. However, what goes up may sometimes come crashing down. 2020 was the year of the first emergency lockdown for COVID-19 and the beginning of the end for Robina's salon. COVID-19 was the demise of many small businesses, specifically those within the LGAs (local government area) of 'concern'. Unfortunately for Robina, that included her salon. By the end of 2020, her yearly revenue was at a total loss, and she was barely able to afford her rent for the salon and other necessary expenses, which didn't even include the bills that were piling up at home. Once again, Robina was pushed into a corner due to another situation that was neither her fault, nor in her control.

THE BLOSSOM

During times of struggle, people often shut out the world around them. When the winds of life become too strong to bear, some will build walls, and others – like Robina – will build windmills. She looked back at her life; living in a war-torn country, fleeing persecution, being smuggled and seeking refuge in another country, flying across the world to try and assimilate into what felt like a whole new planet, watching her mother struggle to provide and support her five children, becoming a mother to only lose a piece of herself forever, to now having something she worked so hard for being ripped from underneath her feet. At this point

Robina's burning flame exploded into a full-force inferno, causing her to take one of the largest leaps of faith in terms of her career. COVID-19 gave Robina the opportunity to realise that no idea is too far-fetched and no dream is unattainable, that through perseverance, consistency and patience, everything and anything is possible. Robina decided that the salon had served its purpose and it was time to put her energy into something that allowed her the freedom to work where she wanted, when she wanted and how she wanted.

Robina believed Panemorfi had the potential to go far, so with a heavy heart, she bid farewell to the comfort she once knew and embarked on a journey that would ultimately change her life for the better.

EVERY GOOD TREE BEARS GOOD FRUIT

Though it has not been an easy road, Robina was no stranger to hard work and the fruits of her labour were slowly beginning to show. Attempting to create a successful business while trying to be a present mother for her teenage daughter and baby boy and a loving wife to her husband has proven to be a difficult task, but Robina hasn't felt happier and more sure of herself. Thus far, Robina has been able to successfully establish Panemorfi, supplying wholesalers nationally and internationally. With the help of her team, Robina was able to secure their first exclusivity contract with an international wholesaler, followed by another contract with one of Australia's largest wholesalers, breaking into the ecommerce market through another leading wholesaler, all within the first two years of operating the business.

'Difficulty is actually the atmosphere surrounding a miracle, or a miracle in its initial stage.' – LB Cowman

ROBINA SAVIDIS

Robina is a boisterous young woman, full of life and ready to take on whatever curveball life has to throw at her. She has been in the beauty industry for twenty-three years, starting with an apprenticeship at her dream salon, working independently in her parent's garage when she was just a teenager, to eventually owning her own salon for ten years which was followed by the creation of her baby, Panemorfi Skin Care. Robina juggles being a wife, mother and businesswoman, all with a smile on her face. She is no stranger to hard work and believes there is no other way of getting there, her life motto being, 'You can't go over it or under it, best to break it down and go through it.'

Her early beginnings are something that Robina carries with pride and are something she believes have made her the person she is today. From a young age, Robina was no stranger to struggle. From fleeing persecution, seeking refuge in a foreign country, experiencing the loss of a child and enduring financial hardship as a small business owner during COVID-19, Robina is living proof that your past or your circumstances do not dictate your future. Robina often says, 'You can never control what is happening to you or even around you, but you do have the ability to control how you react to it, and that's what matters most.' These experiences and her mother's moral values taught her that courage and determination go a long way to making a huge difference to the course of your life.

OUTWARD BOUND
SARAH CREMONA

Ever since I was a little girl, the longing to become a mother has been a gentle yet persistent flame burning within me.

This is my journey of unearthing through challenge, removing the masks, discovering my true self through matrescence and emerging into a life authentically aligned with purpose.

My days as a child were spent outside, pushing dolls around in prams, and as the eldest daughter of fourteen cousins, I was surrounded by babies. I was a daddy's girl who loved riding on the back of his motorbike and sitting beside him in the big red truck on road trips to restock his fruit shop.

When asked the million-dollar question, *What do you want to be when you grow up?* my response was always, 'A teacher.' From the outside looking in, I grew up in what some may call an 'ideal upbringing' in a small coastal country town in New South Wales, Australia.

I was known for being strong-willed, busy and tough. While some may have viewed this as being too much, it was me. I was determined and curious, never satisfied with 'that's just the way it is', which led me towards rebellion throughout my teenage years.

With my parents, being business owners in our small town, it was common to hear phrases like 'your reputation is everything', with no ill intent behind them and unknowing how they would resurface throughout my parenting years.

Upon finishing high school and receiving an average final examination score, I felt a pang of rejection, telling myself I wasn't smart enough. I kept this hidden, filled with shame and buried deep within, advising others that university wasn't for me.

I couldn't bear the thought of not being good enough.

Before leaving for Massachusetts, USA, as a nanny, after receiving my qualification in early child care, I recall the sombre goodbye as I walked through the departure gate and down the ramp, with my dad sternly and lovingly advising, 'Off you go and don't look back,' as we both sobbed. I took his advice, too scared to turn around for the fear that I may not actually board.

This was the end of my world as I knew it and the beginning of a completely new one full of uncertainty.

During my time in the US I learned about diversity, opportunity, abundance and wealth, with weekends spent exploring the eastern states of NYC, Maine and Boston. Summer vacations were spent on an exclusive private 'neck' off the mainland and it was here my eyes were opened to possibility; the feeling inside told me I desired more for myself.

It was from here I created a deep-rooted belief that achieving success was through money, so shortly after returning home and meeting my husband Rick, we found ourselves in the big smoke of Melbourne, climbing the corporate ladder, people-pleasing, chasing money and happiness outside of ourselves. That was until the most welcome surprise of our firstborn son shook our worlds completely – for all the right reasons.

It was as if overnight my entire identity and perspective shifted from a career-oriented woman, wearing Wittner heels and pencil skirts, to a fierce protector and dairy cow, thrilled with home decor and fiddle-leaf figs – rearranging the entire house to maximise filtered light.

Nothing about the life I knew before made sense anymore, only the love I had for my son.

And I was okay with that.

FACING THE SHADOW

Three years later, we were blessed with our daughter, who arrived with eyes wide open, ready to take on the world. Birthing her was magical, however, adjusting to life as a family of four and all that followed was confronting.

We relocated interstate and I found my sense of self in a fragile state, struggling with postnatal anxiety; the woman staring back at me in the mirror barely recognisable – and honestly, I didn't love her.

I loved my children more than anything. My entire world was shaped around meeting their needs, but in trying to meet their every need and be the 'perfect' mother, I neglected myself. I built walls around me as protection from having to deal with what was occurring within, supressing my emotions with food, judging, blaming, playing victim and keeping my husband at a distance. I felt a level of resentment for his life not changing, yet mine seemingly overturned.

I believed seeking help and being vulnerable meant I was weak, and that being seen as not having everything put together would mean I was failing. So, I pushed through.

Amidst the mixture of beautiful life chaos and my own inner confusion, I found myself struggling to control my thoughts. One fleeting moment, I considered the possibility of a minor car accident that would result in my hospitalisation and a chance to rest, to have someone take care of me. This realisation was a sign of my difficulty in expressing myself, using my voice and asking for help.

The scary thing was that, on the outside, no-one had any idea. I considered myself strong, so my struggles compounded until one night as I rocked my daughter to sleep, something inside me snapped. I was standing in her nursery with my body aching and exhausted, mind overwhelmed, shoulders slouched and anger building in my chest.

I knew I couldn't continue like that, and I realised no-one was coming to save me. I had to save myself.

One realisation, a moment of courage and immediate action that night in our study, with a whiteboard in front of me, I began accessing the raw emotion behind my pain, gaining clarity around who I wanted to be, how I wanted my children to remember me, why it was important and what it would mean by achieving this.

Being able to contribute towards something greater than myself fuelled my soul, and recalling our wedding vows, which promised we'd 'together repair one small part of the world', I realised I had so much more to give in all areas. I was my only limit. Me.

The clarity I saw that night felt powerful. Not only did it provide insight, but the purpose, the why and the emotion behind it were the true catalyst for change, being accessed from a place of meaning and desire.

I had been defining motherhood by societal versions of how a mother should be, do, have, not have, combined with my own inner stories of expectations of myself in motherhood. I realised that although I was a mum, and that was my most important primary role, I was so much more than that too.

Having visited a clairvoyant seeking answers around this time of unravelling, she told me I had a young spirit with me and I was going to become a 'mum coach'. I scrunched my nose up at the thought, being a career I'd deemed a bit 'woo-woo'. I considered demanding a refund, yet the people-pleaser in me thanked her and I drove away planning a zero-star review on Google (which never happened).

I landed a new job in the public sector thinking it was my long-term career path, one that ticked all the boxes of security, safety and financial stability. I was proud of myself for securing this role, but happiness was found there for around nine months before I began asking myself, *There has to be more, right?* And that there was. A whole lot more.

SARAH CREMONA

EMBRACING UNCERTAINTY

I thought I'd lost myself since becoming a mum, but then again, I never really knew myself. Not anything more than surface level, anyway.

Birthing my three children rebirthed something inside of me; an insightful concoction of unshakable love and polarity – the very best kind.

Drum roll ... Incoming third child. Our son entered the world in a way I can only describe as *too much and too fast* via emergency C-section. Shortly after he was born, both him and Rick were taken from theatre and there I was, in a cold and sterile square box ... alone with my thoughts.

In the moments to follow, the blue curtain in front of my face felt as though it was suffocating me, yet I was too scared to move except to wipe away the tears beginning to soak through my pillow. Anger rose in my chest as I tried to push it back down. Afraid of what would appear, I shook my head and asked myself, *What the actual fuck just happened to me?* With teeth gritted, hands clenched, I looked around in that vulnerable moment, and no-one was there to validate what had happened. Acknowledging the fear, I needed to be held and I needed my baby, yet I was alone to make sense of what was.

As we nursed each other through the *fourth* trimester, I was forced to let go of control, which allowed Rick to take the reins and shine. I learned to invite compassion into my life, to rest and accept that it's not possible to control everything. I learned that good enough is okay and the best lessons appeared through uncertainty, discomfort and vulnerability; plus they did not mean I was weak, instead it's okay to say 'I need help' and accept it.

This transition for our family was equal part challenging for everyone; my daughter couldn't bear to see me physically hurting, labelling my C-section scar 'Mummy's crack', shortly after sharing, 'I don't want to be a mummy because I don't want a crack like yours.'

We did the best we could with what was available to us at the time, meeting them at their level with compassion, connection and open arms.

Writing about the birth brought me a sense of comfort, in a creative way, allowing emotional release. Prior to this, I was unaware of the concept of birth trauma, but my body's reactions made it clear that something significant had occurred that couldn't be ignored.

Becoming a mother of three was a transformative awakening and it was clear I was being offered an opportunity to evolve.

So that I did.

One evening, I stood at the top of the balustrades on the second floor of our townhouse, feeling numb after another difficult bedtime, where tears were shared by all, including myself. I took a deep breath as my inner world shrunk and I asked for help from something greater than myself – the universe? My higher self? Anything. I surrendered. It was time for professional help.

After attending a few sessions with a perinatal psychologist with minimal results, I navigated towards alternate methodologies including life coaching, EFT, reiki, breathwork and naturopathy.

I participated in an online life coaching workshop, taking notes as I breastfed my baby. Impulsively I raised my hand when the facilitator asked for a volunteer to demonstrate with, and in front of two hundred students, I was guided through a realisation that our perceived problems are often not the problem, but rather, it is our thoughts and perspectives of them. He helped me identify my unresourceful patterns of unrealistic expectations, involvement and seeking validation from others where it cannot be given, and sharing when I couldn't reach the outcome myself, that I had a lack of self-respect.

Ouch!

As I sat there, my ego bruised, I couldn't help but feel the weight of so many eyes on me. There I was, a mid-thirties, incredibly stubborn Aries woman, my first instinct to defend myself and run away, but instead, I found myself frozen in a state of shock.

I knew the only thing I could do in that moment was to 'be there', as my ballet teacher used to say, so I sat with the discomfort and felt what needed to be felt.

The beginning of navigating self-trust where those walls I had built up around me in that one moment came crumbling down and there I met parts of myself that were living unconsciously … For the very first time.

This experience gave me language, validation and permission, in a way, to begin stepping into my personal power, releasing stories that no longer served me and exploring who I truly am underneath everything.

Fuelled by newfound passion for understanding human behaviour, I commenced studying and founded my business as a conscious motherhood coach and mentor.

Since activating this space, I feel a deep sense of purpose and fulfilment. All the years of stacking skills, knowledge and experiences aligned, allowing me to create a life by design, contributing on a greater scale with purpose.

The growth I've since accessed for myself has brought immeasurable value to our family and those surrounding us, where our lives are thriving because I decided to rescue myself, befriend uncertainty, surrender control and respect myself enough to begin taking responsibility.

Giving this gift to myself has also gifted to those around me.

EMERGENCE

'Did you feel like you were heard growing up?' my reiki practitioner asked.

She uncovered a physical energy blockage in my throat that had worsened over the years, especially when speaking in public. I realised I had manifested this dis-ease as a form of self-sabotage, a way of keeping myself small, stemming from past experiences of feeling silenced, judged and for being assertive.

I never gave much thought to the phrase 'your reputation is everything' until examining my insecurities over recent years. I realised that, without any conscious awareness, I had internalised the idea somehow, that it was more important for others to think well of me than for me to think well of myself. Since creating awareness of these patterns and beliefs, I've expanded my world, minimising the impact of past experiences and reshaping my perceptions.

And to my surprise, recently I felt compelled to review those clairvoyant notes and found that my dream career, 'mum coach', was in fact predicted many years ago.

No need for a refund after all!

RISING ABOVE LIMITATIONS

I used to define success by the amount of money I made and failure by external measures, but in a roundabout and empowering way, I ended up reaching my childhood dream. I'm a mother, a teacher and so much more.

I can proudly say I am what I wanted to be when I grew up. It just took a gentle swaying of my own inner pendulum to unearth and access those deeper parts of myself that held the answers, allowing me to evolve. An exploration towards trusting myself as I step forward having created a life by design, where I radiate my light and share my wisdom with others, allowing them to do the same for themselves.

This is my story thus far; a journey of becoming and a determination towards healing one small part of the world where it is most needed: mothers.

When mothers decide to tune into their own inner world, they reclaim their power, aligning with the woman they desire to be, to improve the future for themselves, their children and their children's children.

Now that's what I am here for.

SARAH CREMONA

Sarah Cremona has become a leading figure in the conscious motherhood space in a short amount of time, who wears many hats as a mother of three, wife, coach, mentor, speaker & birth trauma advocate. She is a professional life coach, trained in NLP and meta dynamics.

Sarah's journey as a women's mentor began after becoming a mother for the third time, through compounding struggles the only way forward was backwards; through healing, which meant addressing the limits of her mind and body, aligning them to move forward with a strong foundation to support her future growth, both personally and professionally.

In the first year as a coach and the founder of her business, The Mumma Nest, Sarah was nominated as a top five finalist for the 'Rising Coach of the Year' award within the coaching community of approximately four thousand students.

She continues to share her journey thus far and insight on numerous speaking panels.

The Mumma Nest was founded with a deep understanding of the

unique challenges and experiences that arise for women transitioning through motherhood and beyond, and it's Sarah's mission to provide women with the necessary resources, guidance and support to make personal transformations, which in turn will enable them to effectively guide and support their children, breaking unresourceful patterns that may have been passed down through generations.

Sarah says that by having access to practical tools throughout motherhood can make all the difference, especially when motherhood brings a lot of uncertainty.

With firsthand experience of the difficulty in prioritising her own needs and seeking help, she encourages women to proactively explore and take care of their emotional and mental well-being, rather than waiting for it to become potentially a reactive, clinical matter.

Sarah's unique ability to connect with her clients on a personal level, and understand their individual needs, is a key factor in her success as a coach. She approaches each client with a non-judgmental and results-focused mindset and is committed to supporting the authentic and whole woman in front of her.

By encouraging self-awareness and challenging her clients' limits, through tailored one-to-one private coaching, group coaching and workshops she empowers her clients consciousness of thoughts, behaviours, values, and emotions allowing them to access more presence, acceptance and certainty in their life which gives them more connection, love, happiness and freedom.

To Sarah, conscious motherhood is about tuning into our inner world firstly to better connect and support our children, also learning from the lessons they have to share with us about ourselves. She sees challenge as opportunity for expansion, it's then up to us whether we choose to see them that way.

Website: www.themummanest.com

SARAH CREMONA

Email: sarah@themummanest.com
Instagram: @the_mumma_nest

LEADING WITH HEART
SHARON COLLON

I ran my fingers along the wall as I walked down the stairs. I truly loved this house. It always felt special to me. It wasn't my house, although I had wished it was. It was a beautiful home. A home that thirteen-year-old me thought was perfect – both the country-chic interiors and the family. I was the babysitter. Called in for some much-needed respite on afternoons and weekends, so the parents could have a well-earned break from their two small boys.

The mother was a school teacher, and I remember thinking how lucky these boys were to have such an incredible mother. I spent a lot of time in their home and got to know her quite well. From the exterior, they had it all, but as I spent more and more time with them, I began to realise the mother, as incredible as she was, was miserable.

I didn't notice this at first. It was something I grew to know after spending years with the family. I imagined she woke up every day, resolute that *today* would be the day everything changed. She could fix this if she just tried harder. If she just had more patience, she could make her family a happy one. But inevitably, the day would track along like all the others and she would feel exhausted and burnt-out before the sun had gone down.

As I continued down the stairs, I announced, 'The boys are finally asleep,' with a big sense of pride that I could, most of the time, get them to do what I needed them to. She met my gaze. She had that look. You know, the feeling when you're upset but holding it all in, but if someone dares to ask you if you're okay, you'll burst into tears; tears that you're not sure will ever stop. Even at thirteen, I knew this feeling, so I didn't ask her if she was okay. I just stood on the other side of the kitchen bench and changed my expression to concern. She said, 'Do you think something is wrong with Thomas?' She continued, 'I spend a lot of time with kids, and I don't know any children as naughty as him. Everything is a battle. Why can't he be like his brother? Why does he make everything so hard?'

I didn't know what was wrong with Thomas. Sure, I could see him struggling in certain situations, but I didn't know anything about ADHD back then.

Without me answering, she seemed to resign herself to the situation and spoke softly to no-one in particular, 'You know, I just don't think some people are meant to be happy.' The silence that followed made her words stick in my brain enough for me to vow that when I became a mother, I would try *really* hard to enjoy it.

Life is a collection of little moments; they pass by so quickly we can miss the significance of them as we busily race onto the next thing. Even then, I had deeply felt for the exhausted mother and her child who was struggling.

I was slumped on the kitchen floor, my shoulders rolled forward, with my legs out in front of me. I looked like a sad rag doll. I wasn't aware I was crying but my eyes stung with the salt of tears. I smelt dinner burning on the stove and heard a thump and knew the sound; the boys had put another hole in the wall. All three of my boys were gorgeous kids but our life was chaotic. The fighting was getting out of hand. I was tired. Tired in my bones, tired in my soul. All the boys had ADHD and were each challenging in different ways.

Everywhere we went, I received negative feedback about them and everywhere I turned to for help, I was met with a brick wall. I listened to the screams of the boys and dreamt of running away. I knew though that I could never leave them. I loved them so much. I just wished things were easier. I woke up every day determined that I could make things better, but each day ended the same.

When I had met Anthony, my husband, he had been open that he'd had a pretty terrible time in school. The trauma and the stigma of having ADHD had seen him banned from the classroom, excluded socially and finally asked to leave the school in year ten. I could hear the pain in his voice as he spoke of this time. I looked at my own three children with the same diagnosis and was filled with dread that Anthony's stories would become theirs too.

It was bigger than this though; our whole family was affected. We were suffering and we couldn't find support. For some people, home is their sanctuary, a place they can retreat from the world. For me, it was a war zone. There was no safe space.

ADHD is a spectrum neurological difference that causes problems with emotional regulation, frustration tolerance, executive functions and working memory. There are positives too, people with ADHD tend to be spontaneous, creative and out-of-the-box thinkers.

Depending on where your child sits on the spectrum, parenting kids with ADHD can be *a lot*. I thought having a husband who also had ADHD would make things easier, as he would be able to understand the children. However, over time I came to realise that this wasn't necessarily the case. Actually, it made things significantly harder.

I felt totally out of my depth in our family that had four ADHD brains (add some Tourette's, oppositional defiance, sensory processing and specific learning disorders in there too). Traditional parenting strategies didn't work. Every day I would wake up with enthusiasm to do things differently. Maybe if I had more patience myself, maybe if we could all stop yelling at each other … But each day would end the same. I would be in tears.

I sighed and thought, *You know, I think some people aren't meant to be happy,* and I realised I was now the exhausted mum in the kitchen I had met all those years ago.

Who was the voice for these families? Where could I find help for families like mine? We were sinking and I knew it.

When my first son was diagnosed with ADHD, we were given a photocopied pamphlet. I can remember walking out of the specialist's office wondering how on earth I was going to raise a fully functioning human based on this pamphlet. I did not have the skills to give this child what he needed.

I set about researching as much as I could about ADHD. I tried everything we could to help him. We spent about $30,000 on every therapy, treatment and diet available at that time. A lot helped, but our home life was absolutely exhausting. I looked around for support and was shocked to realise there wasn't much. There were strategies for the child, but very little to support the whole family. We were lost. We were overwhelmed. We were tired.

The stress of living in a battleground had a terrible effect on my health and in 2016 I was diagnosed with psoriatic arthritis, an autoimmune condition where your body attacks its own healthy tissue. For me the most distressing part of living with this condition is the chronic pain. Nerve pain is the worst thing I have ever experienced; nerve pain that runs up the back of my head and nerve pain in my pelvis. A part of me could not believe I could be raising three children with extra needs and be living in such severe amounts of chronic pain.

To be up all night rolling around in pain, crying, but then still need to get up and pack lunches? This disease is degenerative. It sits on my shoulder like an evil angel constantly whispering limiting beliefs in my ear. There is no sugar-coating it – it changed me. I went from being an extroverted person to a more introverted one. I learnt to guard my time and energy fiercely and not waste time on things that didn't matter. I mention this because I believe that having a chronic condition has fundamentally shifted my leadership style.

Perhaps in the early days, I was an impatient leader. I had more of a headstrong approach to things. I liked things to be done quickly and efficiently. I didn't have time for time-wasters. I always wanted to be perceived as strong. I believed if you wanted something enough, you could make it happen. Those who were not succeeding needed to just try harder. I believed results were always about effort. But having a chronic condition, that was for the most part invisible to the outsider (and hard for others to understand), taught me that life is so much more complex. Sometimes people are battling with things we can't comprehend. It gave me a greater understanding of how my children and husband might feel with their ADHD brain. They, like me, needed to approach things differently to succeed. There is not one *right way*. We didn't need to try harder, we needed to try differently.

We do not need more problem-solvers in this world. We need more listeners. This was the fundamental catalyst for me changing my focus from just treatment of the boys to strategies that would help our whole family. We needed to change our approach from treating the boys as a problem to fix, to listening to their needs and changing their environment, to work with their brains and focus on making day to day life easier for our family.

I started to audit our home life. I looked at the times in the day when we struggled and worked collaboratively with the boys to brainstorm ideas for what might make things easier. I ran experiments on my household to see what the four ADHD members did in certain situations. I documented everything. I noted what worked and what didn't. I began to notice there were certain things we could do to make things easier for all of us.

I was obsessed with anything that saved time, saved my energy and created more time for joy in my family. Even through my exhaustion, I could see I was onto something. I knew what I was doing was working. Our family life was improving. It was never going to be perfect, but it was much more functional. I wanted to share what I'd learnt with other families who were also feeling lost and unsupported.

Over the years, I became a spokesperson for the exhausted parents of kids with ADHD; advocating for their children and my own and creating resources to make day-to-day life easier by working with the ADHD brain.

Whilst I have always liked to think of myself as someone who has leadership qualities, I didn't for one second think it would be doing what I'm doing now. My company was born out of necessity and a deep desire to help other families like mine. It wasn't intentional; for us it was survival.

Lessons that I have learnt about leadership from working with people with ADHD:

FOCUS ON HOW YOU WANT TO FEEL

It's so easy to get bogged down in the details. How you want the future to look. How you are going to achieve your goals. Most motivation is based on emotion and if you focus on how you want to feel *as well as* how you want it to look, it's easier to motivate yourself to get there. People with ADHD lead with their emotions. I think sometimes neurotypical people ignore this part of themselves and it can get in their way. Humans are emotional beings, acknowledging emotion with honesty instead of pushing them to the side can help us lead with true purpose.

IT IS BETTER TO JUMP

If you wait until you are ready ... you will be waiting.

So often we want to wait until we are ready. We feel like we have to get all our ducks in a row. Sometimes it's better to take risks and acknowledge that sometimes you will win and sometimes you will learn. So many times in life, I have jumped before I was ready. It is that feeling like when you jump into the icy backyard swimming pool. There is a second when your feet leave the safety of the pool's edge. The moment before you hit the water, your head screams, 'No!' but it's too late to back out. Once you are in the water, your body adjusts. I have felt this way a lot. As soon as I hit 'go' on a webinar with 1,200 people, my feet are leaving the edge of the pool. I have a moment of 'No!' however, as soon as I am with my audience, swimming in the webinar, I always think, *I'm glad I did this.* Don't wait till you are ready. Sometimes the water is okay once you are in. My clients with ADHD have taught me that you can take risks and that there are not too many failures you can't come back from. Taking the risk is worth it.

FOCUS ON THINGS THAT INTEREST YOU

People with ADHD can focus. In fact, they can focus incredibly well, they just cannot necessarily choose what they focus on. They find it difficult to focus on things that are not interesting to them. I have learnt so much by witnessing this. In today's world, we have this notion that we have to be an expert in everything. We read books, get tutoring, obsess about what we are not naturally good at. For example, I am terrible at numbers. I used to beat myself up about not being able to manage my business accounts and finances. Until I realised the reason I was finding it so difficult was because it doesn't interest me. I learnt from my beautiful ADHD community that it's better to focus on things that interest you, because interest and engagement equals a zone of genius. Do not waste time hiring a tutor or doing courses on things that do not light you up. Focus on things you are naturally drawn towards and outsource the things you find dull. You can save so much energy this way. Recognising that people have different zones of genius can allow you to help those around you to reach their true potential.

USE YOUR EARS MUCH MORE THAN YOUR MOUTH

There's an old saying, 'You have two ears and one mouth for a reason – use them accordingly.' This does not come naturally to me. Nor does it to some leaders who think their primary role is to do and fix, rather than listen and observe, then to coach and empower. When someone discusses a problem with me, my brain automatically starts problem-solving. I instantly want to make it better for that person. I want to rush in and make a list of action items to get them out of distress. I have learnt through training as an ADHD coach, that jumping to problem-solving and not dedicating enough time to truly listening to the person makes the person feel invalidated. We need to listen between the words. We need to understand how the person is feeling. What it is truly like in their shoes. Most people know the answer, they know what they need to do, they just might not be ready to do it. What they need is a sounding board. They need to say their ideas out loud to process them. Most people do not need more advice. Over the years, I've learnt to use my ears more than my mouth. When you truly listen to your clients, to your team, to your family, they will often tell you the answer and solution themselves.

GOOD LEADERS WILL RECOGNISE THAT PEOPLE PROCESS INFORMATION DIFFERENTLY

We tend to assume that people process information the same way we do. But good leaders recognise that people process information differently and to get the best from their team and clients, it is important to recognise and accommodate their processing modalities. David Giwerc,

MCAC, MCC, founder and president of the ADD Coach Academy (ADDCA), explains the different modalities. They are:
- Conceptual – You need to get a global understanding with all the pieces clear.
- Auditory – You need to hear instructions or what is being said.
- Kinesthetic – You need to move so you can focus and understand.
- Visual – You need to see some object to concentrate on or comprehend.
- Verbal – You need to talk to work out thoughts and feelings.
- Emotional – You need a strong positive emotion to focus and learn.
- Intuitive – You receive spontaneous insight or sense information in flashes. You feel compelled to do something that feels right.
- Tactile – You need to touch or feel an object to learn.

Which processing modalities work for you?

People are so unique and their own experiences shape how they receive and share information. Understanding this has shaped my leadership journey. American Psychologist, Dr Ross Greene, promotes a concept understanding that *people do well if they can.* No-one chooses to fail or struggle. So, if someone is struggling, a great leader will review how we can help make things clear for them. How can we give them the skills and support they need to succeed?

BE KIND. ALWAYS

Years ago, I stood with my beautiful elderly grandma on top of Bulli Lookout. We had been going there for Devonshire teas for as long as I can remember. We looked down at all the houses below and out to the beautiful blue sea. She gestured to hundreds of houses we could see and said, 'See all those houses. Inside all those houses are people struggling with things we will never know about or understand.' It felt sombre for my grandmother, who was usually so upbeat. She continued, 'People do the best they can with what they know.' It has always stuck with me that we should be kind. We do not know where people are on their journey. We do not know what people are dealing with behind closed doors. It is imperative that we are kind to each other.

To the exhausted mother crying on the kitchen floor, thinking maybe some people aren't meant to be happy, you deserve to be happy and I believe you can be, if you choose to, by doing your best with the cards you have been dealt, and the best leaders will help others do the same. Perhaps, what the world is crying out for is more leaders who lead with their hearts. Women who, whilst building their own empires, also hold the hand of those around them so that others rise too.

SHARON COLLON

Sharon lives in Sydney with her husband, three boys, two cheeky boxer dogs and a quirky Scottish-fold cat. She is happiest near the ocean, listening to an audio book or podcast.

Sharon would describe herself as an extraverted introvert who is somewhat of a germaphobe. She is superstitious about the colour red. She loves listening to people's stories and learning about what makes them tick. She is a collector, a collector of memories. Both good and bad. Her favourite memories are those moments when you laugh so hard it is impossible to stop.

Sharon is a business owner, ADHD coach, podcaster, author and advocate. She is passionate about helping people with ADHD have functional and fun lives. Sharon uses her lived experience, thirteen years of research and training at ADDCA to help and support those living with ADHD.

When her first son was diagnosed with ADHD she felt incredibly alone. She had heard her husband talk of the trauma of growing up misunderstood with ADHD and was determined to change the storyline for her own children. She searched for help. There was information about how to help the child, but there was nothing on how to support the whole family. The journey of raising her beautiful boys with ADHD was isolating and exhausting. The stress severely affected her health.

She realised that she was only surviving each day and things had to change. She began researching ADHD and developing systems to work with the ADHD brain. She realised that she could change the environment around her children to work with their strengths. She loves anything that makes life with ADHD easier!

Sharon began to realise through working with families that often the parents had ADHD too. So trained as an ADHD coach to be in a position to help the adults directly.

Sharon's company, The Functional Family, has assisted over thirty thousand families. She has created online support groups where parents can ask questions, connect and support each other. She offers one-on-one coaching, parent mentoring, a regular blog, podcast and a membership and an incredible six-week online program, ADHD and Families.

She wants to help families get back their time and energy, but most importantly create space for the good stuff!

The Functional Family is grateful to be acknowledged with many awards including AusMumpreneur awards, Local Business Awards and Cook Community Award.

SHARE YOUR DREAMS WITH THE WORLD
SONIA MARTA

What's your favorite memory? Imagine it.

That's precisely how I felt when I showed my little munchkins my work. There are, quite frankly, no words to describe how I felt in that moment, which in more expressive words could be put as 'I found my purpose in life'. But hold on a second, let's not rush to the middle of this climax.

Let me press play from the start.

DISCOVERING THE WORLD

I'm still in awe when I look back to when I was a baby and recall how I never crawled. No walking on all-fours … ever. Since I can remember, I have observed every situation, every person's actions and speech with such amazement that I took every detail and applied it to me, so when I tried it, I would nail it for the first time.

Take walking as an example. I refused to crawl until I felt I could walk, and then I just went on and did it. Not sponsored by Nike, by the way. Sure, at the time, it had taken me 365 more days than all the other tiny creatures wriggling around me to get around with my own two feet. But when *I* gave it a shot, I dived deep into the pool and started swimming *sans problèmes*. If my parents hadn't figured out how much determination lay simmering within me, I have no clue what would have. Since then, the ones dear to me know all too well that when I set my mind to something, there's no stopping me, no halting or taking U-turns. Straight ahead is the only route.

Oh, and in the meantime, I would analyse and study every book I was given. I mean books with buttons, hole punches, textiles, glitter and even musical ones. And then one day, they no longer sufficed to fulfil my free time, so I looked at my little body and decided, *Hey, I'm more than ready to walk. No Nobel Prize is awarded for nailing this newborn stuff at first shot. What on Earth am I waiting for?* Tell me I was part of the *Baby Boss* spies without telling me I was part of the *Baby Boss* spies (the movie). I should've applied for an audition. Too bad I couldn't speak at the time.

Even in kindergarten, I instantly loved poems and short stories. The gift (curse as well) of kindness and being a people-pleaser bloomed. I knew the little volcano I was, and still am, is no ordinary mountain, but a very fixed mount, ready to release its flaming lava, so determined that there lies no obstacle in my way I cannot overcome.

I had made a friend and spent all my time with her. Nothing would give me more short-term happiness than sharing my not-so-neatly packed morning snack. I also fed her one of the two hard-boiled (not my preference) eggs my mom made the evening before while I was at that kindergarten.

CREATE YOUR WORLD

Remember how I said I was deeply attached to my rhyming literature from an early age, right? Well, not even a year later, I had come home with a fiery desire inside me, after a vividly eventful day (mundane as I would see it now) after school. I had eaten a terrifically savoury meal that my grandmother had carefully crafted before I climbed the stairs to my room to ask my mom the favour that would kickstart my voyage. 'Mom, I want you to grab this pen and this paper and help me write a poem.' I looked into her eyes to ensure she knew how serious I was.

She tried to put her rebuttal on centrestage. 'Writing a poem is easier said than done! It's not easy to say pie! Let's read one instead.'

You can already foretell what I will say (or write) next. But I'll say it anyway. And so it happened that the first verse I wanted to produce had turned from thought to reality. And from a one-time thing, it turned into a habit. Over the next nine hundred days – just kidding, I'll stick to a simple 'three years' – I came home, got comfy and turned straight to the next blank piece of paper my mom and I would create for our next set of rhymes. I stuck to a simple topic: everyday activities. One could've been about my first time seeing a squirrel, the next about my first time sleeping after lunch at kindergarten, for instance. Before I knew it, I stared at hundreds of these pieces of paper stacked over each other.

Simultaneously, I would look at movies that made my childhood, over and over again, on repeat. Not only that, but because, at the time, I was yet to learn English, and these were in the same language, I would listen to the songs, analyse and learn the lyrics, and then seem like a *petite* expert. My parents recognised my passion and drive for the arts, so they moved me to a British school where I could adequately learn English.

Listen to your children and take them seriously. You'll be amazed by their creativity and how many new paths will unfold.

Skip forward a beat, and I'm already in year four, part of the 'creative writing club' – a brainstorming session with one of my favorite teachers, Miss Orla. Every week, a forlorn picture, to say the least, would look me in the eyes, and I'd be tasked with writing a short story about a page related to it. These fourth periods on Wednesdays would be like a switch I could turn on and let my simmering creativity go wild.

SONIA MARTA

Looking back, I realise how much of a lead role the ones who've taught me over the years played in my journey to becoming who I am today.

This also was rooted in the idea that struck me one day; all of the poems I had written deserved to make other children smile just as broadly as the work of other poets made me smile. 'I want to publish them,' I told her, awaiting a positive reply. Call it déjà vu already. I suppose you can tell once more what happened. I wonder what my bets would have been if I had gone into hypnosis. Maybe not as bright as delusional. Haha, get what I did there? No? Oh, man!

It took around two years of blasting through rejection emails to knock on the doors of a printing house that accepted our work.

Right, where was I? Oh yes, meanwhile, my first 'big thing' was morphing into reality; I had set my expectations and standards to a new record, as if I had just hit the hammer on one of those fun park machines and the bar lit up, flashing before my eyes to the most outstanding high score. I figured if doing what I loved was so rewarding and could blossom munchkins' passions and talents, why in the world had I not started sooner? I am kidding, I am joking; it was more of crying than figuring *anything* out, really … happy tears, though (obviously). I was just so overwhelmed and proud and ecstatic to actually be able to hold my childhood highlights that, well, I had gone through a pack of tissues! I'm exaggerating – relax!

Year five was when I discovered another one of my interests, or shall I say, when I unravelled another 'present'. As I write this, I wonder, is it too late to assimilate this to the 'Twelve Days of Christmas' song? Think about it, 'For the second blossoming, I so happened to find performing arts was another passion of mine …' You've got to give me some credit – sung on the right rhythm, it's pretty bewildering. Okay, votes are in; the original still takes home the trophy.

In year five, I auditioned for the winter production, and I got one of the main characters. The show was *Cinderella*, and I would be godmother – *Bibidibabidiboo!* After, I started getting involved in many extracurricular events related to theatre, and it was an excellent decision!

You deserve to know the story of my first project. I visited the headmaster, asking if I could hold my author session in the school. He gave a big thumbs up.

The memory of it is still raw – I recall it being World Book Day, and the school, as usual, would bring in other authors who had freshly started their writing journey. I held my session like a professional after the writer who was visiting that year. My hands were waving excitedly, I was telling my colleagues about how the idea of the book was brought to life, icy chills were running down my back, and the dimples on the children's tiny sweet faces, their broad smiles and giggles.

I realised it was, in fact, *me* presenting, and there was this wave of overwhelming warmth, gratefulness, and the look all the darling youth had, grasping the moment. 'This was going to be the beginning of something I will adore and always be dear to me.' It was the only thing I could have said as so many emotions washed over me.

The moment I question writing, it is one of my 'things'; I look back to when children I had visited got in touch with me telling me that they published a book thanks to me inspiring them. All ifs or maybes shattered into pieces.

Being a published author by age ten made me realise that there is nothing I can't accomplish if I set my mind to it.

And that's the end of that mixtape. Jump two years forward, and déjà vu hit once again. I looked back to the emotions I felt when seeing how many people's eyes lit up and decided it was time to write my own work in English. I had read so many books and movies, flipped page after page, pressed play and cried at so many movies when inspiration struck. 'I am going worldwide,' with a smirk and a burning dream. I was not going to let anyone stop me from doing so. Reaching out to such a vast audience, I was dumbfounded by all the messages of praise and thankfulness I received, all the support and all the motivation that kept me going. There were encouraging messages from people pursuing all professions, like authors, teachers, parents, actors, and most importantly, children.

I had written about change and continuing to believe in yourself. I perceived it as a relatable topic to the children moving to a new house or environment, those who encounter an unexpected change in their life.

For many, a change is fearful and seems awful, but many times it pans out to be just what we need, contributing to the foundation of who we are and leading us onto the path of who we will become.

When I admired YouTubers, I grabbed a camera and hit play. I took action while I let inspiration guide me into the unknown. I like to cancel out the noise and haze the world around me, envisioning myself where I want to be and what I want to do and morph my ideas into actions. There is a quote that helps me stay on course when I feel like I'm sliding off my train tracks by Tiago Forte author of *Building A Second Brain*, 'There's a phase in your life when you have to be productive, and a phase when you have to be creative. I see it as a pendulum: productivity, creativity, productivity, creativity. Go too far to either end of the spectrum, and you start hitting diminishing returns.'

Be an inspiration. Be bold.

The familiar sight of books welcomed me as I entered the airport's bookstore. I was rushing to get a last-minute gift for a visiting friend. I had set my mind on grabbing her a children's book about Bucharest, thinking of the joy I experienced while I flipped through the books my mom gave me about cities like London, Rome, Paris, Zurich and Madrid. To my surprise, there were no books about Bucharest. I turned to my mom and told her, 'You know what? I will write a book about my city.' I could not believe there wasn't a sole book about my hometown. Yet there were tens, even hundreds, of books for other iconic cities.

After the holidays, we made this project come to life, leading us to the launch of the first book about Bucharest landmarks. I was featured in *Forbes* and asked to be a moderator for a session with Chris Riddell, author of the series *Goth Girl* and the illustrator of JK Rowling's books, later on for the spooky season.

I started exploring various projects and extracurricular events outside school and discovered, thanks to the trip to Virgin Radio Miss Momirleanu organised, my French teacher, a person very dear to me, my love for broadcasting, especially radio, and my interest in performing arts thanks to Luis.

Exploring various interests of mine, I realised how passions are like a fireplace. You must keep the fire burning, never letting it be put out.

My messages are for anyone willing to pursue their passions and parents willing to raise successful children.

For Children	For Parents, Grandparents and Tutors
Explore as many activities as possible and think of what brings much joy. What do you like to do and you don't know when the time flew by.	Pay attention to what your child loves and create opportunities for them to test their skills.
Explain to your dear ones what you like to do and why. Be serious about it.	Listen to them as they are your business partner and encourage them on their journey.
Be bold, be different.	Help and support your child to find their unique voice and discuss it.
Look for opportunities that make you happy; ask the teachers for that role, that presentation you want to make.	As adults, parents or business owners, support young children and teens as they take the real world very seriously and are willing to present their ideas.
Dare to dream big!	Encourage children to dream big, and support them in their journey! Give them the wings to fly!

SONIA MARTA

I am an avid reader and love the world of books, especially fiction. My first book was published when I was ten years old, on Children's day in 2018. Since then, I have met more than two thousand children on my journey, visiting schools and kindergartens talking about the importance of reading and creativity. I partner with World Vision and donate books to schools and high schools in rural areas, including a session with children during their English lessons, inspiring them to follow their dreams.

In 2022 The Rapping Astronaut story won third place at the Outstanding Creator Awards in USA, for both children's motivational and inspirational books and illustrated and picture books category. In the same year it was launched the ebook in Ukrainian and I expanded the physical books distribution in the Carturesti Network, the most extensive bookstore network in Romania.

I am one of the youngest authors in Romania, at 14 years old, having already three books published. I am proud as I have inspired a few other children to publish their books after participating in my sessions or reading my stories and discovering that you can be a child author.

WOMEN LEADING THE WAY

A few achievements I am proud of are the certificates I received at Wordfest, winning either first or second place, in 2021 and 2022, the OSCAR of IBSB in 2021 for the best horror movie produced, directed and having me as a lead actor, participation. Other activities worth mentioning are related to my participation and winning various certificates to Kangaroo, Spelling Bee, or certificates for community service collaborating with SOS Children's Villages in Romania, World Vision or other educational institutions like kindergartens, schools or even universities.

I am constantly writing for the school's magazine, The International Voice, and for other blogs or magazines when I'm invited. The latest article was published in January 2023, in The Relatable Voice, by Lucia Matuonto, creative director at worldauthors.org.

My favourite free-time activities are reading, writing and – besides these – travelling, watching movies and cooking. I am thankful to my teachers at the International British School of Bucharest, who nurtured my talent and supported me.

My books are available worldwide on various platforms.

The Rapping Astronaut:
Print: carturesti.ro
Ebook: Amazon Kindle
Audiobook: Narrated by Shane G Casey – Audible

The Rapping Astronaut – Ukrainian version: bluemasters.gumroad.com/l/rap-ukr

Bucharest City Tour, a Trip with Sonia:
Print: carturesti.ro
Ebook: Google Play Books

USING CORE VALUES TO LEAD

LEADING WITH EMPATHY, INTEGRITY AND BOUNDARIES

STACEY BARRASS

Welcome and thank you for taking the time to sit down with me. I know your day is jammed with a never-ending to-do list, so let's get chatting about why we're both here.

Let's start with what 'leadership' means to you.

Do you know your leadership style and what it is that drives you to lead? Do you understand your core values and how, by tapping into those values, you can be the best version of yourself as a leader? What if identifying those values could raise your leadership to the next level?

I'm pretty sure you're asking, *What's with all the questions?* But by asking these questions, you'll discover how to identify your leadership style and understand what makes you tick, what drives you and what makes your heart sing. It's essential you know the core values that drive you on a daily basis.

To be honest, I had no idea about my leadership style when I started my business journey! What I did know was I didn't like to be a follower, so becoming a leader was the only way for me. Sure, I liked working for others – both in small business and large multinationals. I enjoyed being part of a team, and like a lot of people, Friday night drinks were always a hit. I learnt that being around like-minded people makes my heart sing.

So, how did I discover my leadership values of empathy, integrity and boundaries? To get there, we need to go back – way back to childhood where my beautiful little brain was growing and moulding. It was sponge-like, and I'm sure, working hard at consuming all of life's beautiful moments. I have some memory issues, so let's go with what I know.

I am a survivor of childhood sexual abuse. I grew up very confused about the world, and my frustrations cultivated and morphed into introversion and isolation. I lived in my imagination and created stories of a dream life I was desperate for. This escapism allowed me to distance myself from the ever-present recurring flashbacks and visions that no child should have.

As I developed into a young teenager, my world and social circle became smaller, until I found a well-known escapism tool – alcohol! A traumatic childhood, alcohol and a small town where promiscuity was worn as a badge of honour – what could go wrong?.

Searching for someone to help me understand what love, acceptance and understanding really meant, I was in a revolving circle with other teenagers trying to find their way through. It was dysfunctional at best, with most of us manoeuvring through peer pressure, meeting parents' expectations to do well at school, and us, simply trying not to die in fast cars with hoons who loved ripping burnouts and donuts into the bitumen of rural streets.

Sharing my well-kept secret with a school friend was the second of ultimate betrayals. I learned firsthand how an intimate secret can spread like wildfire through a state secondary school. Kids are mean. They are vicious and can behave in a downright unconscionable manner. This secret, now disclosed to 150 of my non-closest friends, made my life an absolute misery, day in and day out. Bullying, violence and isolation sat with me on my lonely concrete bench at the edge of the school courtyard – every, single, day. Not one person ever asked if I was okay. Not one person showed empathy towards me. Why? At the mere age of sixteen, I didn't comprehend or understand the depth of lack of empathy in the world.

At my young age, I didn't know what it meant to have depression or anxiety. I'm sure I suffered from them both considerably; depression rising from my abuse and anxiety due to the impending avalanche of bullying I received each morning walking through the school gates. I could not take another day of the mental and physical anguish. It was a load that would have broken my soul if I'd stayed any longer.

A NEW PATH

Creating a new path for myself, I started to rewrite my story and found a full-time job as a receptionist in Melbourne's CBD. From this point, I suppressed all my abuse, feelings and insecurities; I grew into an extremely angry adult. I was a child who had been bullied daily, and this trauma unfortunately curated into me becoming a bully. I became a woman who was mean and judgemental. Yes, I was the mean girl. The snide girl. The backstabbing, gossipy girl. I became my bully. This just sent me into a deeper journey of isolation. Would you want to be friends with me? Nope, and for very good reason. This was not the path I had dreamed of; definitely not what I wanted for myself, my family and my friends.

Through many years of self-discovery and personal development, I have identified that I have an enormous heart and enjoy supporting and encouraging those who have experienced, and continue to face, barriers in life. This, literally, makes my heart sing. I can feel it smiling when I'm aligning my actions with my core value of empathy.

A quick story, if you will indulge me. I was attending a conference in

WOMEN LEADING THE WAY

2019 with a room full of extremely successful and brilliant women. I was in awe of their stories and their successes, as well as their humility. In the bathroom, I met an amazing woman who looked so sad and ready to cry. I stepped over to her and asked if she was okay. She shared with me that she felt intimidated and overwhelmed. She felt that a group of women had been looking at her in a way that made her feel she didn't belong. She didn't know anyone and wanted to leave. In that moment, I gave her a hug and told her she deserved to be there as much as anyone. But then, my bully stepped in. I asked her to tell me who they were; I was going to go back into that room and take matters into my own hands. I was ready to rumble – so to speak ...

Um, hadn't I changed my path? Would this action make my heart sing? No way, definitely not. I calmed down and told my new friend I had her back and if she felt uneasy at all during the function, to find me and I'd be her best wing-woman ever. THAT. MADE. HER. FACE. BEAM. Seeing her face light up like that made my heart start to sing. This is exactly where I was meant to be. 'You don't even know me,' was her reply. 'Sure I do. You're my dunny buddy.' We both started laughing and walked back into the crowd of amazing women. By showing the smallest amount of empathy, I was able to make both our hearts sing.

I have steadily grown into the woman who stands up for those who feel they don't have a voice. Those who have been treated unfairly or violently. Those who feel undervalued, not worthy, diminished or unimportant. Those being judged – for any reason whatsoever.

EMPATHY

Empathy is defined as 'the ability to understand and share the feelings of another'.

I've discovered that empathy is my key value.

Identifying with the mean girl in the room, I understand why and recognise that trauma has been inflicted for her to not realise her worth, her humility, her sense of womanhood and her ability to drop into her heart. Unable to truly accept herself and those around her with vulnerability and humility, it's possible the mean girl, or woman, hasn't found the ability to show empathy to herself.

Bringing a sense of openness, acceptance and complete love to all is difficult for a woman with trauma, however, living woven in chains and locks and completely unable to expand your heart with true conversations with other women is not a life worth living.

So how can I show my team, clients and stakeholders what it is to lead with empathy? By showing up, and being the one who steps in with vulnerability and openness, I am putting myself out into the world, saying, *I'm here, completely raw and open.* It's akin to standing on the end of a platform, 300m above the Grand Canyon, about to step off without a parachute. *Are you completely out of your mind, why would you put yourself in that position?* Because the journey through leadership with empathy opens your world in an abundant way that is inconceivable until you experience the love and fulfillment you once only dreamed of.

Opening conversations with, 'How are you?' not just because it's a polite question, but because you truly care, your empathy will shine through. When you show you care about her journey to date and her challenges, that you are there for her, no matter what she is about to disclose to you, she will feel safe to disclose what is happening in her life, with honesty and transparency. When she responds with an open heart, trusting in your sincerity, you create an amazing connection. It's a deeper connection than you could ever imagine.

Question: Can you imagine walking into a room full of women, not feeling one ounce of nerves or juggling lines of doubt about whether what you're wearing is appropriate or whether anyone will talk to you, knowing they will accept you wholeheartedly?

Imagine that time. You walk straight in, lock eyes with the first amazing woman smiling at you and approach with a calm, confident, empathetic aura, as you introduce yourself. Is your heart singing? Are you smiling? Imagine feeling completely yourself, 100% sure you are there because you are amazing.

INTEGRITY

'The quality of being *honest* and having strong *moral* principles.'

Delivering integrity in business is easy once you understand honesty in its true essence.

Look at the above statement as one of simplicity. When you understand honesty in its true essence and how it underpins you and your decisions, moving forward, decisions become easier to make. The decision process becomes clearer when alignment of integrity and action collide.

Do you do what you say and say what you do? Do you talk a good game and deliver as promised? Or are you a quiet achiever who gets on with the job? Either path will work as long as you do it with integrity. Consider asking team members, family and friends where they see your level of integrity.

In business, I continue to deliver integrity through transparent, open conversations with everyone I meet. This can be joyous, celebratory and high-five exuding opportunities. Alternatively, these conversations can be clunky, uncomfortable and slightly confronting. Team members receive honest feedback (with enthusiasm and encouragement) when they are delivering true outcomes that make their hearts sing. This is also the case when I deliver areas for improvement (with empathy and care). Avoiding honest conversations can tilt you from your foundation of integrity and lead you into murky waters where your moral principles (or values) may be compromised.

I have been able to be an effective leader by creating an environment of trust, honesty and integrity. Modelling integrity to those around you, will encourage others to raise to the occasion and deliver the same behaviour. This assists in creating psychological safety within your cohort. Leading with integrity creates a safe space for everyone to share without judgement or negativity.

A quote from Douglas MacArthur sums it up: 'A true leader has the confidence to stand alone, the courage to make tough decisions and the compassion to listen to the needs of others. He does not set out to be a leader but becomes one by the equality of his actions and the integrity of his intent.'

Question: Are you seen as a leader with integrity? If so, do you lead by example? What values does your behaviour represent and what behaviours would you like to improve?

BOUNDARIES

Leading with your heart (empathy) and doing so with integrity (doing what you say and saying what you do) doesn't mean having a lack of boundaries.

Boundaries give a source of strength to your ability to deliver time after time, day after day, and with clarity to those around you.

A boundary is a simple identifier that can be used, both personally and professionally, to determine what you are willing to accept as part of any relationship. For example, do you set boundaries on your time? We all have twenty-four hours in a day – are you allowing that time to be utilised to pursue a path that makes your heart sing or is in line with your purpose? Are you allowing others to utilise that time for what they want from you? My boundaries are in place to ensure my children's needs are a priority, my team can rely on me for actionable items, and also to allow some free space for my own personal projects (my 'love to' work, i.e. volunteering, keynote speaking).

Sometimes, a simple request of your time can be answered with, 'I'd love to do that, though my diary is a little crammed. However, I can make some time next Tuesday in the morning or Friday in the afternoon.' This is a simply a way of guarding your time and creating a boundary so both parties get the outcome they are looking for.

Question: Has aligning your purpose to desired outcomes assisted you in maintaining firm boundaries? Is what is being asked of you in alignment? Will it deliver an outcome that makes your heart sing, create business opportunities or growth in your industry? Do you reduce your pricing to suit your client, or do you hold firm with your boundaries and belief in your value?

Have you tapped into your leadership style yet?

Do you know what makes your heart sing?

How would you like to lead?

You are your own leader. You can make it all happen and lead in whatever manner you wish. Your starting point is to look at your values and whether they align.

I'll leave these thoughts with you.

What is your leadership legacy?

STACEY BARRASS

Stacey has built an impressive thirty-year career over a number of industries, however, nothing has made her heart sing more than her current role as the founder and managing director of Goddess Cleaning Group. This registered social enterprise is in its twelfth year and has supported more than 150 men and women who have faced barriers to employment.

With a beautiful tribe of three boys who are now twenty-one, eighteen and thirteen, she has juggled single parenting with business building. Knowing the constant challenge of raising children, racing to appointments and attending extra-curricular sports and events, Stacey understands the balancing act required to enable her to have the best of both worlds. Being present at all times.

In 2019, she was announced winner of the Victorian Business Excellence award at the AusMumpreneur Awards for her commitment to building a strong, female-led business. Stacey has been featured in several local publications and across many social media platforms for her support of women from disadvantaged and domestic violence backgrounds.

WOMEN LEADING THE WAY

Prior to her current role at Goddess Cleaning Group, Stacey worked in several industries, including ten years within the building and construction arena. Through her passion for construction, she has been able to build a strong builders' cleaning division working with many boutique development companies across Victoria.

Building on her passion for social enterprise, Stacey has guided the business through the accreditation of social enterprise with Social Traders and also received registration with the NDIS as a preferred provider. As a mentor to women, Stacey is a determined individual who is committed to supporting those that need the work platform the most. She has spent the last twelve years creating a social enterprise and is currently most passionate about expanding relationships within the social procurement network.

After stepping down from the role of vice-chair with the amazing NFP St Kilda Mums and five-year tenure on the board, Stacey has chosen to allocate a number of hours a month renovating an old farmhouse in South Gippsland with her partner Bruce. Ask her about her secret talent! She knows how to drive a tractor!

LOOSENING THE GRIP OF ANXIETY
SUE STEVENSON

What if there was a way to loosen the grip anxiety has on our world right now?

If only I'd known what I know now when I was an anxious child and parent raising my kids, I wouldn't be here writing this story; I'm certain of that.

I can't change or remove my own or my daughter's suffering, but I can, at least, share my experience, and maybe it will resonate with what you, or someone you know, is going through.

For most of my childhood I believed there was something wrong with me, yet, I was quite the chameleon, wearing my 'good girl, people-pleasing' mask to hide the thousands of times my belly felt gripped by a vice. I was too frightened, embarrassed and ashamed to admit how I really felt inside. Although I had six siblings, there were many times I felt completely alone. I would feel so overwhelmed, I'd hide in the bathroom, close my tear-filled eyes and imagine the world swallowing me up, wishing the pain of my inner turmoil would go away. But it didn't.

I spoke to *no-one* about this until I was in my forties. Until then, I had no idea it was anxiety that had gripped me and made my life confusing and taxing for all those years.

I developed the coping strategy of internally shutting down and supressing uncomfortable feelings when I was away from home, yet my family knew the slightest trigger could escalate my emotional state from zero to a thousand in seconds. I hated feeling stressed and anxious and I became frustrated and impatient when my family mocked or teased me, or when I felt like my thoughts and opinions were simply dismissed. In those moments I felt powerless; and oftentimes I felt like I just didn't matter. Sometimes I'd get so angry because, from my eyes, the situation seemed so unfair. I'd do and say things I often regretted afterward, especially when my parents punished me for my behaviour. I'd then feel intense embarrassment, guilt and shame, and I felt like I was a massive disappointment to my parents.

Unfortunately, in my adulthood, similar patterns also appeared when my kids pushed my buttons. I could be calm and kind toward the students I was teaching all day long, yet, for my own kids, some days I had little patience at all. There was no space left to stuff anymore emotions in. Instead, regretfully, I'd react and lose my cool, dumping my emotions onto my kids or my husband.

How little I understood about what was really going on. Back then, I truly believed it was their fault for upsetting me. Until one pivotal moment back in the year 2000 when my 'big feeling' daughter was sixteen. After years of struggling to manage her increasingly intense mood swings, and while in the heat of yet another argument, things escalated to the point where everything got out of hand. We both said and did things we regret. She ended up screaming that she hated me and I was too controlling. In her rage, she leant forward, glared directly into my eyes and yelled, 'I just want to kill you.'

In that moment of shock, fear, panic and despair, I then did something I'm not proud of; I told her to pack her bags and get out. I didn't feel safe in her company, and I felt like I couldn't handle being around her highly reactive and volatile emotional state anymore. I had reached my threshold. I had unsuccessfully tried to support her, with what I later discovered had been *anxiety* controlling *her* for all those years.

We were both very emotionally charged and after she made a few phone calls, while watching her storm off, the reality of what had happened started to set in. Had I lost my daughter for good? Was this it? I felt gutted.

I had become the mother I never wanted to be.

A plethora of emotions overcame me in that moment. I felt I had completely failed as a parent.

On one hand, I was blaming my daughter for her extreme behaviour and on the other, I was incredibly disappointed and angry at myself.

For many days I found myself helplessly crying in a heap not knowing how to dig myself out of the dark hole I found myself in. Until I came to the realisation that this wasn't about my daughter needing to change. I wasn't a victim; this was about me needing to change.

If I wanted to rebuild my relationship with the daughter I still loved immensely, I knew I had to dig deep and find the strength and courage to step up and change myself. After all, this was the same beautiful, emotionally sensitive little girl who used to tell me she loved me 'so much it hurt'. I had to find a way out of this mess.

That's where my own journey of self-healing and inner growth began, and what an incredible journey of reinventing myself it has been.

Let's fast track to now having divorced my children's father, whose compulsive gambling habit had depleted me of not only money, but also energy, trust, harmony, love and joy.

I now have my daughter well and truly back as an integral part of my life, gifting me with three beautiful grandchildren. I am truly grateful for the painful yet many rich life lessons she has taught me along the way.

With over fifty years of lived experience, thirty-two of those educating and supporting kids, I have observed the negative impact anxiety has had on them. The following concerning data, I believe, is an issue that can, and must, be mitigated.

WOMEN LEADING THE WAY

6.9% of Australian children and young people (aged four to seventeen years) had suffered from an anxiety disorder in the past 12 months.[1]

This statistic is even more concerning because it excludes all undiagnosed anxiety in kids, and we must consider the fact that anxiety is linked with many other mental health issues, such as depression, ADHD, ASD and conduct disorders that so many kids are experiencing.

Additionally, this data was released prior to the COVID-19 pandemic.

In the first year of the COVID-19 pandemic, global prevalence of anxiety and depression increased by a massive 25%.[2]

Never was the significance of increasing mental health and anxiety rates more evident to me, than when one morning, our school principal called an extraordinary staff meeting to deliver the devastating news that a third young person in a two-year period in our school community had taken their own life.

This was the final catalyst for me to pluck up the courage to leave my safe teaching job and start my own business. Using my CALM confidence formula, I am able to support and transform the lives of families who have been suffering in the grip of anxiety.

I'm proud to say I have discovered the formula to reducing anxiety, and I'm now a woman on a mission to reduce the suffering anxiety causes in kids and adults globally.

I encourage you to follow these steps so you can begin to loosen the grip of anxiety and start seeing the results this formula can bring, even when faced with adversity.

Clarity + **A**lignment x **L**ove + connection –> **M**indful actions = **CALM** Confidence

---

[1] Lawrence D, Johnson S, Hafekost J, Boterhoven De Haan K, Sawyer M, Ainley J, Zubrick SR. (2015). The Mental Health of Children and Adolescents. Report on the second Australian Child and Adolescent Survey of Mental Health and Wellbeing. Canberra: Department of Health.
[2] World Health Organisation March 2022

STEP 1: CLARITY – CLEAR THE BRAIN FOG

Without being able to think clearly, we simply cannot function at our best.

When I look back at that moment when I asked my daughter to leave, I knew I was at a crisis point in my life, and so was she.

I was riddled with guilt and shame for not being able to manage my daughter's behaviour and emotional state, and at the time, I had no idea how to get out of the mess we had found ourselves in.

I sought professional help, but it proved to be what I describe as 'unhelpful help'. I felt lost and confused.

In a moment of despair, I stopped and had a hard look at myself. How had I got to this point? And BOOM, the penny dropped. I suddenly had clarity. This was all about me needing to change.

In the words of the great Dr Wayne Dyer, 'Change your thoughts – change your life.'

I reflected upon the challenging times in my life when I had stepped up despite feeling gripped by anxiety and worried sick about what the future held. I remembered my husband's two suicide attempts and how we got through that, as well as seeing my mother progressively lose her battle to ovarian cancer. I thought about the time I needed to overcome my intense fear of public speaking when I began my practical teacher training. Although conquering that fear was no walk in the park for me, I did it, which meant I was consequently able to enjoy a thirty-two-year career as a teacher.

It was clear to me that I needed to start seeing things through a different lens and act quickly, because I was not prepared to lose my daughter.

And so began my mission to find a solution, rather than staying stuck in victimhood.

Rather than try to change or control my daughter, I decided to:

Focus on what I could control.

Open my mind to new ways of responding to my daughter.

Explore what was possible rather than impossible.

Face some hard truths by putting my arrogance aside and accepting there was a lot I didn't know.

Challenge my beliefs. In my childhood, I 'learned' that adults are automatically entitled to respect. What a terrible belief that has proven to be. *Both* my daughter and I deserved respect, and I was fast learning we needed to love and respect ourselves first – another light-bulb moment for me!

I was getting more clarity around what had been missing for my daughter. Sadly, I'd been automatically expecting her respect without making sure her needs were being met first.

I can now see, that for years, I had struggled to know how to meet my 'big feeling' daughter's emotional needs. I had been telling myself the same old unhelpful story; that she was high maintenance. Again, I had blamed her. *Aaaaarrrrgggghhhh!*

I needed to release old faulty thought patterns to clear the brain fog and free up space to think clearly.

Although I used to think I could juggle many things at once, I now realise when I have too many tabs open, I'm stuck in a perpetual cycle of busyness, overwhelm, stress and confusion. I call this *too muchness*.

Key tip #1: Simplify and declutter your life to simplify and declutter your mind.

When I notice I've slipped into 'too muchness', I do a tidy-up.

I find this helps declutter my mind by letting go of what I don't need. This simplifies my thinking so I can get back to thinking clearly and moving forward, focusing on one thing at a time. Sometimes I've decluttered by sorting out my wardrobe, my desk, my handbag and even my emails.

Imagine the freedom and relief after a big mind tidy-up!

Disorganised thoughts –> stress & anxiety –> more disorganised thoughts –> more stress & anxiety

STEP 2: ALIGNMENT – ALIGN WITH YOUR SOUL

'The world we have created is a product of our thinking.' – Albert Einstein

Although this quote supports step one of my formula, I believe we must also pay attention to our soul.

One huge life lesson I've learned in recent years is that to live authentically, I must honour my soul and do what makes my heart sing.

I've spent too much of my life worrying about what other people think or say, i.e. how I *should* be living my life according to others.

I'm still a work in progress but here are some ways I align with my soul that you might like to try: Detach yourself from the noise and busyness going on around you and tune into YOU. Step back, take a few deep breaths and pay attention to what you really need right now.

You don't have to meditate for hours a day. I simply stop several times a day and mindfully reconnect with what my soul needs in that moment. Sometimes I step outside and breathe in the fresh air for five minutes or stop and have a cup of tea in the sunshine. Grounding myself by reconnecting with nature certainly helps too.

Rewrite your belief blueprint and create your own masterpiece that matches your vision, your dreams and your soul – no-one else's.

Walk to the beat of your own drum. Only you know what's right for you.

Focus your energy on what authentically matters to YOU, what *you* need, value and desire, while building upon *your* strengths.

Catch yourself if you're ever gripped by 'not enoughness'. The truth is, you are enough, and you always were.

Key tip #2: The more you honour your soul, the more your life will flow and fall into place for you.

Instead of swimming against the current of someone else's river, find your river, jump in and go with the flow.

STEP 3: LOVE AND CONNECTION – LOVE AND TUNE INTO YOURSELF AND OTHERS

Put simply, anxiety is fear playing out and the antidote for fear is love.

For four decades, I was driven by fear, feeling relentlessly anxious. I now understand why feeling stressed and under pressure felt like 'my normal'.

I had heard about the importance of loving yourself but to me this seemed like a foreign concept. Indulging in the occasional bubble bath or massage just didn't cut it because afterward, I'd immediately slip back into busyness, pressure and being hard on myself. That racing mind of mine never slowed down for long.

Fortunately, I've now learned that self-love means far more than massages and bubble baths. It's about being kind to yourself, which is something I now intentionally practise every day.

So, if you're feeling anxious, I encourage you to ditch self-doubt, and instead, slow down and shift into self-love.

Here's how:

Listen to your cheerleader instead of your self-critic.

When you're feeling frustrated, annoyed or impatient or you're being hard on yourself, you're certainly not coming from a place of love for yourself or others. Instead, your ego self, aka 'self-critic', deeply embedded in your unconscious mind is trying to protect you because it doesn't want you to change. It's driving you from a place of fear.

When you're facing a challenge that you want to overcome, tell yourself, *I love me. I've got this! I'm worthy of this!* This is how your cheerleader speaks to you, building you up, rather than knocking you down. Notice the fear, anxiety and stress subside when you're in a place of self-love.

Stop and breathe deep slow breaths. Practise this often, whether you're anxious or not. Mastering purposeful deep breathing can really calm your body and mind when you're feeling stressed or anxious.

Stop and allow yourself to feel.

Put simply, in childhood, most of us were taught to suppress emotions that were deemed negative or bad according to our parents or other significant adults. How many of us were told 'don't cry' or 'settle down'? Yet, we're all emotional beings and every emotion, despite how bad you might think it is, needs to be fully processed, otherwise it simply stays stuck as trapped energy in your body, causing ongoing discomfort and anxiety.

Blocked energy is why many of us disconnect ourselves from others and have behaviour patterns we don't seem to be able to change.

Tune into others so you get to connect deeply at their level.

Here's what I've learned. *It all starts with us.* When I learned how to tune into my own emotional needs and how to fully accept and process my emotions, I became significantly better at tuning into what my daughter needed.

Key tip #3: SLOW DOWN TO SPEED THINGS UP!

Get off the hamster wheel and give your mind and body time to slow down. Ditch old fear-based habits, breathe deeply and slowly, and embrace self-love.

STEP 4: MINDFUL ACTIONS

When I look back at how stuck I used to be, I realise I was simply reacting to what was happening around me.

If you ever find yourself thinking you have no choice or control over who you are or how you function, challenge that thinking. That way of thinking is the reason so many of us stay stuck in the grip of anxiety.

It wasn't until sometime after I'd reached crisis point in my relationship with my daughter that I realised my thinking needed a complete overhaul.

I needed to reprogram the way I'd been thinking to change the way

I was behaving.

I needed to relinquish trying to control or blame others and start taking responsibility for my own choices and life results. It was time to shift the focus onto myself and my actions.

It wasn't until I became an observer of myself that I became aware of what I needed to change in me. This then meant change was now possible.

Key tip #4: If we don't change things, things don't change.

I strongly believe that being mindfully aware of my thoughts, emotions and actions enables me to take charge of them. It puts me back into the driver's seat in my life, no longer automatically driven by old childhood programming that kept me stuck and conflicted. Thankfully for those close to me, particularly my daughter, I've let go of trying to gain control over my life by trying to control others.

When I hit rock bottom in my relationship with my daughter, all those years ago, I never imagined it would be the catalyst that would change the trajectory of my life. I'm so grateful we have both been able to discover how anxiety negatively impacted our actions and that we have been able to free ourselves from its crippling grip – and you can too!

SUE STEVENSON

Sue Stevenson is a mother of three adult children, two adult stepchildren and is a grandmother of six. After enjoying a thirty-two-year career working in schools, Sue is now the founder of U-Turn Anxiety and is on a mission to reduce anxiety suffering in one million kids.

As an anxious child, a parent of two anxious children, a teacher and educational leader in health and wellbeing, Sue has seen firsthand the impact anxiety can have on young people and families. She is acutely aware of the limited resources available to those who need high-quality anxiety support.

Knowing anxiety rates have risen significantly over time, Sue is extremely committed to sharing her skills so we can collectively turn things around and reverse that trajectory.

She believes we must empower adults and children with the skills to not only cope, but thrive during times of adversity in our lives, without allowing anxiety and fear to control people's thoughts and actions.

Through Sue's online and face-to-face programs, workshops and presentations, Sue empowers parents, educators and kids with the tools they need to reduce anxiety, so they all get to thrive with courage and calm confidence.

Hence the birth of her CALM Confidence Formula.

Sue believes we must focus on going below the surface to address the root causes of anxiety, rather than only treat the symptoms and problems that come from anxiety – those surface behaviours we see playing out.

If we really want to loosen the grip anxiety currently has in our world right now and break the cycle of repeated fear-based generational unconscious programming, we must educate and empower the adults who are raising and guiding our future generations.

Sue firmly believes we must shake up our leaders, so they start directing more resources into prevention and early intervention, rather than resorting to waiting until people are at crisis point before they get help.

If you want to empower yourself and loosen the grip of anxiety for yourself or someone you care about, here's where you can get started on your journey toward thriving with CALM confidence, surprising yourself with a level of joy and fulfilment you didn't even realise was possible.

Website: uturnanxiety.com.au
Email: suestevenson@ktbm.com.au

LinkedIn   Instagram   Facebook   Book a complimentary call with Sue

FORGING MY OWN PATH
DR TANYA UNNI

It was 2020 and I felt on top of the world. I was entirely in command of my working life as an entrepreneur, community leader and proud businesswoman.

The year began with the promise of rich business opportunities and exciting new endeavours. I represented Australia in Loka Kerala Sabha, a global expatriate meet organised by the Government of Kerala. Not long after, I was in Dubai as part of a business delegation with the Gold Coast City Council.

Whilst in Dubai, rumours began circulating about a virus and the requirement to wear a face mask for the Arab Expo. Despite this, I continued pitching unique business opportunities that had the potential to propel me to new heights. Everything was seemingly picture perfect.

But alas, life had different plans for us. As soon as we arrived back in Australia, the news about COVID-19 had well and truly spread throughout the nation, casting confusion and widespread fear. Like most of us in Australia, my initial reaction was complete disbelief. At that point in time, none of us truly knew the impact or devastation it would have on families or businesses.

The nation went into a spiral, implementing lockdowns, strict social distancing, curfews and masks mandates. In the medical industry, we were at the epicentre of a virus with enormous magnitude and great uncertainty, trying to protect our patients, staff, doctors, and of course, our businesses. I couldn't fathom how a 'recession-proof' industry could face such an impactful and frightening situation. Yet, it didn't take me long to realise that during a time like that, there was only one hat I could wear if we were going to make it through. And that was my leadership hat; to help guide and support our team through the unpredictable times.

Throughout my business and entrepreneurial journey, I have made a conscious effort to remain a 'participating and reformer' style of leader. On very few occasions I have been a disciplinarian.

This unprecedented situation required me to implement new goals and strategies to adapt to the situation. Issues at hand were varied, urgent and important. Having just under one hundred people associated with our business as employees and contractors, I felt immense pressure to ensure our company ran as smoothly as possible, so I could continue paying wages on time. Despite the odds not being in our favour, our goal was to retain all our employees and contractors, and if possible, support even more people from the community.

My business partner, who is also my husband, is adept at crisis management, which allowed us to implement a crisis management team and plan promptly. To begin our new ways of working, we called a brainstorming session to hear and connect with our team. With this, we were able to identify pain points, brainstorm solutions and delegate responsibilities in record time. The outcome was professionally outstanding and personally rewarding.

This proactive approach ensured we could primarily serve our community and support more patients. We were able to connect with patients who were stuck at home and unable to access medical care, and our team was able to extend personalised services to our most vulnerable patients. This was achieved by simultaneously managing the safety of our employees, protecting the welfare of our nurses and doctors and ensuring their mental and emotional wellbeing was a priority. Our medical team was literally the frontline army in this war between humans and the virus.

Once our goals were set, strategies identified and tasks delegated, it was time to take a step back and leave our plan in the capable hands of our team. Our mantra was to trust our teams' ability to implement and carry out the plan successfully … and to this day, I still sincerely believe this is one crucial juncture in every business leader's journey. It is equally important to take a step back in the execution stage as it is crucial to step in during a crisis. Unfortunately, this is where many business owners falter. I firmly believe that trusting your team's capabilities reaps more benefits than micromanaging. A leader rises and shines, not by trampling their employees down and walking all over them, but by gliding along their soaring wings.

I believe each one of us has leadership skills. Women, especially, are natural leaders in that they are constantly performing incredulous miracles at the commonest of hours. This is evident in the ease with which women carry out tasks in the house, the numerous decisions they make for their families, and how kids are mentored, supported, and at times, disciplined. We encourage children when they fail; we cheer for them when they try. We praise them and reward them when they achieve and meet their goals. This is, in fact, the essence of leadership. It is no different from what we do in daily life.

Along the way, we have come to believe that obtaining various degrees and deep industry knowledge are prerequisites for becoming a good leader and synonymous with success. However, from my experience, this couldn't be further from the truth. What you truly need to excel as a leader is courage, a sense of adventure, self-confidence and self-assurance.

Our dynamic team was able to work coordinately at each stage. Within a matter of weeks, we were able to start many new initiatives, including a twenty-four-hour dedicated telephone line for patients, drive-through COVID-19 testing sites, an established partnership with a pathology centre, and new protocols and procedures for car park consultations. Among all these initiatives, I take the greatest pride in the drive-through vaccination and mobile vaccination clinics for people with special needs. For all of this, I was at the frontline working alongside my team. I was not going to leave my team to do the hard work alone, especially if it meant asking them to risk their lives in the middle of a pandemic.

The career path of a businesswoman is never rosy. Apart from the usual struggles of any business leader, women have to fight their own battles. Even though I was unsure if I should share this, my journey is truly relatable to many women. I realised early on that being a lady in the entrepreneurial world meant people would not always take my business seriously – often being dubbed as a 'side hustle', 'time pass', or in my case, 'a waste of time and money'. Unfortunately, it is a lonely journey and I knew this right from the early days of entrepreneurship. As a practising doctor, doing anything outside my trained medical field is often not appreciated, supported or encouraged.

If you are not in the clinic seeing patients as a doctor, you are taking a day off.

When you only take consultations on certain days of the week, you are a part-time worker.

Unfortunately, it doesn't matter how many hours you invest in business idea generation, product innovation or market research. It is hard to explain to those around you that time spent 'on' your business is far more valuable than being 'in' your business.

Being a natural problem-solver, I often take on reformer-style leadership. I love meeting new people, taking notes, contributing solutions to issues, working on concepts and developing ideas. A great example of this is my personal skincare brand. From ideation and conceptualisation to implementation, a great deal of deliberations, research and brainstorming was required. While I was constantly fed negative comments like 'the market is overcrowded', or 'it'll be an expensive journey with no return', I continued to work hard and believe in my dreams and vision. What made a difference in my journey was the clarity in my thoughts and that I set realistic goals each year. I never planned to think small or to settle for anything less than where I saw myself. And while times can be challenging, industries can shift and consumer expectations are continually changing, I knew that to be a true leader, I had to be a disruptor, a change-maker and a reformer. I was prepared to take a path not walked by many, knowing every decision I made could be critical and that there would be few mentors to guide or support me along the way.

My skincare and wellness business is run by a small team who take on various roles per the hour's need. Today, I'm proud to see my brand being launched internationally. As of 2023, Dr Tanya Skincare will be available in India and UAE, in addition to Australia. While there are still miles to travel before I sleep, I'm proud of how far we've come and see great value in stopping to celebrate the wins, big and small.

To me, the formula to being an exceptional leader is straightforward:

Clarity in communication – Ensure each team member understands your business' values and ethos. Make the goals of the company known and your expectations of them clear. Do not leave room for confusion, as your team members are the ones who will carry your message to future team members. It will also influence how they interact with customers, directly influencing your brand image.

Instil confidence in people – Trust the instincts of team members, let them learn through trial and error and be receptive.

Positivity – I truly believe you can conquer the world with a winning mindset. This only happens through positive thinking, setting your intentions, practising positive affirmations and ignoring negativity. Surround yourself with positive people who will inspire and motivate you.

Fairness – This is extremely important. As a leader, you set standards for your team, and they look up to your leadership style. Remember, all eyes are on you, meaning how you show up to your team will influence how they interact. Under any circumstances, it's important to be fair in your decision-making. By doing this, you will gain the respect and trust of your team.

Honesty – The honesty one exhibits in life will become the foundation of their business. If you're honest with your team, you will get the same in return.

Humility – A business leader must remain humble and approachable. There are always lessons to be learnt and corrections to be made. As a business leader, you will experience many ups and downs. Remember, during the highest peaks of your success, you should be the most humble. Your success isn't just owing to your talents; you are enjoying the fruits of your team's hard work too. Be the leader your team members aspire to be, encourage them to take leadership, mentor them and reward them. Being humble will always take you further, so be sure to share your success with your team and acknowledge their hard work. To me, these are the most inspiring leaders who are paving the way.

DR TANYA UNNI

I grew up in Kerala, a state on the south-western Malabar Coast of India. While it's recognised as one of India's most popular tourist destinations and named by *National Geographic Traveler* as one of the ten paradises of the world, there's one thing that makes my hometown even more special: it's the birthplace of Ayurveda, the ancient practice of medicine built on the belief that health and wellness require a delicate balance between mind, body and spirit.

Ayurveda – 'Ayur' meaning 'longevity' and 'Vedic' meaning knowledge – originated in India more than five thousand years ago. This philosophy believes many diseases are preventable when people find balance across all areas of their health – from how they think and what they eat, to their lifestyle choices and habits.

I was lucky to grow up with this practice and belief system deeply ingrained and intertwined in my daily life, self-care practices and rituals. This is fundamentally who I am and what has shaped, influenced and inspired my personal and professional beliefs as a woman, wife, mother, entrepreneur, businesswoman and doctor.

Growing up, I was blessed to come from a home that encouraged both creativity and academics, allowing me to tap into deeper parts of my multifaceted self. While dancing and entertaining are where I feel most alive, my passion and love for medicine are equally crucial to who I am.

My love towards medicine and caring for people came from my greatest role model, my muthessa (grandpa). His selfless nature, commitment to cure and service mindset had an everlasting impact on me as a little girl. Aside from admiring his professionalism and passion, he also taught me values deeply ingrained within me to this day. At a time in my home country where it was considered normal, coming from a middle-class, educated family, to afford helpers at home, he taught me the importance of treating everyone equally regardless of their socio-economic or caste situation. He helped me look at people beyond their social status and to always treat others with respect, dignity and compassion.

Staying true to my commitment to walk in my grandfather's shoes and fulfil my purpose to serve and assist people, I decided to study medicine in 1997. When I first started studying, I couldn't stop thinking about how I could help people and find solutions to their problems. Thankfully, this passion has continued to intensify over time. I was also lucky enough to meet my best friend, life and business partner, and my now husband, during medical school.

I was fortunate as a young doctor to work in London for a period, where I was trained by one of the finest educational institutions in the world. This experience had many highs and lows, but I am forever grateful for every single aspect of my journey, as it helped me to understand more about myself and my passions. It also greatly expedited my professional growth and encouraged me to dig deeper into medicine and holistic health.

After seven years, we decided to move to Australia, seeking new opportunities and challenges to grow. Within three months of arriving, I started my own business, which was just the beginning of a rewarding and fruitful journey. Today, I am the proud owner of eight medical centres, a skincare brand and clinic and multiple health businesses. With over eighteen years of experience delivering premium medical care to my patients, I'm excited to continue incorporating my expertise and passions to find new ways to help people improve all areas of their health, to live healthier, happier and more confident lives.

PURSUIT OF YOUR PASSION THROUGH PERSEVERANCE AND PRIDE

DR VANESSA ATIENZA-HIPOLITO

My leadership journey didn't start in primary or secondary school. I dreaded leading. I never raised my hand to volunteer. I was never selected to lead groups or tasks at school. Not even in university and medical school. I never initiated conversations with people. I was introverted, shy and dreaded public speaking. I hated it and would be so sweaty and have panic attacks when I was required to recite or perform in public. Many times, my fingers would freeze during solo piano recitals and organ competitions. I dreaded those moments because they would cause me to stop and make mistakes in front of, what was sometimes, a big audience. It was embarrassing.

Anyone can be a leader, and being a leader in any workplace or community starts first with leading yourself from within. You must be in charge of your thought process, your energy and how you show up in this life with purpose. For me, it starts with self-love and a lot of deep inner work towards self-love and self-compassion.

It gives me so much joy to share my journey as a self-aware leader.

This is my journey of how I started to lead myself from the inside out. As a leader with a type-A personality and control freak, it can be frustrating if things don't go to plan.

Here are my nine steps on how I take ownership of my LEADERSHIP aka SELF-LEADERSHIP, using my DR VANESSA framework:

D – DIRECTOR

I am the architect, co-creator and CEO of my life. I am the one, and only, person who is in charge. I am the driver of my growth.

As a busy medical doctor and business owner, I was struggling to balance my family life and my professional career. I used to work full-time and felt I was failing as a mother and wife. I was beating myself up for not being present for my family. I even sabotaged my health through emotional eating. I didn't like what I saw in the mirror, especially after my second child, and I felt I had lost control of who I was; I wanted to reclaim the 'old' me. *Atomic Habits* by James Clear and *The Slight Edge* by Jeff Olson were two books I'd recommend that helped me build my mental strength.

R – REINVENT

In my quest to get back to my pre-wedding body, I made a pact with myself that I would be a better version of myself by 1% every day. I began by being in charge of my nutrition and learned how to meal plan, acknowledging the importance of meal preparation for the week. My physique improved with small consistent habits, discipline and goal-setting.

Since I started to transform and create healthy habits, I was able to slowly accomplish my first 5km, then 10km and 12km run, as well as the first of many half-marathons and full-marathon races. I am especially proud I was able to do two run-cations by finishing my half-marathon events in Budapest and Bordeaux. I am at my fittest, strongest and happiest in my forties than ever before, even compared to my twenties.

V – Victory

I began to find joy and happiness with these personal achievements. I had never done sports and was an average student during my childhood. I did not know the feeling of winning competitions and receiving academic or sports awards. I was inspired by Mel Robbin's book *The High 5 Habit*. I was able to create a habit of being my own number-one cheerleader. I celebrated all my small and big wins. I have also enjoyed receiving my finisher medals, which I call my *blings*. Imagine, a sedentary life and not knowing how to swim as an adult before having kids, I have now run marathons, swam in the ocean, joined triathlons and completed half-ironman events, swimming my longest (3.6km) open-water event last year. I wrote about these stories in my contributions in *Global Girls* and *Courage and Confidence* anthology books. I found my happy place. It gives me so much joy and happiness every time I swim in the morning, three to four times a week, while the rest of the world is still sleeping.

Growing up, I was taught to be humble and modest with my achievements. In fact, most of the time, I even downplay them. It was only when I started to receive awards and recognition for my work as a doctor and entrepreneur that I realised I should not be ashamed of my achievements. I was recognised for my work at the AusMumpreneur Awards, honoured to be named the Breast Radiologist of the Year at the Radiology Awards 2022, and a finalist at the Australian Women's Small Business Champion Awards. These awards are reflections of the hard work, resilience, commitment, passion and dedication of my team and the impact they provide to the community. I now acknowledge that this needs to be celebrated and indirectly markets and leverages the value of my expertise and my business.

A – APPRECIATION AND GRATITUDE

In my quest towards deep inner work and self-awareness, whilst training for my marathon and half-marathon races, I stumbled upon the audiobooks by Rhonda Byrne, *The Secret* and *The Greatest Secret*. I even watched the documentary many times and loved *The Secret – Dare to Dream* movie. I wanted to learn and practise the law of attraction, so I also bought *The Secret Gratitude Book* in 2019, when I was in Chicago. I remembered what Oprah had said in her show: to count your blessings and make a list of five things you are grateful for every day. I can't quote her exactly, but it got stuck in me. I forgot all about that journal in 2019 and wrote randomly in 2020. In 2021, I found myself writing consistently, almost every day. My list was getting longer over time. The more I wrote about my appreciation and gratitude every morning, the more I became aware of the blessings magically showing up in my life.

I went deeper into my appreciation mode when I was preparing for the AusMumpreneur finalist interview. Daily journalling and writing my thoughts and prayers opened up creativity I didn't realise I had. Every day, I am grateful to wake up knowing my purpose in life. Every day, I am thankful for those who love and support me, especially my family, relatives, friends and network. Through journalling, I discovered I have a voice and I was able to amplify my voice through my being an author. All my books and blogs are products of my journal-writing. I can only unlock my zone of genius and unload my thoughts through my creative writing from pen to paper.

N – NEGATIVE SELF-TALK

Looking back when I was training for half-marathons, marathons and endurance open-water swims, I was on the journey towards self-discovery and took a deep-dive into self-ownership of my thoughts. I used to beat myself up when I was too slow, or at the end of the pack and one of the last finishers in the race. I would compare myself to the other forty-year-old-plus age-group athletes. I hated being last and criticised myself for being slow and unfit. I was so judgemental of myself, which eventually took away the joy of racing.

I realise now, I don't need to compare myself to others who have been running and swimming all their lives. I probably have forty years of catching up to do before I can outrun or outswim this age group. Slowly, I began to practise self-acceptance and forgave myself for not being kind to myself. Since then, I have started to enjoy my running and morning swims again. I was able to build up my self-belief and self-confidence. From zero swimming skills, I was able to overcome my panic attacks in the ocean and progress my swim distance. I learned to be my inner compassionate coach. Despite the challenges of balancing work, home and self-care, swimming taught me a lot of lessons: how to PAUSE, reset, rejuvenate and recalibrate. My morning swim taught me the importance of prioritising exercise to win my day.

E – ENERGY

How do I even manage to make time to do these things? I don't have the time, of course. As a female solopreneur, I am also a mother with parenting responsibilities, an Uber-mum with domestic duties, choir member, social swimmer and triathlete, plus now an author. How do I balance motherhood and my professional career? It can be challenging for sure. My schedule is always fully booked – so how can I even fit in swimming or any type of exercise in my already busy life? I could tell you that I don't have time for all of these, but for my mental health, I make time.

I used to get overwhelmed and feel burnt-out. I would go home from work, or often after overtime, always feeling tired, exhausted and depleted. When I'm at work, I always give 200%. By the time I get home,

I'd have nothing left to give to my family. I would regularly beat myself up for being an 'angry and cranky' mother. I hated myself for that. I was looking for solutions and answers on how I could avoid this from happening. By the time I got home to my beautiful family, I would snap easily at small things and my kids or my husband would reflect all the negative energy I created. It felt like a vicious cycle. For many years, it was like this every day, and I felt sad and guilty for my behaviour.

It was life-changing when I discovered the power of meditation. Being aware and mindful of the energy I give out at home, at work and outside work, was a game changer. I started to learn how to prioritise rest and recovery. Every day after work, particularly after a big and exhausting day, I go home, straight to my room to sleep. When I have nothing left in the tank, I have nothing to give to my family. Rest and recovery for me are now my non-negotiables. It is essential for me to recharge, so I can show up refreshed, feeling relaxed and in a positive mood. Luckily for me, I do not cook; my husband Glenn is the chef in the house. By the time I wake up from my power nap, I can show up to my family fresh and back to my happy, vibrant and high-vibe energy. I can be present when I am in a good mood. Besides, a happy wife creates happy kids, a happy family and a happy life. My family have noticed the change and I have noticed the transformation of my family's positive energy too. The change is also reflected in my kids' schoolwork, sports, music and their relationship with their friends. We are more connected and our bond is stronger than before.

Nowadays, I make it a priority to be in charge of my morning routines, by prioritising prayers, meditation, journalling and writing my gratitude list. I was able to practise consistent mindfulness and self-awareness through Gabrielle Bernstein's books, podcasts and YouTube videos.

I make a conscious choice to show up with a positive and happy attitude at work. I only choose to focus my time and energy on projects and activities that will give me joy. Joy is a choice and has a ripple effect on my life, family and the people around me.

I make a concerted effort to make ME-time my priority, so I can show up in this world in my highest and BEST SELF.

S – SELF-EDUCATION AND SELF-INVESTMENT

I am a lifelong learner, a doctor, a leader and a student of this so-called LIFE. Luckily, I love and enjoy reading and watching online webinars, masterclasses, courses and YouTube videos on self-help and personal development.

I invest a lot of time and energy in looking after myself. I make time for myself as the highest priority, so I can take care of my family, serve my patients and serve my community.

As a specialist breast radiologist, I make time to attend medical conferences preferably face-to-face and also via virtual events. I make time to fit in any learning opportunities in the nooks and crooks of my already busy life.

The greatest investment I made last year was choosing Dr Olivia Ong, the author of the book titled *The Path From Burnout to Freedom* as my coach. Luckily, I was enrolled in her *Radical Resilience 12-week coaching program*. Facing the unknown feeling of post-COVID fatigue, I am grateful and appreciate that she held my hand during this challenging period of my life. It is a privilege to be a co-author of this book with her.

S – SERVANT LEADER

I constantly ask myself:
- How can I be a better leader?
- How can I serve my patients better?
- How can I prepare myself as a leader when I scale and open up my new branch next year?

- How can I make my team's work less stressful and manageable?

I constantly strive to figure out ways for my team to be happy and enjoy their work, knowing they are helping me save lives. Our mission is to serve the women of Western Australia. I am always asking myself and my team how we can improve our service and make our patients happy, knowing most of the women we see every day are scared and anxious about having their breasts scanned. The book *Start with Why* by Simon Sinek inspired me to go deeper into my why so I can inspire my team and the people around me.

I feel blessed and fortunate to be offered a half-scholarship by the Women's Business School Accelerate program last year. I am grateful for Katy and Peace that I was part of this six-month cohort. It opened up opportunities for me to assess and reflect on what was working and not working for me on a personal and professional level. This program prepared me to scale-up my business so I can be of service to more patients.

In addition, I am also fortunate that I have a platform to share my stories and lived experiences through my anthology books. I pray that my chapter will serve and inspire readers.

A – ACTION PLAN

As a self-aware leader, I wake up every day with intention. I plan my day and am mindful of what I do, say, act and think about, at home and work.

My daily thoughts, words and actions are reflections of my self-leadership. *The Everyday Hero Manifesto* book by Robin Sharma taught me about self-mastery.

My nutrition plan taught me to be the DIRECTOR of my life.

My running taught me to REINVENT myself.

My medals from running, swimming and triathlons taught me to celebrate my VICTORIES.

My journalling taught me to APPRECIATE my blessings and spiritual abundance.

My swimming taught me to have positive self-talk and avoid NEGATIVE thoughts.

My meditation taught me to show up with positivity and with high-vibe ENERGY every day in all aspects of my life.

My self-care time and solitude taught me to SELF-INVEST and only focus on projects and activities that bring me joy and happiness.

My why is to be of SERVICE.

How is my chapter even relevant to being a leader? For me, success is an inside job and being a self-aware leader is the key to achieving my goals and dreams.

My ACTION plan is to only focus my energy on what gives me joy and happiness.

My call to action for you today is: how are you going to take charge of YOU?

DR VANESSA ATIENZA-HIPOLITO

Dr Vanessa Atienza-Hipolito FRANZCR is a clinical director, specialist of breast imaging and intervention and business owner at Women's & Breast Imaging (WBI), Cottesloe, Western Australia.

She is a passionate educator and is an adjunct clinical senior lecturer at Curtin University, University of Western Australia and Edith Cowan University.

A highly respected breast imaging specialist, Dr Vanessa is also an accomplished speaker, author, multi-award-winner and finalist, wife, mother and triathlete. Like many women she faces the stressful challenge of juggling the demands of a career and family whilst taking care of her own physical and spiritual wellbeing.

A bright and engaging role model, she always strives to be the best she can both professionally and personally. She is also committed to help others do the same by sharing the experience and wisdom gained from her own amazing personal journey.

Dr Vanessa saves lives. It is her personal mission to save as many lives as possible by spreading her message of preventative medicine and detecting breast cancer early using advanced mammogram and ultrasound screening technologies such as used at her business at WBI.

Dovetailing well with her message of physical wellbeing, Dr Vanessa also enthusiastically speaks on self-care, self-compassion, resilience and overcoming difficulties, providing practical strategies that are easily applied to everyday life.

Website: drvanessaa.com
Link Tree: linktr.ee/drvanessaatienzahipolito

PERFECTLY IMPERFECT
WADZANAI NENZOU

I'm a big believer in the power of education. I agree with Nelson Mandela when he said, 'Education is the most powerful weapon which you can use to change the world.' Over the years I have seen the power education has to empower humans to live their best lives. My vision for the world is a world where every woman has the knowledge to empower herself financially, to live life her way and be the best version of herself. This will in turn empower her family, community and the world at large.

Why exactly is this a focus of my life? For me to best explain it, let me take you back to a young girl in Zimbabwe. I grew up in a middle-class suburb in Harare. My mum was a nurse and my dad worked in the insurance world. Both my parents come from large families and grew up with seven siblings each.

I grew up with the importance of education to better myself being drummed into me. Both my parents had come from the countryside and moved up in social and economic class through getting an education and good jobs. I therefore grew up focused on getting a good education and making something of myself.

I noticed as a child that there were some women who seemed completely reliant on others for their livelihood, whether that be their husbands, parents or other relatives. I also noticed that some women had their own jobs and a little more security, although even those women felt culturally restricted in their choices.

As a little girl, I didn't like this. I was too young to really know why, but I just knew it was wrong and I wanted more for these women. Even then, at that young age, I knew deep down that women were victors. I decided that when I grew up, I wanted to have a good job and take care of myself financially. As I grew older, I also hoped that one day I might be able to play my part in helping women empower themselves to become financially secure.

The journey from making this decision and becoming a financial educator and investment scams fighter is a long journey dealing with perfectionism, impostor syndrome and a scarcity mindset. It is a journey filled with developing life philosophies to help me live my best life.

PERFECTIONISM

There is a top I bought a few years ago which says on the front, *Learn to love yourself babe you are perfectly imperfect.* I remember looking at the message and thinking, *This is something I and most people struggle to do.*

Throughout my life, I have struggled to fully accept myself, warts and all. I have gotten to a point in my life where I now love and accept myself and my flaws, but it has been a long road to get here, and it is still not perfect. It's something I will always continue to work on.

An example of my perfectionism is best highlighted by how long it took me to start investing in shares. I have been working in the financial services industry since 2006 and have all the relevant qualifications. I have also worked in various parts of the industry in investing and financial advice. I had plenty of knowledge to invest in my first direct share many years ago, but because I wanted to know everything possible about share investing before taking the step, I only made my first direct share investment in the last few years.

Another good example is that for years I wanted to do something towards the financial empowerment of women. But I wanted to make sure my life and own finances were perfect before I started. I thought I had to tick all the boxes to make sure I was worthy of being a financial educator. I finally realised, however, that being an educator doesn't require perfection, it needs knowledge and the ability to teach people in a way they can understand. As the years went by, I was continually told by my clients that I explained financial elements in a way they could understand. I realised the natural talent I had to simplify financial elements was exactly the skill I needed to start educating women about investing.

Over the years, I have learnt the root cause of perfectionism is fear and insecurity. My new mindset around perfectionism is, 'Done is better than perfect.' You can spend years waiting to be perfect, or you can take a small step now and another tomorrow, and with time you improve and accomplish something.

IMPOSTOR SYNDROME

Feeling like an impostor when it comes to showing up in your career or business is something many people struggle with. Wikipedia defines impostor syndrome as 'a psychological occurrence in which an individual doubts their skills, talents or accomplishments and has a persistent internalised fear of being exposed as a fraud'. As I slowly became known as a financial educator and investment scams fighter over the years, people in the industry started asking me to speak at events and to be interviewed in podcasts. At first, I felt like an impostor. I remember thinking, *Gosh, if only these people knew what a mess my life can be sometimes.* I always made it clear when I ran events that I wasn't some 'all-knowing financial guru' and that I was also on a journey to financial empowerment. This is true, of course, because no-one is all knowing, but I said this mainly to cover my behind – just in case they discovered I was an impostor. I could then say, 'Hey, I told you so.'

Slowly, through the testimonials I have received from the ladies I have taught and other comments from many lovelies, I have realised *I am enough*. I realised that with my flaws and 'not knowing everything', I still have a lot to offer this world. Things I find easy to do or understand, someone else may struggle with, and focusing on educating these people makes a huge impact in their lives.

SCARCITY MINDSET

Growing up I remember always having a mindset of 'not having enough'; not having enough clothes, money, popularity or material toys, you name it. In hindsight I had plenty, but I was big on comparison and thinking other kids had more than I did. For as long as I can remember, I have always had a scarcity mindset. This has shown up in the past by how I spent my money or how I have shown up in the world.

When it comes to starting my business and educating women financially, this mindset has reared its ugly head in so many big and little ways. I remember when I initially was thinking of starting out as a financial educator, I looked around and saw some amazing people already in the financial education space teaching women. I remember thinking, *What can I offer when others seem more skilled?* This meant I waited years to get started because I didn't think there was space for me.

This was a scarcity mindset, thinking there wasn't enough room for me in a specific industry. As time went on, I realised every one of these people financially educating ladies were doing it in their unique way which spoke to specific ladies. They didn't speak to all ladies, just ones who connected with them. I then realised that my way of educating and showing up in this space would be totally unique. There would be ladies who gravitated towards me because of this, and sure enough, that's exactly what happened.

Remember you are unique and what you have to offer this world is different to anyone else. You could be in the exact same business, and it doesn't matter because how your business shows up will never be the same as anyone else.

As I have matured and got to know myself more, I have philosophies or ways of thinking that I try to live by in my personal life and as a financial educator. I'm not perfect all the time, of course, but I try my best. In the next part of this chapter, I will share these with you.

SEE THROUGH CONNECTING PHILOSOPHY

A lot of people over the years have been impressed by how I seem to get along with a variety of people, both personally and in my business. They have noticed I have friends and acquaintances of all ages, genders, nationalities, races, sexuality and political viewpoints, and they always ask me how I do this.

For example, when I went on a guided tour around New Zealand, I got along with a beautiful lady from Cambridgeshire, England, and years later, we travelled Scotland and Barcelona together. In 2016, I went on a guided tour of Vietnam and made friends with two lovelies from Switzerland, and about eighteen months later they showed me around Switzerland. I also first met one of my friends and mentors in the bathroom at a jazz concert in Melbourne. She has helped me gain clarity in my business and personal life.

When it comes to connecting with other humans, I call my personal philosophy *see through connecting*. I truly believe most people in this world are genuinely good. As humans, we are so much alike and yearn for someone who views us and interacts with us in an open non-judgemental manner, and I try to do that. I take people as individuals not as stereotypes. I see through the artificial elements to the individual underneath. I also genuinely love people and am highly curious about connecting with people. When you are genuinely open with people for the majority of the time, they are open right back.

This is how I try to connect with humans both in my personal and business life, and it has allowed me to make wonderful friends from all over the world and build a business I'm proud of.

CARPE DIEM – SEIZE THE DAY!

If you are to ask my loved ones about one big aspect about me, they will mention that I know how to truly live life to the fullest. I'm a lover of life. I try to truly savour this life as much as possible. I have fun and joy in my life on a regular basis. This is a mindset that is part of my personality and has also come from losing people I have loved over the years.

2016 was one such year, when it was once again made very clear to me that life is short. It doesn't matter if you live to be one hundred years old, a human life in the wide scheme of things, and this huge galaxy, is less than a drop in the ocean. My beautiful sister-in-law Tsitsi died suddenly in a car accident at the very young age of thirty-four. I was absolutely devastated. My whole family, especially my dear brother and their kids, were crushed with grief because my sister-in-law was honestly a one-of-a-kind beautiful soul. Her death reconfirmed what I already knew but had taken for granted; that life is short, and any day could be your time to go.

From that day, I do not go any day without being grateful to be alive, and I live accordingly. I also made a promise to live my life to the fullest in honour of Tsitsi who herself loved life and was one of the kindest people I knew.

This philosophy shows up in my passion to educate ladies. At the end of my days, I want to know I did my best to share my knowledge and skills to positively impact the world. Living a life of purpose and service is part of seizing the day and that's what has truly allowed me to fully show up in my business.

BOUNDARIES ARE EVERYTHING

It took me nearly forty years of being alive before I realised how important boundaries are in living your best life. The Queen of boundaries, to me, is Nedra Glover Tawwab, a psychologist based in the US. Through her social media posts and her book, *Set Boundaries, Find Peace,* she has changed my life.

According to Nedra Tawwab, 'Boundaries are rules, expectations, needs and desires that help you feel safe and comfortable in life and in your relationships.' Nedra suggests that the boundaries we are missing are ones we need to put in place for ourselves – often we lack boundaries in our relationships, not only with others, but ourselves too.

Having clear boundaries in my life is a work in progress. However, ever since I started having clearer boundaries in place in my personal and business life, my life has greatly improved. One big improvement coming from setting clear boundaries and sticking to them has been an increase of peace of mind in my life. When I was younger, there was a lot more drama in my life than I have now, mostly because I now have very clear boundaries regarding drama and the people I choose to have in my life.

DAILY GRATITUDE ROUTINE

My life, exactly as it is right now, is the same as winning the lottery. Others in the world would love to have my life. Every day I remember this. It's a bit of a mantra to remind myself how blessed I am and how much I have to be grateful for.

In the last decade, I have learnt to constantly think about things I'm grateful for. This practice highlights to me how wonderful my life is. I have gotten very good at this practice of gratitude and even when I'm going through tough times, I still find myself counting my blessings. It reminds me of the hymn 'Count Your Blessings' by Johnson Oatman Jr. The lyrics always move me.

Having this gratitude practice in my business has really helped me see how far I've come in my quest to educate as many people as possible. In business it's easy to compare with others and to feel inferior or not as successful. However, when you count all the blessings in your business, it helps you get through the inevitable challenges that come with running a business.

CONCLUSION

My journey has been filled with struggling with perfectionism, impostor syndrome and scarcity mindset. I'm a work in progress, but improving in all three areas, and have been able to show up more in my personal life and in my mission to educate women.

On my journey I have discovered my life philosophies such as:
See through connecting.
Carpe diem.
Boundaries are everything.
Daily gratitude.

These core philosophies have helped me build a life and business I'm very proud of.

Life is messy and imperfect, but through it all, if you just show up as the perfectly imperfect human you are, you will shine brightly in this world as a one of a kind gift.

WADZANAI NENZOU

Hi, lovelies, I'm Wadzanai Nenzou aka Wadzi, nice to meet you.

I'm the founder, CEO, investment scams fighter, financial educator, speaker, commentator, panellist and writer at Heronomics – a mission-driven education company that is passionate about people, especially women, building their wealth without losing their hard-earned money to investment scams.

Growing up in Zimbabwe, I saw the limited choices open to many women due to lack of personal wealth. But I also saw the opposite, the better choices women had when they had personal wealth. Even as a young girl, I knew I wanted more for myself and other women.

I believe in a world where every woman has the knowledge to empower herself financially, to live life her way and be the best version of herself. I believe that a global sisterhood, bringing women together to learn, share stories and connect with each other about money will make a vital difference in fighting poverty and bringing prosperity to the world. I believe in the power of women taking total personal responsibility for their lives and coming together to lift each other up, because when women positively come together, magic happens.

I'm a financial services professional with over seventeen years' experience in the Australian financial services industry. I have worked in the areas of financial planning, superannuation, investments, banking and compliance. I hold a Master of Accounting from Swinburne University, Bachelor of Commerce from Deakin University, Diploma of Financial Planning from ASFA and a Graduate Diploma of Public Policy from RMIT University.

Over the years I have had the pleasure of being interviewed on the ABC News *Breakfast Show* about investment scams. I have been spotlighted by Bendigo Bank in their Bendigo Bank life coach podcast on how investing is for everyone and was honoured to be one of the investing experts for *Yahoo! Finance* Australia's Women's Money Movement Investing event. I have also been a featured expert in the *Yahoo! Finance Australia* Women's Money Movement newsletter and been interviewed by *Yahoo! Finance Australia's* editor-in-chief for their Rich Thinking interview series. Last but not least I have been interviewed by Incubate Foundation, GirledWorld and Ladies Talk Money as an investing educator.

I'm also deeply passionate about the advancement of African-Australians and volunteer my time to collaborate with organisations such as Incubate Foundation to provide mentorship to African-Australian young people and women. I also volunteered my time for two years as a board member for the African Think Tank, an organisation focused on the advancement of African-Australians. I had the honour of graduating from the African Think Tank's African Leadership Development Program in 2016, where I received a great foundation of becoming a leader in the Australian community.

In my spare time I love to laugh, connect with other humans and have interesting conversations. I also love travel, hiking, music, dancing, reading, TV shows (with special love for animes, period dramas, fantasy and crime dramas), movies, listening to podcasts, listening to audio books, eating good food, going to nice bars, going to the theatre, the countryside and life as a whole. Yes, my life is full to the brim of great things!

Website: herconomics.com
Facebook: facebook.com/herconomics
Instagram: instagram.com/herconomics
LinkedIn: linkedin.com/company/herconomics & linkedin.com/in/wadzanainenzou
Twitter: twitter.com/herconomics

THIS BOOK CHANGES LIVES

Proceeds from the sale of this book go to providing marginalised women in business with scholarships to enable them to receive support, mentoring and education through The Women's Business School.

Aligning with the United Nations SDG goals for gender equality, The Women's Business School scholarships are awarded to women in remote and rural areas, First Nations women, migrant women, survivors of domestic violence, women with disability and chronic illness and those facing financial hardship.

We believe that investing in women is the most powerful way to change the world, and these scholarships provide opportunities for deserving women to participate in an incubator program for early stage startups and businesses and an accelerator program for high-potential entrepreneurs ready to scale their companies and expand globally.

You can read more about the work of The Women's Business School Scholarship Program and how they're changing the world here:

thewomensbusinessschool.com/scholarship

ABOUT PEACE & KATY AND SPEAKING OPPORTUNITIES

Peace and Katy are the dynamic duo behind AusMumpreneur, Australia's number-one community for mums in business; The Women's Business School, providing dedicated education for aspiring and established female founders; Women Changing the World Press, amplifying the voices of thought leaders, female founders and women changing the world; and Women Changing the World Investments, providing opportunities for capital for female founders.

Peace Mitchell is a TEDx speaker, international keynote speaker, retreat facilitator and workshop presenter.

If you want your audience to be captivated by a heart-centred, warm and engaging thought leader and speaker then look no further.

With experience delivering keynote presentations on connection, business success, magic and productivity, there's nothing Peace loves more than engaging with your delegates to make your event a huge success.

If you've got an online or in-person event coming up and want to create a magical, warm and engaging atmosphere, please get in touch.

peace@womensbusinesscollective.com
+61 431 615 107

ABOUT THE WOMEN'S BUSINESS SCHOOL

The Women's Business School is a business school designed exclusively for women. Providing opportunities for innovative female founders to scale their startup, connect with fellow founders and gain advice and guidance from successful entrepreneurs and experts. Through the award-winning incubator and accelerator programs, founders receive world-class entrepreneurial education from a team of high-level experts and entrepreneurs as well as mentoring, advice and access to successful female entrepreneurs across a range of industries. If you're ready to take your business to the next level apply today!

thewomensbusinessschool.com

ABOUT AUSMUMPRENEUR

Australia's number-one community for mumpreneurs. The AusMumpreneur Awards are a national event recognising and celebrating Australia's best and brightest mums in business. Held annually, these awards recognise the incredible women who are balancing business and motherhood and creating innovative, high-quality and remarkable brands across a range of industries.

ausmumpreneur.com

ABOUT WOMEN CHANGING THE WORLD PRESS

Women Changing the World Press publishes thought leaders, female founders and women who are committed to making the world a better place through their words and actions. We believe that investing in women is the most powerful way to change the world and we are passionate about amplifying women's voices, stories and ideas and providing more opportunities for women to share their message with the world. If you have a story that the world needs to hear get in touch today.

wcwpress.com

ABOUT WOMEN CHANGING THE WORLD INVESTMENTS

At Women Changing the World Investments our mission is to revolutionise the way women founders can access capital to grow their businesses and in turn grow their communities of influence. Investing in women, their ideas and their innovation is the way we make real change in the world.

We are committed to:
- Changing the experiences and trajectory of funding for female founders and entrepreneurs.
- Advancing the normalisation of funding female founders.
- Ensuring all women have a seat at the table, especially women of colour, First Nations women, women with disabilities and those who identify as women.
- Changing the tone of the conversation about capital raising for female founders.

We do this through:
- Providing real, appropriate investment for female founders who share our values – when women's success is empowered and facilitated,

families, communities and our society benefit.
- Providing real opportunities for investors who share our values. We also support the ambition of women to invest in viable, success-orientated businesses and be a part of growing our economy.

As part of this capital, we provide appropriate resources, connections and skill development to ensure they are supported through their growth as a founder and the growth of their enterprise.

We are committed to creating change and incubating new opportunities for collaboration, connection and economic growth by investing in brilliant, high-potential, women-led companies.

Our work has an immediate beneficial impact on the female founders we support, as well as creating lasting legacy work through amplifying the work of women entrepreneurs and changing the way venture capital can be accessed by women.

wcwinvestments.com

ABOUT WOMEN CHANGING THE WORLD AWARDS

The Women Changing the World Awards recognises, acknowledges and celebrates the trailblazers, changemakers and visionary action-takers. Providing a platform to amplify the achievements, accomplishments and work that women around the world are doing to make a difference in big and small ways. We believe that by elevating women, their ideas and their impact we can create a ripple effect that not only celebrates these women and the incredible work that they do but also inspires others to take action and make the world a better place in their own way too.

wcwawards.com

Printed in Australia
Ingram Content Group Australia Pty Ltd
AUHW021239140324
391739AU00001B/1